CHILDREN'S PLAYS
for
CREATIVE ACTORS

Children's Plays
for
Creative Actors

A collection of royalty-free
plays for boys and girls

by

CLAIRE BOIKO

Publishers   PLAYS, INC.   *Boston*

MANUFACTURED IN THE UNITED STATES OF AMERICA

Preface to New Edition

This is the heyday of the young actor. Television and motion pictures have brought the young professional actor to the attention of a vast audience of children. Now, as never before, boys and girls want to "get into the act." Most of the plays in this book were written to include all the children in a class or drama group who want to perform. By using choral verse, mime, dance and music, many kinds of performing talent can be recognized. Teachers also have a wide variety of subject matter, mood and style from which to choose.

In various productions throughout the country, the plays have proved adaptable to many different mediums. "Small Crimson Parasol" for instance has been presented as a musical play, a television script, and a puppet show. Other dramas have been tape recorded for classroom study, or performed as live radio shows.

Although primarily directed at classroom production, the plays have also proved useful to such community groups as Boy Scouts, Girl Scouts, The Police Athletic League, summer camps and playground drama groups.

Claire Boiko

Contents

CONTENTS   ix

CHILDREN'S PLAYS
for
CREATIVE ACTORS

Small Crimson Parasol

Characters

STORYTELLER
SUKOSHI
HONORABLE MOTHER
KIRAI, *the butterfly*
CHOTTO, *the tortoise*
ZIN-ZIN, *the tiger*

HONORABLE GRANDMOTHER
WOODCUTTER
YIN ⎱ *property boys*
YAN ⎰
KABUKI CHORUS

TIME: *The present.*

SETTING: *Japan.*

BEFORE RISE: *The* STORYTELLER *enters in front of the curtain, and bows very low to the audience. He is carrying a book under one arm, and a rolled scroll under the other.*

STORYTELLER: Ko-ni-chi-wa. Welcome to Japan. I am Ojisan, the storyteller. I go from street to street in the villages calling, "Come, boys and girls. Come and hear my stories!" Then, out of the cottages and up the narrow alleys come the children of Japan, to hear me tell the old tales and the new tales. Today I have a new tale for the children. I have borrowed it (*Bowing again*) from you. I hope you do not mind. As a matter of fact, you American boys and girls borrowed this story from a German folk tale teller named Jacob Grimm, and he in turn borrowed it from—who knows? You just cannot keep a good story at home, can you? Now, with the help of my Kabuki Chorus, I will tell you what happened to Little Red Riding Hood when she came to Japan. (*He holds up book which has "Little Red Riding Hood" printed on it.*) Little Red Riding Hood became Small Crimson Parasol. (*He unrolls and holds up the scroll which has "Small Crimson Parasol" printed vertically in oriental block letters. The curtain opens behind him on a bare stage. Kneeling on mats, down left, is the* KABUKI CHORUS. *One member has a gong, one a drum, and one a flute or recorder. Others have wood blocks.* YIN *and* YAN *stand down right, holding large gold discs.*) It was many, many suns ago. (YIN *and* YAN *hold up discs and slowly revolve them counterclockwise, then exit right slowly.*)

CHORUS:
Many, many suns ago . . .
In Japan, on the island of Kyushu,
There is a mountain capped with snow.
Below the mountain lies a green valley.
In the valley is a meadow of tall grass.
On the meadow is a cottage.
(YIN *and* YAN *carry on a screen with a Japanese scene painted on it and place it down right, then exit.*)
In the cottage long ago,
Lived an Honorable Mother.
(HONORABLE MOTHER *enters left, walking slowly as the* CHORUS *taps wood blocks in rhythm with her steps. She bows to audience and stands beside screen.*)
With the Honorable Mother
There lived a small daughter.
(SUKOSHI *enters left with small mincing steps, with the wood blocks tapping in rhythm. She carries a closed red*

parasol. She bows to audience and to MOTHER, *then goes to join her.*)
This is Small Crimson Parasol.
She has a feather head.
(SUKOSHI *giggles behind her hand.*)
She has a wandering eye.
(SUKOSHI *looks all around, wide-eyed.*)
Listen, well, Sukoshi-san,
Listen to your mother.

HONORABLE MOTHER (*With finger pointed at* SUKOSHI): Listen to me, Sukoshi, my child. It is time for you to visit your Honorable Grandmother. (YIN *and* YAN *carry on a straw basket and a small tea table set with cups, teapot, etc., and place them in front of* SUKOSHI *and* MOTHER, *then exit.*)

SUKOSHI: *Ah, so deska,* yes, Mama-san.

MOTHER: Bring her this basket with pickled octopus and seaweed cakes.

SUKOSHI: Ah, good. How delicious. Pickled octopus and seaweed cakes!

MOTHER: Pay attention, Sukoshi. Do *not* go through the bamboo forest. There is darkness there. There is danger there. There are *tigers* there.

SUKOSHI (*Smiling and nodding*): *Ah, so deska,* Mama-san.

MOTHER: Go now, my dear little Sukoshi, before the sun grows hot. Do not linger to pick the flowers. Do not chase the butterflies. And do not sit dreaming upon the stones of the field. And please, child, take your small crimson parasol. It may be quite warm—and then again —it might rain.

SUKOSHI: *Ah, so deska,* Mama-san. (*She bows to* MOTHER, *opens her parasol, puts the straw basket on her arm, and takes small mincing steps to the sound of the wood blocks, toward center stage.* MOTHER *kneels at the tea table and holds position.*)

STORYTELLER: And so, Sukoshi set off with her small crimson parasol on the journey to visit her Honorable Grandmother. But alas—

CHORUS: But alas—

STORYTELLER: Sukoshi was a very scatterbrained little girl. As soon as she saw the cool, green bamboo forest, she forgot all about her Honorable Mother's warnings and went straight into the woods! (*Her steps slow, then speed up.* YIN *and* YAN *carry on a bamboo tree from left and place it down right, and then exit.* KIRAI, *the butterfly, holding fans, enters and stands beside tree.*)

CHORUS:
No! No! No!
Do not take this path, Sukoshi-san.
Do not go into the forest, Sukoshi-san.
No! No! No!
(SUKOSHI *stops by the tree.* KIRAI, *the butterfly, opens her fans, and slowly waves them back and forth as if beating her wings.*)

SUKOSHI: Ah! How beautiful. It is a flower. A lovely, waving flower. I will pick the flower for Honorable Grandmother. (*She puts down her parasol and tries to grasp* KIRAI.)

KIRAI (*Haughtily*): Stop! Don't touch! (*She flutters her wings as flute plays.*)
No-thank-you-very-much.
I am no earthly bud,
No blossom of the mud.
I'm here—I'm there—
I'm Empress of the air.
Small foolish child, use your eyes,
I am Kirai, the butterfly,
The Monarch of the summer skies.

SUKOSHI (*Bowing deeply*): I beg your pardon, Imperial

Majesty. I was confused. The shadows teased my eyes.
Please excuse this unworthy Sukoshi!

KIRAI: Very well, but don't let it happen again. And now,
I am late for my appointment with the cherry blossoms.
Let me pass, child. (KIRAI *dances off as flute plays and*
CHORUS *speaks.*)

CHORUS:
Butterfly, flutter by,
Flash and flitter,
Skip and skitter,
Skim and glide,
Seek and hide,
Flash and flutter, butterfly!

STORYTELLER: An encounter with a haughty butterfly. Do
you think that stopped our Small Crimson Parasol? Not
a bit. She went on, further into the forest. (YIN *and*
YAN *bring on second bamboo tree, and place it at cen-*
ter, then exit. CHOTTO, *the tortoise, enters slowly on*
hands and knees from right, accompanied by slow drum
beat from CHORUS. *He stops at center when he sees*
SUKOSHI, *and folds himself inside his shell.*)

CHORUS:
One foot, two foot,
Three foot, four—
Now a little,
Then a little,
Again a little more.
Easy does it,
Slow as mush,
Never hurry,
Never rush.

SUKOSHI: But what is this? (*She touches the shell.*) I do not
need my eyes to tell me. My fingers know what this is.
This is a great cool stone. I will take this great cool

stone to Honorable Grandmother for her garden. (*She tugs at* CHOTTO, *who thrusts arms, legs, and an angry head out of his shell.*)

CHOTTO (*In a deep, slow voice*): Here! Here! What are you doing?

SUKOSHI (*Jumping back in alarm*): Oh! I thought you were a stone.

CHOTTO: A stone? Humph. I am Chotto, the tortoise. You need your eyes examined, child. (*Drum beat sounds again, as* CHOTTO *starts to lumber off left.*)

Leave me alone.

I am *not* a stone.

A stone is a no one.

I am Chotto, the slow one.

Biding my time,

Making my way,

Inch after inch,

Day after day.

So, leave me alone.

I am not a stone!

SUKOSHI: I beg your pardon, noble tortoise. (*She picks up her parasol and minces along as wood blocks tap.* YIN *and* YAN *carry on third bamboo tree and place it left of center, then exit.* ZIN-ZIN, *the tiger, enters from left on tiptoe, and hides behind the tree.*)

CHORUS:

Listen, listen. What is that?

(*Flute trills.*)

Only a bird in the treetop high.

Hush, hush! Who goes there?

(*Wood blocks tap.*)

Only a child on the forest path.

Listen, listen. A sound in the bush.

(*Drum beats faster.*)

Look! Look! A shadow falls!

(The gong sounds. ZIN-ZIN *rushes out, snarling.* SUKOSHI
hides behind her parasol.)

SUKOSHI *(Peeking over the rim of parasol)*: Oh! Oh! You
look like—! You look like—!

ZIN-ZIN *(Swaggering)*: What do I look like, my little tid-
bit?

SUKOSHI *(Straightening up)*: You look like a tiger. You
sound like a tiger. But you cannot *be* a tiger.

ZIN-ZIN *(Astonished)*: What? I've never heard of such a
thing. Why can I not be a tiger?

SUKOSHI: Because.

ZIN-ZIN: Because why?

SUKOSHI: Because I *think* you are a tiger, that's why. Today I have made two mistakes. Number one: I mistook
a butterfly for a flower. Number two: I thought a tortoise was a stone. Now then, listen carefully. If I think
you are a tiger, I must be mistaken. You are really
something else. Do you understand?

ZIN-ZIN: Not very well. *(He shakes his head, puzzled.)*
What am I then?

SUKOSHI: Hm-m-m. You have tan fur and black stripes.
You have four feet and a long tail. Therefore you must
be a zebra! How nice to meet you, zebra. I shall tell my
Honorable Grandmother about you.

ZIN-ZIN *(To audience)*: Ah, a grandmother! Two nice fat
tidbits for Zin-Zin! *(He licks his lips. To* SUKOSHI) Of
course I am a zebra, you clever child. You are not afraid
of me, are you?

SUKOSHI: Oh, no.

ZIN-ZIN: Then let me come with you to your Honorable
Grandmother's cottage. I will protect you from the
wicked tigers that might spring out at you.

SUKOSHI: How kind of you to go out of your way for me.
Thank you, Mr. Zebra. (YIN *and* YAN *take off the trees
as* ZIN-ZIN *and* SUKOSHI *march in place, and wood blocks*

and drum sound the rhythm. YIN *and* YAN *bring on another Japanese screen and place it down left, near the* CHORUS. HONORABLE GRANDMOTHER *enters and stands in front of screen, hands folded.*)

CHORUS (*In dismay*):
Oh! Foolish Sukoshi!
Oh! Wily, wicked tiger!
Oh! What will happen now?

ZIN-ZIN (*To audience, licking his chops*): I will tell you what will happen now. I will get this small, silly child into the cottage with her grandmother, and then I will have a feast. Now how shall I do this? Ah, I have an idea. Oh, I am a clever tiger, I am! (*To* SUKOSHI) Look! Look out at the sky.

SUKOSHI (*Peering out over audience*): What is it? What do you see?

ZIN-ZIN: I see a flight of birds, white birds with silver crests, over there. Look into the sunset until you see them! (SUKOSHI *shades her eyes and holds her pose.* ZIN-ZIN *creeps over to* HONORABLE GRANDMOTHER *and pushes her behind the screen. The gong sounds again.*) There. Into the closet with you until I can finish your granddaughter. Grrrow! (*He beats his chest.* YIN *and* YAN *carry in kimono, kerchief, quilt and small blanket.* YIN *dresses* ZIN-ZIN *in kimono and kerchief while* YAN *spreads quilt on the floor.* ZIN-ZIN *lies on the quilt and* YAN *covers him with the blanket.* YIN *and* YAN *exit, and* ZIN-ZIN *speaks to the audience.*) There I am. Am I not a clever tiger? Do I not look like a grandmother? Listen to me moan. (*Moaning loudly*) Oh, Sukoshi. Where are you, Sukoshi? (SUKOSHI *rushes to* ZIN-ZIN *with small running steps, accompanied by taps of wood blocks.*)

SUKOSHI: Honorable Grandmother! What is the matter? Are you ill?

ZIN-ZIN (*Feigning an old woman's voice*): Yes, my dear. I must have eaten a green mushroom.

SUKOSHI (*Wringing her hands*): Oh, let me run for help. There is a woodcutter nearby.

ZIN-ZIN (*Growling*): No! (*In old woman's voice*) I mean, no, dear child. Stay with me. I shall be much better soon.

SUKOSHI: Very well. (*She kneels by ZIN-ZIN's head, looks closely at him and turns to the audience.*) Oh. I do not like to hurt the Honorable Grandmother's feelings, but she looks so strange today. (*To ZIN-ZIN*) Honorable Grandmother, what furry ears you have.

ZIN-ZIN: Just so. All the better to hear you with, my dear.

SUKOSHI (*Staring into his eyes*): And, Honorable Grandmother, what green, glittering eyes you have.

ZIN-ZIN (*Staring back fiercely*): Just so. All the better to see you with, my dear.

SUKOSHI (*Seeing his tail twitch*): What is this? (*She pulls edge of blanket aside and reveals his long tail.*) Why, Honorable Grandmother, what a long tail you have. Tail? Grandmothers do not have tails! (*She pulls off the blanket.*) Zin-Zin! Where is my Grandmother? Help! Help! (*The gong sounds. ZIN-ZIN springs up and makes clawing motions. SUKOSHI furls her umbrella and uses it like a sword.*)

ZIN-ZIN: Do not try to escape me. I am going to make two bites of you. Grrrow! (*The wood blocks tap rapidly as the* WOODCUTTER *enters from right, carrying his axe.*)

CHORUS:
Hurrah! Help is coming.
Hurrah! It is the woodcutter.
Hurry! Hurry! Hurry!

WOODCUTTER: Get away. Get away, you demon tiger, or I will chop off your evil head!

ZIN-ZIN (*Quavering*): What? Chop off my head? You have

made a mistake. I am not a tiger. Tell him, Sukoshi. I am a zebra. (SUKOSHI *shakes her head. He turns to the audience; pleading*) You tell him. Tell him that I am a zebra.

WOODCUTTER: A zebra indeed! I know you, you slinky rascal. You are Zin-Zin, the scourge of the forest.

ZIN-ZIN (*Falling to his knees*): Mercy, mercy! I have not hurt the old grandmother. She is in the closet. (SUKOSHI *brings* GRANDMOTHER *from behind screen.*) Mercy! Oh! (*He sobs and bows very low.*)

WOODCUTTER: Is this Zin-Zin, the terror, begging for mercy? Very well, you moth-eaten good-for-nothing. I will have mercy. But listen well. You are to go deep into the bamboo forest, and you are never to bother any human folk again. Do you understand? (ZIN-ZIN *nods.*) Now, swear this oath. I cross my heart and hope to die—

ZIN-ZIN (*Trembling*): I cross my heart and hope to die—

WOODCUTTER: I will never, *never* annoy a human being ever again, for as long as I live!

ZIN-ZIN: I will never, *never* annoy a human being ever again, for as long as I live.

WOODCUTTER: Good. Now, scat. Scat, I say! (*The drum sounds as* ZIN-ZIN *bounds off left.* GRANDMOTHER *hugs* SUKOSHI, *and the* WOODCUTTER *leans on his axe.*)

CHORUS:
Scat! Scat! You mangy cat.
Never return again.
Good! Good! You chopper of wood,
You saved the silly child.

STORYTELLER: And so, the tiger went deep into the green bamboo forest. Never again did he show his whiskers in the meadows of Kyushu. The woodchopper received a medal as big as his head from the Emperor of Japan. (WOODCUTTER *kneels at center.* YIN *enters, carrying a medal on a pillow, followed by* YAN, *who places medal around* WOODCUTTER's *neck. Then all three exit.*) And what about Sukoshi, and her Small Crimson Parasol? (SUKOSHI *crosses to* MOTHER *at right, twirling her open parasol over her shoulder.*) Sukoshi was a sadder but wiser child.

CHORUS: Sadder, but wiser.

STORYTELLER: Never again did she go deep into the forest.

CHORUS: Never again.

STORYTELLER: Never again did she chase the butterflies.

CHORUS: Never again.

STORYTELLER: Nor did she pick up the cool stones of the field.

CHORUS: Oh, no.

STORYTELLER: And I assure you, now she knows the difference between a tiger and a zebra.

CHORUS: She knows! (SUKOSHI *and* MOTHER *kneel, and raise the teacups to their lips.*)

STORYTELLER: Small Crimson Parasol went home to her Honorable Mother. And there she lives, to this very day, happily sipping tea.

CHORUS:
In the cottage on the meadow,
In the valley below the mountain,
Below the mountain, capped with snow,
On the island of Kyushu, in Japan,
(YIN and YAN *enter, holding the large gold discs.*)

STORYTELLER:
Many, many suns ago.
(*He bows.*)

CHORUS (*Bowing low*):
Many, many suns ago.
(YIN and YAN *hold up discs and slowly revolve them counterclockwise, as the curtains close.*)

THE END

Peter, Peter, Peter!

Characters

PETER PARMENTER	SKINNY
JOEY	THE BRAIN, *a girl*
MACK	PETER PRIME
MRS. PARMENTER	PETER THE SECOND
MISS OOLONG	PETER THE THIRD
MADAME PLUNK	MR. WHISTLE

SCENE 1

TIME: *Afternoon.*

SETTING: *A street. The scene may be played before the curtain.*

AT RISE: PETER PARMENTER *enters left, whistling. He stops at center.*

PETER (*Looking at wrist watch*): Three-thirty-five. Hm-m-m. Now what did I have planned? Let's see. At five o'clock I'm supposed to help Mother put up screens. But right after school I was supposed to do something, too. Now what was it? And who was it with? (JOEY *enters right, carrying baseball bat, as* MACK, *with knapsack on his back, enters left.*)

JOEY: Hey, Peter, go get your ball and bat. We're playing over at the empty lot.

PETER: Hi, Joey. Say—did I promise you I'd play ball today?

JOEY: Sure you did. Just after lunch you said, "Hot dog! A ball game. I'd rather play ball than swim in a pool full of ginger ale!"

PETER: I did? Hm-m-m.

MACK (*Tapping* PETER *on the shoulder*): Wait a minute, Peter—

PETER: Oh, hello, Mack. What's the matter?

MACK: Don't you remember? Right after lunch you said you'd explore the back woods with me.

PETER: I did?

MACK: Aw, come on, Peter. You said exploring is the most fun in the world. You said you'd rather explore the back woods with me than eat a pumpkin pie ten feet wide.

JOEY: Listen, Mack. He said he'd play ball. Come on, let's go, Peter. (*He pulls* PETER *by the right hand as* MACK *gets hold of his left and tugs.*)

MACK: Oh, no! Daniel Boone and I are going exploring.

PETER: Hey! Ouch! Stop, you guys. (*To audience*) Now what? I want to go both places.

JOEY: You know something, Peter? There's something fishy about the way you always promise to do things and then wiggle out.

PETER: I'm sorry, Joey. I get so busy sometimes—hey!—fishing! That's what I promised to do after school—go fishing with Skinny.

MACK: You mean you promised somebody else . . . ?

PETER: Yes. Before breakfast.

MACK: Well, if you promised Skinny before breakfast, I guess he comes first.

JOEY: Listen, Mack, it isn't much fun exploring by your-

self. Come on with me and play ball. We really need a
first baseman.

MACK: O.K., Joey. I might as well. So long, Peter. When
you catch up with yourself, let me know.

JOEY: Yes, Peter. Drop me a post card sometime when you
aren't too busy breaking appointments. Come on, Mack.
(*They exit right.*)

PETER (*Calling after them*): Don't be sore, Joey . . . !
Mack . . . ! I really do want to play ball. I really do
want to go exploring. (*Stands center, bewildered*) And
doggone it, I really want to go fishing, too! (MISS OO-
LONG *enters left, primly.*)

MISS OOLONG: Peter! Peter Parmenter! How would you
like to earn a shiny half dollar?

PETER: Boy! Half a dollar? Sure, Miss Oolong. What do I
have to do?

MISS OOLONG: I want you to cut my lawn for me. My
garden club is arriving at six this evening, so I want
you to come at four o'clock promptly.

PETER (*To himself*): Four o'clock. Gee. That means less
than half an hour of fishing with Skinny. I can't even
catch a sardine in half an hour. But I need that fifty
cents. Skinny will understand. (*To* MISS OOLONG) Sure,
Miss Oolong. I'll do it for you.

MISS OOLONG: Splendid. That's what I like about you, Peter Parmenter. You are so full of enthusiasm. Now, you
will trim the borders, dig out the crabgrass, rake up the
grass cuttings and put the mower back *exactly* where
you found it, won't you?

PETER: You can rely on me, Miss Oolong. I'll be there at
four on the dot.

MISS OOLONG: Grand! You know, there ought to be more
little boys like you, Peter Parmenter. (*She starts to exit
right as* MADAME PLUNK *enters left.*)

PETER: Yes, ma'am. I think there ought to be more little boys like me, too, Miss Oolong. (MISS OOLONG *exits*.)

MME. PLUNK (*Speaking with a French accent*): Yoo hoo, Pierre. Pierre, I have something important to tell you about ze violin lesson this afternoon.

PETER: Good afternoon, Madame Plunk.

MME. PLUNK: I have ze most exciting lesson for you zis afternoon. Maestro Scarlatti, ze famous cellist, is here from Italy for just today. He wishes to attend the lesson of my most talented pupil. Of course, that is *you*, Pierre.

PETER (*Modestly*): Well, thank you, Madame Plunk.

MME. PLUNK: Not only will he supervise ze lesson, but he will play a duet with you!

PETER: Yippee! A duet with Maestro Scarlatti. A chance like this comes about once in a lifetime.

MME. PLUNK: Sometimes never—

PETER: Boy! A duet with Maestro Scarlatti. I'd rather play the violin with him than see the entire World Series from the pitcher's mound of Yankee Stadium.

MME. PLUNK: One other thing, Pierre. Maestro Scarlatti can only arrange to be at my house at four o'clock. Therefore I must insist that you arrive at my front door on ze dot of four o'clock.

PETER: I'll be there. On the dot. I wouldn't miss this chance for anything.

MME. PLUNK: Very good. I shall see you very soon. (*She exits right. MR. WHISTLE enters left.*)

MR. WHISTLE: Say, Peter. I will be seeing you at four o'clock today, won't I?

PETER: Mr. Whistle! Hi, there. I didn't know there was a Scout meeting today.

MR. WHISTLE: There isn't. Don't you remember? You promised me last night that you would come over and nail shingles on the new clubhouse.

PETER: That's right, sir, I did. I remember. I promised.

And I want to, sir. Truly, I do. B-but couldn't I come
over at five o'clock? Or after supper?

MR. WHISTLE: Look, Peter, we have to have this clubhouse
finished by five. We're dedicating it at five-thirty. And
I'm short-handed as it is. Please be there at four. I'm
counting on you. (*He exits.*)

PETER (*To audience*): How did it happen? All I ever said
was—"Sure I'd love to"—and now I'm really in a jam.
(*He starts right.*) I'd better get over to Miss Oolong's
place and start that grass. (*Changes his mind and starts
left*) No, I'll go over to Mr. Whistle and explain about
Madame Plunk. (*He changes his mind again and starts
right, bumping into* SKINNY *who is entering right, with
two fishing rods on his shoulder.*) No, on third thought,
Mr. Whistle will be so angry that I think I'll go to
Madame Plunk and explain about Mr. Whistle. Oops!
Skinny! Oh, gee, Skinny. I forgot all about you.

SKINNY (*Sighing resignedly*): That's the story of my life.
Pete, you are always forgetting about me. O.K., Peter.
Who did you promise what to?

PETER: Honestly, Skinny, I *am* sorry. I'm just about ready
to jump out of my skin, I'm so busy. Things piled up
like a snowball going down the steep side of Everest
today. Wait a sec—you can help me.

SKINNY: Aw, no, Pete. I want to go fishing. The catfish are
jumping in the fishermen's laps down at the creek today.

PETER: Please, Skinny. I'm desperate. Listen—would you
like to earn fifty cents mowing a lawn for Miss Oolong?

SKINNY: Oh, no. Not Miss Oolong. She's too particular.

PETER: Then, would you consider going over to Mr.
Whistle's place and helping him put up shingles?

SKINNY: I've already helped him saw the wood, sandpaper,
and paint the clubhouse. He said I was helpful enough
for six Scouts today, and he wanted to see the rest of the
pack help out.

PETER: What am I going to *do?* I'm due in three places at four o'clock—

SKINNY (*Grimly*): Four places. You forgot fishing with me. Listen, Pete. I think I know somebody who can help you with your problem.

PETER: Who? How?

SKINNY: I'm not sure, exactly, but this person has a fantastic brain. This person has more ideas in thirty seconds than most people have in thirty years. Do you want to give it a try?

PETER: Sure. What do I have to lose?

SKINNY: O.K. Follow me. About face! (*As they start off left,* PETER *takes a fishing rod from* SKINNY. *They shoulder the rods like rifles.*)

PETER: Hup-two-three-four.

SKINNY: Hup-two-three-four.

PETER (*In a singsong*): I'm all mixed up, there is no doubt—

SKINNY (*In a singsong*): I'll see that you get straightened out—

PETER: Count off—

SKINNY: One, two. Count off—

PETER: One, two.

BOTH: One, two, three, four. . . . Mixed up! No more! (*They exit as curtains close.*)

*   *   *

SCENE 2

SETTING: *The home of The Brain. Up center is a machine, labeled "Super-Duper-Duplicator." Folding screens stand at either side of it.*

AT RISE: THE BRAIN, *hidden behind an enormous book titled "Atomic Physics Made Difficult," is seated in chair down right.* SKINNY, *who now has a baseball with him, and* PETER *enter. They both carry fishing rods. They stand as if in front of a door.*

SKINNY: This is the place. (*He pantomimes knocking on door.* BRAIN *rises, keeping book in front of face, and pantomimes opening door.*) Hi there, Brain. This is Peter Parmenter. We need your help.

BRAIN (*Lowering book, revealing her long pigtails and horn-rimmed glasses, which have slid down on her nose*): Oh, it's you, Skinny. How can I assist you?

PETER: Hey, it's a girl! I thought you said this person was "a brain."

BRAIN: Humph! Apparently you do not believe that a person can be a girl and have a brain, too. Please enter and allow me to demonstrate my remarkable mind. (PETER *hangs back.*)

SKINNY: Come on, Pete. It's all right. This is Jane Jackson, better known as "Jane the Brain." Just tell her what your problem is and watch her fizz. She's better than UNIVAC. Aren't you, Jane?

BRAIN: Indubitably.

PETER: Well, it seems sort of odd—but I'm desperate, and I'll try anything. You see—er—Brain—er—Jane, for about a year now I've been so busy I haven't had time to catch my breath. Every day it's the same rat race. If I'm not helping the teacher clean the blackboards, I'm running errands for the grocer, or fixing the neighbor boy's tricycle. If I'm not practicing the violin, I'm giving concerts, going to my Scout meetings, or delivering papers.

BRAIN: And you think there ought to be two of you.

PETER: You took the words right out of my mouth.

BRAIN: Elementary, my dear Peter. In fact, you sound busy enough to be quadruplets. Would that suit you?

PETER: Who, me? Quadruplets? Impossible.

BRAIN: Never say "impossible" to Jane the Brain. As the famous scientist Alberta Einstein once said, "What woman can imagine, woman can do." Come with me. (*She takes them to Duplicator.*)

PETER: What is that?

BRAIN: Let me demonstrate this entirely original mechanism: the Super-Duper-Duplicator. Has either one of you gentlemen a spheroid?

PETER: A what-oid?

SKINNY: She means a *ball.* I have one. Here. (*He tosses baseball to* BRAIN, *who holds it up.*)

BRAIN: Very good. Now, notice. I am going to place *one* ball in the hopper of the Duplicator. Then I shall set the dial for an integer of three. (*She does this.*) Then I shall crank the proto-separator. (*She cranks. A gong rings four times, and four balls bounce out of the machine.*) Now look. Here are three exact triplicates plus the original ball.

SKINNY: Fantastic!

PETER: Unbelievable!

BRAIN: Actually, this is a rather simple feat. As the great inventor Thomasina Edison once said: "The simple appears difficult, but the difficult does not always appear simple." Now, Peter, will you kindly step in the machine here?

PETER: Who, me? Hey, wait, I want to think this over.

BRAIN (*Pushing him behind screen*): Take a deep breath. It doesn't hurt a bit. (*She sets the dial, and four loud gongs are heard.*)

PETER (*From behind screen; giggling*): Hey—that tickles!

BRAIN (*Pulling down on crank*): Now we shall see. (PETER PRIME, PETER THE SECOND, *and* PETER THE THIRD *march out from behind screen, original* PETER *behind them.*)

SKINNY: Wow! She did it!

PETER: Hey—who are these guys?

THREE PETERS: We are Peter Parmenter.

BRAIN: These are your triplicates, Peter. I split your atoms very neatly if I do say so myself!

PETER PRIME (*Removing cap*): Pleased to meet you, Peter. I'm Peter Prime—the Scout Peter. I'm in charge of cookouts, badge work, good deeds, sports, birdwatching and anything in the outdoor line.

PETER THE SECOND (*Removing beret*): Delighted to make your acquaintance, old sport. I am Peter the Second— the artistic Peter. I practice for you, give concerts, sing in the choir, do beadwork, basket weaving, paint pictures and recite the whole of *Hiawatha* for the PTA.

PETER THE THIRD: Hi. I'm Peter the Third. I'm the handy Peter. My job is to run errands, fix bicycles, mow lawns, paint dog houses and put up screens.

PETER: This is great! Come on, Skinny, let's go fishing.

SKINNY: All right. Tell the fellows where to report, and we'll take off.

PETER: Listen—er—Peter—er, all of you.

THREE PETERS (*Saluting*): Yes, sir.

PETER: I want you to go to my Scoutmaster and help him. Then you go to my violin teacher's for my music lesson. After that, straight home to help my mother, and then to Miss Oolong's house.

THREE PETERS: Very good, sir. (*They salute again and march off right.*)

PETER: Say, thanks a lot, Jane. What do I owe you for all that work? I have only two comic books and a couple of trading cards. You can have them.

JANE: Please, no remuneration. I'm always delighted to assist. As that famous scientist, Lady Ida Newton said, just before she discovered gravity, "There's no friend like a genius!"

SKINNY: Come on, Pete. Let's go. Let's get a spot on the

creek before it's all fished out. (*They shoulder the rods
and exit whistling, as the curtains close.*)

*   *   *

SCENE 3

BEFORE RISE: PETER *and* SKINNY *enter and seat themselves
on edge of one side of stage, feet and fishing lines dangling over edge.*

PETER: This is the life, huh, Skinny? A fishing rod, a pal,
and hours and hours of good old empty time.
SKINNY: I wonder how the three musketeers are doing over
on your street. (PETER *and* SKINNY *lean back, pull hats
over their faces and pretend to sleep. The curtains
open.*)

*   *   *

SETTING: *The street where Peter lives. There are three
homes, marked by signs. Down right is "Plunk Residence"; at center is "Parmenter"; and down left, "The
Whistles Live Here."*
AT RISE: MADAME PLUNK *is seated at music stand, holding
violin.* MRS. PARMENTER *is seated by telephone, and* MR.
WHISTLE *is working on shingles. They freeze in position
as the three* PETERS *enter right.* PETER THIRD *carries
handyman's pail.*)

PETER PRIME: You know, fellows, the original Peter didn't
tell us which house was which. Where do we go from
here?
PETER SECOND: Let's see. Plunk residence, here. Parmenter,
there . . .
PETER THIRD: Parmenter. That's our last name. I go there
first.

PETER SECOND: That's the Whistles' house over here. "Whistle" sounds more musical than Plunk. I'll try that house.

PETER PRIME: O.K. I'll go see Scoutmaster Plunk. (PETER PRIME *goes down right and knocks at Plunk door.* PETER SECOND *crosses left and waits in front of Whistle house as* PETER THIRD *goes up center to Parmenter house; they hold positions.*)

MME. PLUNK: Who is there, please? Oh, it is you, Pierre.

PETER PRIME (*Saluting*): Hullo, ma'am. Is Scoutmaster Plunk there?

MME. PLUNK: *Scoutmaster* Plunk! Oh, ho, ho! Pierre is making a funny joke. (*She takes him by the sleeve.*) Come in now, and have your violin lesson.

PETER PRIME: Oh, but, ma'am, you have the wrong Peter. (*She thrusts a violin in his hands.*)

MME. PLUNK: Now, let me hear your pretty, pretty scales—

PETER PRIME: But, ma'am! I can light a fire with two sticks; I can follow a trail of bent twigs, and I can hike ten miles in my bare feet. But I can't play a violin.

MME. PLUNK: What? You cannot play a violin? When I have personally spent three years teaching you? Well! Madame Plunk will call your mama this instant. (*She picks up telephone as* PETER PRIME, *perplexed, holds violin. They hold pose as* PETER SECOND *knocks on Whistle door.* MR. WHISTLE *answers the door.*)

MR. WHISTLE: Hi, Peter. Just in time. How about doing your favorite job—hammering nails in these shingles.

PETER SECOND (*Going to table with* MR. WHISTLE): Hammer nails? With my hands?

MR. WHISTLE: Well, you don't usually hammer them with your nose!

PETER SECOND: You don't understand. I might spoil my touch. I'm surprised that a violin teacher would even suggest such a thing. Now, may I have my music, please?

MR. WHISTLE: Music? Music? What's the matter, Peter? Aren't you feeling well? You look a little pale. Open your mouth and say "ah."

PETER SECOND: Oh, a singing lesson today. (*He takes a deep breath and sings "ah" up the scale loudly.*)

MR. WHISTLE: Good grief. The heat has been too much for you. I'm going to notify your mother that you are not well. (*Shaking head*) Not well at all. (*He picks up telephone as* PETER THIRD *walks into Parmenter house. Telephone rings at Parmenters'.*)

MRS. PARMENTER (*On telephone, not noticing* PETER THIRD): Hello? Madame Plunk? Isn't Peter there yet? Oh, he is. What? He won't play the violin? He says what? He'll catch a woodchuck for you? Oh, dear. That doesn't sound like my reliable Peter at all! Just tell him to come home this instant. I'll—I'll *speak* to him. I'm sorry he has been impertinent, Madame Plunk. (*She hangs up with a bang. The phone rings immediately.* MME. PLUNK *hangs up phone and exits.*) Hello? Oh, Mr. Whistle. Peter? Peter is at your house? But—but, he must have run all the way from Madame Plunk's. *You* are having trouble with Peter? You think he may be sick? He won't hammer nails? But he loves to hammer nails. Oh, dear, he must be sick. Please send him right home. I'll *speak* to him. Thank you, Mr. Whistle. (*She hangs up phone and shakes her head in bafflement as* MR. WHISTLE *hangs up phone and exits.*) Oh, Peter, Peter, Peter!

PETER THIRD (*Coming up to her*): Did you call me, Mother? (MRS. PARMENTER *twirls around and yelps in surprise.*)

MRS. PARMENTER: *Peter!* How—how—how—?

PETER THIRD: You sound like an Indian, Mother. I came right home to help you paint, scrub, weed, hoe, and put up the screens.

Mrs. Parmenter: You are volunteering to put up the screens? But you *hate* to put up the screens. Oh, dear! (*She puts a hand on his head.*) You must be sick. There must be an explanation for this.

Peter Third: Oh, you bet there's an explanation. It's a dilly! (*They hold pose, while* Skinny *and* Peter *rise and stretch, then pull up lines.*)

Skinny (*Sniffing*): I smell dinners cooking all along the street. Must be suppertime. We'd better get home, Pete.

Peter (*Sniffing*): Mm-m-m-m. Hamburgers. I'm as hungry as a wolf. See you later, Skinny. (Skinny *goes off right,* Peter *exits left and re-enters upstage where he stands unnoticed on the other side of his mother.* Peter Prime *and* Peter Second *cross to stand beside the original* Peter.)

Mrs. Parmenter: Well, young man. I am waiting for that explanation.

All Peters: You see, Mom, it's like this—

Mrs. Parmenter (*Doing a triple take*): Ah-h-h-h! I've had too much sun! Oh-h-h! I think I'm going to faint— (*She weaves toward* Peter Third, *who helps her to chair.*)

Peter Prime: Wait. Don't faint, Mom. I'm the Scout with the first aid. Quick, Peter, get some smelling salts. Peter Third, you fan her. (Peter Third *fans her vigorously with a newspaper, as* Peter *takes smelling salts from the table drawer.*)

Peter (*Handing smelling salts to* Peter Third): Here. I guess we were too much for her. She probably got to thinking about buying four pairs of sneakers every month, and she just keeled over.

Peter Second: I'll sing her a soothing lullaby. (*He sings at the top of his lungs*) Lullaby, and good night, good night, dear old Mother. . . . (*The other* Peters *hold their ears.*)

Peter: Hey, pipe down. You sound like the noon whistle.

Boy! What a mess this turned out to be. (SKINNY *and* BRAIN *enter and knock, and* PETER THIRD *opens the door.* BRAIN *carries reverse duplicator.*)

SKINNY: I brought Jane to look in on you, Peter, to see if you need any help.

PETER: Help! I'll say I need help. Everybody is furious with me. My mother fainted from shock, and you ask if I need help!

BRAIN: Aha! I perceive you have some difficulties here. However, I am prepared to lend you my marvelous mentality again. If you wish, I will put your four selves together again.

PETER: I can't go to your house. How can I leave Mother in this pickle?

BRAIN: I am always prepared for the unexpected. It just so happens that I have with me a portable reverse duplicator. Have you a screen?

PETER THIRD: I'll get it. (*He exits left, bringing back screen, which he sets up.*)

BRAIN: All right. Line up, gentlemen, and go in back of the screen one by one, while I set up a magnetic field. (*She points the duplicator at the screen as the boys go behind,* PETER *last of all.* PETER *takes the Scout cap, artist's flowing tie, and handyman's pail. The other* PETERS *exit backstage, unseen by audience. Three loud gongs are heard.*)

SKINNY: Pete! Are you all right?

BRAIN: You may emerge now, Peter the Only. (PETER *comes out, wearing the cap, flowing tie and holding pail.*)

PETER: Look at me, Skinny. I'm back in one piece. (MRS. PARMENTER *rubs her eyes, as if waking.*)

MRS. PARMENTER: Why, I must have fallen asleep. I had the most peculiar dream, Peter. I dreamed there were four of you. Now, isn't that just impossible?

PETER: It is now, Mom. Listen, Jane, thanks for the use of your brain. It really is fantastic. But I think I'm going to use my own noodle from now on. I have a way to stop my troubles—with a calendar and a clock.

BRAIN: What? You can solve your difficulties simply by using a calendar and a clock? *Im*possible. Er—practically impossible.

PETER: Watch! (*He takes a pencil and paper from pocket, and licks the pencil tip.*) Ladies and gentlemen, you are about to behold the one and only, the original Time Schedule made up by Peter Parmenter on the dot of five o'clock. (*Holding the paper up and demonstrating*) On the top line will be a complete listing of the day's activities. On the side lines, the time of each activity. If I follow this jim dandy document—I may, just *may* keep up with myself.

SKINNY: Say, Pete, you'll remember to leave time for fishing, won't you?

PETER: Of course, Skinny. I'd rather go fishing with you than eat a double dip chocolate cone—a mile high—

SKINNY: With two cherries and a walnut on top!

BRAIN: Well! I must admit that your solution is admirable, Peter. I couldn't have done better myself. As that great female playwright Wilhelmina Shakespeare once said: "All's Well That Ends Well." (*She and* PETER *shake hands as the curtain closes.*)

THE END

Anywhere and Everywhere

Characters

CHORUS, 7 *children*   CONDUCTOR
THREE CAVEBOYS   SKIPPER
HORSES   SAILORS
BICYCLE GROUP, 3 *children*   VOYAGERS
AUTOMOBILE GROUP, 5 *children*   THREE JET PILOTS
TRAIN GROUP, 5 *children*   ASTRONAUT

TIME: *The present.*
SETTING: *The stage is bare, except for chairs for Chorus. The backdrop is a scene of the earth and moon, with a rocket ready to blast off.*
AT RISE: CHORUS *is seated onstage. Each child has a sign.*

CHORUS:
  Where do people go, go, go?
  Where do people go?
1ST SOLO: Anywhere! (*Holds up sign reading "To North Pole"*)
2ND SOLO: Everywhere! (*Holds up sign reading "To South Pole"*)
3RD SOLO: Up! (*Holds up sign reading "To Mars"*)
4TH SOLO: And down! (*Sign, "To Center of the Earth"*)

27

5TH SOLO: All around! (*Sign, "Around the World in Eighty Days"*)

6TH SOLO: In and out! (*Sign, "To Rome and Points North"*)

7TH SOLO: 'Round about! (*Sign, "To the Equator"*)

CHORUS:
That's where people go, go, go.
That's where people go!

1ST SOLO:
How did people go, go, go,
How did people go,
In the world of long ago,
How did people go?

2ND SOLO:
When they had no big round wheels,
When they had no sails,
When they had no shining wings,
When they had no rails?

CHORUS:
Here's how people used to go, used to go, used to go
In the world of long ago,
Here's how people used to go.

3RD SOLO:
When they wished to move, or meet—

CHORUS:
People used their two good feet!

THREE CAVEBOYS (*Tiptoeing in*):
We are three brave caveboys—
We have no wheels,
So we walk on our toes
And our bare, brown heels.

1ST CAVEBOY:
Our feet go a-walking and a-stalking . . .

2ND CAVEBOY:
Our feet go a-gliding and a-striding . . .

3RD CAVEBOY:

Our feet go a-climbing over hills, up trees . . .

CAVEBOYS:

Our feet go a-hiking up plains, down leas.
Feet take us here! Feet take us there!
Feet walk, stalk, glide, slide everywhere. (CAVEBOYS *exit right.*)

CHORUS:

Feet walk, stalk, glide, slide everywhere.

1ST SOLO:

In the world of yesterday, yesterday, yesterday
When Grandpa wished to travel away,
How did Grandpa go, go, go,
How did Grandpa go?

CHORUS:

Grandpa got a horse, of course,
Grandpa got a horse!

2ND SOLO: A bronco.

3RD SOLO: A hunter.

4TH SOLO: A hack horse.

5TH SOLO: A runner.

6TH SOLO: A rider.

7TH SOLO: A pack horse.

CHORUS (*Softly*): Clip-clop, clip-clop, clip-clop . . .

HORSES (*Galloping in*):

Stepping high! Stepping high!
We gallop and fly; we gallop and fly,
Over the path and down the course,
Going far?

CHORUS: Get a horse!

(HORSES *step in rhythm as* CHORUS *chants faster and faster.*)

Clip-clop, clip-clop, clip-clop, clip-clop.
Clippety-clop, clippety-clop, clippety-clop, clippety-clop.

Clippety-cloppity, clippety-cloppity, clippety-cloppity,
clippety-cloppity—
Gallop and gallop and gallop away—
Gallop and gallop and gallop away!
(HORSES *gallop offstage.*)

1ST SOLO:
How do people go today, go today, go today,
In our world of work and play,
How do people go today?

CHORUS:
'Round and 'round and 'round again,
'Round and 'round and 'round they spin.
In trucks, and trolleys, and automobiles
People go on wheels, wheels, wheels!
(*Bicycle bell rings.* BICYCLE GROUP *of 3 children enters.
One child holds handlebars and others hold cardboard
wheels.* NOTE: *A real bicycle may be used if desired.*)

BICYCLE GROUP:
Two wheels, two wheels,
Red or white or blue wheels,
Rolling, roving new wheels,
Two wheels, two wheels!
(AUTOMOBILE GROUP *of 5 children enters. One child,
holding steering wheel and horn, is the driver; other
children carry cardboard wheels.*)

AUTOMOBILE GROUP:
Four wheels, four wheels,
Two and two more wheels,
Make way for more wheels.
Make way for automobiles!
(AUTOMOBILE GROUP *and* BICYCLE GROUP *exit in oppo-
site directions.*)

CHORUS:
Clickety-clack, clickety-clack, clickety-clickety-clickety-
clack—

Get your tickets to Maine and back.
Something's choo-chooing down the track,
Something long and strong and black.
(TRAIN GROUP *of 5 children enters. Children shuffle
along, each with his arms outstretched to the shoulders
of the child before. Leader is dressed as an engineer and
rings a hand bell. The last child is the* CONDUCTOR.)
TRAIN GROUP (*In rhythm*): Whoo whoo! Locomotive . . .
locomotive . . . Whoo whoo!
CHORUS (*Softly*): *Clickety-clack, clickety-clack, clickety-
clack, clickety-clickety-clack* . . .
TRAIN GROUP:

Chuffa, chuffa, choo-choo,
Can't wait! Can't wait!
Many, many passengers,
Much, much freight.
Hear the wheels of steel go 'round,
Listen to the whistle sound,
Busy! Busy! Outward bound.

CONDUCTOR: All aboard! Next stop—Maine! (*Leader rings
bell.*)
TRAIN GROUP (*Shuffling out*): Whoo whoo! Locomotive
. . . locomotive . . . Whoo whoo! (*They exit.*)
1ST SOLO:

Up the rivers, over the lakes, across the wide blue sea,
How do people go, go, go?
Please tell me!

CHORUS:

Up the rivers, over the lakes, across the wide blue sea,
People skim, and sail, and steam.
Ahoy! Helm alee!

(SKIPPER *enters with* SAILORS, *who carry a large cutout
of a ship.* VOYAGERS *follow them.* SKIPPER *blows whistle.*)
VOYAGERS: Ahoy! Helm alee!

SAILORS:

Heave ho! Heave ho!
Heave the mooring. Belay!
Jibber the kibber and anchor the skipper,
We're west . . . west away!

SKIPPER (*Blowing whistle*):

Give her more rudder, matey.
Steady now, as you go—
Flags are red,
Engines ahead,
Let the wild winds blow! Oho!

VOYAGERS:

Let the wild winds blow!
Bon voyage, oh, bon voyage!
Heave the mooring! Belay!
Jibber the kibber and anchor the skipper—
We're west . . . west away!

(SKIPPER *blows whistle again.* VOYAGERS *throw confetti around stage, wave and shout. Then they exit, followed by* SKIPPER *and* SAILORS.)

1ST SOLO:

Through the clouds, through the winds,
Through the sky so blue and high,
How do people go, go, go,
Through the sky so blue and high?

CHORUS:

Through the clouds, through the winds,
Through the sky so blue and high,
People streak and soar and roar
Through the sky so blue and high.

(1ST JET PILOT *enters, runs across stage with arms stretched wide, imitating an airplane.*)

1ST JET PILOT: Zoom! Zoom!

2ND JET PILOT (*Entering in same manner*): Zoom! Zoom!

3RD JET PILOT (*Entering in same manner, taking place in V formation with other* PILOTS): Zoom! Zoom! (PILOTS *circle stage as* CHORUS *chants.*)

CHORUS:
Taxi to the runway,
To the star and sun way,
Jets are going one way—
Up! Up! Up!

1ST PILOT (*As if speaking into microphone*):
Captain Alpha to Captain Beta:
North Pole is near.

2ND PILOT:
Captain Beta to Captain Gamma:
Do you read me loud and clear?

3RD PILOT:
Captain Gamma to Alpha and Beta:
Follow the strato-jet stream.

1ST PILOT: Roger . . .

2ND PILOT: And over . . .

PILOTS:
Each sky-sweeping rover
Is on the beam! (*They circle stage and exit.*)

1ST SOLO:
Beyond the clouds, beyond the wind,
Beyond the back of the sky, sky, sky—
How do people go, go, go
Beyond the back of the sky?
(ASTRONAUT *enters.*)

ASTRONAUT:
Beyond the clouds, beyond the wind,
Beyond the back of the sky, sky, sky.
The rockets fire
And lift me higher.
With a mighty surge
They strive and urge

To take me to the moon, moon, moon,
To take me to the moon. (*He runs off, and other characters re-enter right and left.*)
1st Solo: Ten seconds to lift-off!
Chorus: Ten . . . nine . . . eight . . . seven . . . six . . .
All: Five . . . four . . . three . . . two . . . one. (*Rocket on backdrop begins to rise slowly.*)
1st Solo: Blast off!
All (*Following rocket's rise*): Oooh!
2nd Solo (*Excitedly*):
 She's up! She's steady!
3rd Solo:
 Look at her glow!
4th Solo:
 Rockets ready!
5th Solo:
 All systems go!
6th Solo:
 She's in orbit! Retros, soon.
7th Solo:
 Hooray! She's landed on the moon!
All (*Waving arms*):
 Hooray! We've landed on the moon!
 That yellow old fellow, our neighbor the moon.
 (*They turn and face audience.*)
 And that's how people go, go, go.
1st Solo:
 And that's how people go.
All:
 Anywhere and everywhere,
 Up and down, all around,
 In and out and 'round about,
 That's how people go!
 (*Curtain*)

THE END

The Wonderful Circus of Words

Characters

JAMIE
GRAMMARIAN
FOUR PENNANT BEARERS
PERIOD

WORDS:

ARTICLE

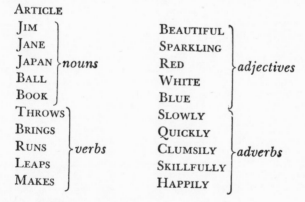

SETTING: *Jamie's living room.*

AT RISE: JAMIE *is sitting at the table, bent over a book of English grammar.*

JAMIE: Let's see. The teacher said to compose ten sentences. I'd better look up the definition of "sentence" in the grammar book. (*He flips pages of book.*) What a bore! (*Reads*) "A sentence is an association of words so ordered as to convey a completed idea." I wish I were outside playing baseball. (*Reads again*) "For example, 'The pencil is on the desk' is an example of a simple sentence." Boy! What a dull subject. Who cares about whether the pencil is on the desk, or the floor, or in the wastebasket. (JAMIE *waves his pencil, then grins as he imagines it is a bat. He holds it bat fashion.*) Batter up! (*He crumples a piece of paper into a ball.*) And the pitcher winds up for a super-special sizzle ball. (*Throws paper upstage*) And the ball streaks across the plate like a meteor . . . And it's a strrrike, ball fáns! A strike! (*As* JAMIE *does this,* GRAMMARIAN, *dressed as a ringmaster, enters and sits on table. As* JAMIE *recovers the paper ball upstage,* GRAMMARIAN *blows his whistle sharply.* JAMIE *turns, startled.*) Who are you?

GRAMMARIAN (*Bowing*): Flammarian Grammarian, Impresario of the English Language.

JAMIE: Where did you come from? I didn't see you a minute ago.

GRAMMARIAN: Oh, I've always been here. Every time you speak to someone or write a letter or read a book, I'm here. Now, Jamie, do I really look dull to you?

JAMIE: No, you don't, Mr. Grammarian. It's the grammar book. It's a lot of old mumbo-jumbo. But you look like a ringmaster.

GRAMMARIAN: That's just what I am. Grammar is the ringmaster, so to speak, of that wonderful three-ring circus, the English language. Once you glimpse the excitement of words, you will never again say that English is a dull subject.

JAMIE: I don't understand.

GRAMMARIAN: Let me demonstrate. (*He strides to center and blows his whistle, as the music of "Ta Ra Ra Boom*

De Ay" is heard. FOUR PENNANT BEARERS *march on, followed by the* WORDS. *Each* PENNANT BEARER *carries a pennant marked "Nouns," "Verbs," "Adjectives," or "Adverbs," and is followed by the* WORDS *in that category. Each* WORD *may wear a name card.* ARTICLE *follows the other* WORDS, *beating time with a small drum. The* WORDS *arrange themselves in four columns, face the audience, and mark time until the* GRAMMARIAN *finishes.*) Ladies and gentlemen, teachers and students! We are about to present the most stupendous, most colossal, most difficult-to-spell language in the entire world! You are about to behold complex sentences full of intricate infinitives, scintillating syntax and red-hot rhetoric. Feast your optics on the first ring as your ringmaster presents that death-defying trapeze act, the Dangling Participles. Hold your breath as the Volatile Verbs, strong men of the sentence, tumble tenses and juggle conjugations. In ring number two, see the Adjectives in bangles and spangles, each one a princess of the polysyllables, and the clowns, those merry mix-ups of modification. And finally, in ring number three, the trained adverbs, each one especially educated to modify his own verb, adverb or adjective. And last but not least the Nouns! Twenty thousand—you count them—twenty thousand exotic, extraordinary Nouns, from "aardvark" to "Zanzibar," brought to you at enormous expense all the way from Noah Webster's Dictionary. Hurry! Hurry! Hurry! The show is about to begin! (*He blows his whistle; the* WORDS *break ranks and mill about aimlessly.* JAMIE *pulls at* GRAMMARIAN's *sleeve.*)

JAMIE: Mr. Grammarian—your words! They are just wandering around. Shouldn't somebody take them in hand —organize them?

GRAMMARIAN: Certainly! That is my task. You see, Jamie, grammar makes sense out of nonsense; (*He blows whistle;* WORDS *begin to arrange themselves back into columns.*) order out of chaos; sentences out of higgledy-piggledy words. (WORDS *are in order again, marking time quietly.*) Attention, words! Prepare yourselves to make a sentence! (WORDS *stop marking time and stand still.*) All right, Jamie. Help yourself to a subject. You may have any of my nouns.

JAMIE: I hate to be so thickheaded, Mr. Grammarian, but I don't know what a noun is. (*At this, the* NOUNS *march forward and range themselves horizontally along the stage as they speak in unison.*)

NOUNS:
A noun is a name
That means the same
As a person, a thing, or a place.

JIM: A noun can be—

JANE: The sky or the sea—

JAPAN: Yokohama— (*She bows.*)

BALL: Mickey Mantle.

BOOK (*Pointing to nose*): Or the nose on your face.

JAMIE: If I choose one of these nouns, will it be the subject of the sentence? What the sentence will be about?

GRAMMARIAN: That is correct.

JAMIE (*Inspecting the* NOUNS): I choose . . . Jim. He looks a little bit like me. I think I could make up a good story about him. (JIM *stands at attention, as the other* NOUNS *go back behind their* PENNANT BEARER, *in column form again.*)

JIM (*Stiffly, in robot fashion*): My name is Jim. I am a Proper Noun.

JAMIE: He's just standing there, Mr. Grammarian. He isn't doing anything.

GRAMMARIAN: You need a bit of action for your friend Jim. Why don't you try adding a verb? (*He whistles.*

The VERBS *line up across the stage. As* JAMIE *inspects them, they pantomime their appropriate actions.*)

JAMIE (*Pointing, as* THROWS, *dressed as discus thrower, throws*): He's throwing. (*As* RUNS, *in shorts and shirt, runs*) He's running. (*As* BRINGS, *dressed as weight lifter, brings dumbbells to him*) He's bringing. (*As* LEAPS, *dressed in Superman costume with cape, leaps*) He's leaping. (*As* MAKES, *dressed as carpenter, pretends to hammer a nail*) He's making something. Say, those verbs are hard workers, aren't they!

GRAMMARIAN: Indeed they are, Jamie. They make statements, give commands, ask questions, and behave like the muscles of the sentence. Watch Jim come alive when you choose a verb for him.

JAMIE: Let's see. . . . Baseball is my favorite sport, so I'll choose "throws." (THROWS *stands beside* JIM. *He pumps* JIM's *arm up and down in throwing motion.* JIM *smiles and winds up.*)

JIM (*Proudly*): Jim throws!

GRAMMARIAN: There! That is a genuine, twenty-four carat sentence.

JAMIE: That's a sentence? But there are only two words.

GRAMMARIAN: Very true, but those two words are all you need to express a complete thought.

JAMIE: But I don't know what Jim is throwing. It could be a rock, a bean bag, a pillow, or a ball.

GRAMMARIAN: What sort of word do you need?

JAMIE: A thing word . . . a . . . a . . .

NOUNS: You need a noun.

GRAMMARIAN: And a small article. (ARTICLE *and* BALL *come forward.* BALL *gives a tennis ball to* JIM, *and takes his place beside* ARTICLE *and* THROWS.)

JIM (*Winding up and throwing the ball offstage*): Jim throws the ball.

GRAMMARIAN: Are you satisfied with your sentence as it stands now?

JAMIE: Not quite. I don't know much about the ball. Maybe it's a big ball, like a basketball. Or a small one, like a ping-pong ball. Or a red and blue one, like a beach ball.

ADJECTIVES (*Stepping forward in line across stage*): You need an adjective. An adjective is a word that describes a noun. Listen to what we can do to Jim. Happy Jim. Sad Jim. Good Jim. Bad Jim. Fat Jim. Slim Jim. Bright Jim. Dim Jim.

JAMIE: Oh, is that what you are? I thought an adjective was something horrible.

ADJECTIVES: We can be horrible. Dreadful, deadly, doleful, desperate, demonic Jim!

JAMIE: Wow! Adjectives pack a lot of power. I'll use the adjective "white." (WHITE *takes her place in the sentence. She gives a white ball to* BALL, *who gives it to* JIM.)

JIM (*Throwing offstage*): Jim throws the white ball.

GRAMMARIAN: A fine, upstanding sentence. You may be proud of it.

JAMIE: Wait, Mr. Grammarian. I'm still not finished. It's that word "throws." The sentence doesn't tell *how* Jim is throwing the ball.

GRAMMARIAN: Is that important, Jamie?

JAMIE: Well, it certainly is. Say you are a pitcher—if you throw the ball slowly, the batter may hit a home run. If you throw clumsily, the umpire may call a ball. If you throw skillfully, you may strike the batter out. See?

GRAMMARIAN: I see. And I have just the words you need. The adverbs. (*He whistles. The* ADVERBS *take their places. Each one performs in pantomime as* JAMIE *inspects him.*)

JAMIE (*As* SLOWLY, *dressed as a turtle, crawls by*): That

must be "slowly." (*As* QUICKLY, *dressed as a rabbit, hops by*) That's "quickly." (*As* CLUMSILY, *dressed as a bear, lumbers along*) "Clumsily"—that's how he's walking. (SKILLFULLY, *dressed as a monkey, juggles balls deftly*) The monkey is juggling "skillfully." (*As* HAPPILY, *dressed as a canary, smiles and whistles sweetly*) The canary sounds as if it's whistling "happily." Well, I like Jim. I want him to play a good game of ball, so I'll choose "skillfully." (SKILLFULLY *takes his place after* BALL. WHITE *gives another ball to* BALL *who gives it to* JIM. JIM *gives an extra special wind-up and throws the ball offstage.*)

SKILLFULLY (*Holding up three fingers like an umpire*): Strike three!

WORDS (*In unison*): Hooray for Jim! Jim throws the white ball skillfully! Jim throws the white ball skillfully!

JAMIE (*Proudly*): There now! That's a sentence. My very first real sentence.

GRAMMARIAN (*Smiling*): Are you quite sure you have finished?

JIM: Jim—

THROWS: Throws—

ARTICLE: The—

WHITE: White—

BALL: Ball—

SKILLFULLY: Skillfully— (*They keep repeating the sentence, one word at a time. After they have repeated it several times,* JAMIE *tries to quiet them down and motions them to stop, but they keep on going.*)

JAMIE: Hey! The sentence is going on and on. I can't stop it!

GRAMMARIAN: Yes, you can. Think a moment. What stops a sentence?

JAMIE: Oh! A period!

PERIOD (*Bouncing out and doffing beanie*): Did someone call me?

JAMIE: Can you stop my sentence?

PERIOD: Young man, I may look small, but I've stopped more sentences than a Philadelphia lawyer. (*He sits down firmly at the end of the sentence. The sentence stops at "skillfully."*)

JAMIE: There!

GRAMMARIAN: There! Now, do you feel happier about learning English grammar, Jamie?

JAMIE: Sure I do. But I've only started my sentences about Jim. I could go on and write a paragraph—or a composition.

GRAMMARIAN: Just a minute, Jamie. Do you know what time it is?

JAMIE (*Looking at the clock*): Nine o'clock! Why, I've never spent more than ten minutes on grammar before.

GRAMMARIAN: I must pack up my circus of words. I have an urgent appointment at the White House this evening.

JAMIE: Boy! The White House! Do you know the President?

GRAMMARIAN: I've known them all, my boy. When Mr. Jefferson first sat down with quill pen and ink, I was at his right hand, guiding him as he wrote, "When in the course of human events—" We did rather well on that document, Mr. Jefferson and I, if I do say so myself. But, I'll be back. This was only a smattering. Wait until you meet the Conjunctions, Prepositions, Pronouns, and Punctuation Marks.

JAMIE: Conjunctions! Pronouns! Punctuation Marks!

GRAMMARIAN (*Whistles*): Attention! Now hear this, all you words. Prepare to embark for Washington. (*WORDS form columns, march in place.*)

NOUNS:
> Apples, animals, aspirin, ants!
> Peanuts, pineapples, pots and plants!
> Saturday, Sunday, Susan, Sam!
> Timbuktu and Amsterdam!
> We are nouns,
> Whose voices sing
> Of person, quality, place and thing.
> (*They march offstage.*)

VERBS:
> Dancing, prancing, jumping, bumping!
> Doing, wooing, howling, scowling!
> Reading, writing, weeding, fighting!
> Being, seeing, fleeing, freeing!
> Verbs command, and act, and ask—
> Verbs can tackle any task!
> (*They march offstage.*)

ADJECTIVES:
> Scarlet, silver, sapphire, gold!
> Toasty-warm, icy-cold!
> Sugar-sweet, fleecy-white!
> Dangerous, glamorous, dismal, bright!
> Adjectives, gaudy as tropical birds,
> Paint a picture with colorful words!
> (*They march offstage.*)

ADVERBS:
> Happily, sadly, snappily, madly!
> Afterwards, almost, rarely, badly!
> Also, always, sometimes, never!
> Forward, backward, seldom, ever!
> Adverbs answer: here? or there?
> How much, how many, when and where?
> (*They march offstage, followed by* ARTICLE, *who has been beating drum.*)

JAMIE (*At desk, writing*): "After Jim threw the white ball skillfully, Red Jones came up to bat. Red Jones was a good batter." No, I need something more interesting than that. I have it! "Red Jones was known far and near as the terror of the pitchers." That's better. "Jim wound up for the next pitch—"

GRAMMARIAN: Come on, Period. We'll have to leave Jim winding up for the next pitch. But we'll return one of these days and see if he's struck out Red Jones. (*He holds up a hoop which is decorated with tissue paper and a circus design in the center.* PERIOD *makes a running jump through the center of the hoop, doffs his beanie to the audience, and turns his back. On his back is written in bold letters, "The End." Curtain.*)

THE END

The Big Shoo

Characters

TOM TUTTLE
ANNIE LAURIE MACKENZIE
LITTLE DAN'L SMITH
BIG DAN'L SMITH, *his uncle*
PHINEAS PHLUSTER, *the Master of Ceremonies*
TATTERSALL, *a scarecrow*
SAMSON, *the Scarecrobot*
PROFESSOR PEPPER, *an inventor*
JABEZ JONES, *a hired hand*
RAUCOUS ⎫
CROAK ⎪
SHRIEKER ⎬ *crows*
CAW-CAW ⎪
RASP ⎭
FARM FOLK

TIME: *Early evening in fall.*
SETTING: *A recently harvested cornfield.*
AT RISE: TOM TUTTLE *stands at center, with his back to the audience, looking up at banner across backdrop, which proclaims: "Harvest Festival Tonight! Come One. Come All."*

45

TOM: A Harvest Festival! Oh, boy. (*He looks right, shading his eyes, and calls loudly.*) Dan'l. Little Dan'l. Come on over and see what I see.

LITTLE DAN'L (*Offstage right*): Where are you, Tom?

TOM: In Phineas Phluster's back cornfield. Come on. Hurry! (*As* LITTLE DAN'L *enters right,* ANNIE LAURIE *enters left, turns a somersault and lands behind* TOM, *who turns quickly and catches her foot.*) I have you!

ANNIE LAURIE: You let me go, Tom Tuttle!

TOM (*Sheepishly*): For land's sakes. It's only Annie Laurie MacKenzie. Shucks, I thought you were at least a six-banded raccoon running across the field.

ANNIE LAURIE (*Brushing herself off*): I was just practicing my over-under flipperino. You ought to get your eyes examined, Tom. Anybody who can't tell a girl from a raccoon is in sad shape. (*Noticing* LITTLE DAN'L) Hello, Little Dan'l.

LITTLE DAN'L: Hi, Annie Laurie. What's up, Tom?

TOM: Just look at this sign, Dan'l. The field is all fixed up for something special tonight.

LITTLE DAN'L: Sure. Haven't you heard about the Harvest Festival? My uncle, Big Dan'l, hasn't talked about anything else for weeks.

ANNIE LAURIE: I've known about the Harvest Festival since August. Why, there's going to be square dancing—

LITTLE DAN'L (*Sadly, to* ANNIE LAURIE): Only if we find a caller in time. (*To* TOM) But even if we can't square dance, there'll be other things to do—races, and pie-eating contests, and corn-shucking, and a greased pole—

ANNIE LAURIE: And a beauty contest.

LITTLE DAN'L *and* TOM: Boo!

ANNIE LAURIE: And Phineas Phluster says there's going to be a mystery contest. He says there's going to be a Great Big Shoo.

Tom: What kind of a shoe? A horseshoe?

LITTLE DAN'L: Maybe he meant a "chew." You know, a bubble gum chewing and blowing contest.

ANNIE LAURIE: He didn't tell me, but he was very mysterious. He wouldn't say another word. He just winked his eye and said I'd see—all in good time. (BIG DAN'L *enters with* TATTERSALL. TATTERSALL *flops about and weeps noisily.*)

TATTERSALL: I can't. I positively cannot. I absolutely cannot. N-O-T. Can't!

BIG DAN'L: Now, now, Tattersall. Don't carry on so. (*Holding* TATTERSALL *up*) Of course you can do it. You'll be fine. Hello there, children.

Tom *and* ANNIE LAURIE: Hello, Mr. Smith.

LITTLE DAN'L: Hi, Uncle Dan'l. What are you doing with the scarecrow?

ANNIE LAURIE: Did you bring him to decorate the field for the dance? I love dancing. (*She does a few square dance steps.*)

Tom: Why is Tattersall crying, Mr. Smith?

BIG DAN'L: All in good time, children. All in good time. Now, Little Dan'l, suppose you help me set Tattersall up properly in the field. (LITTLE DAN'L *takes other side of* TATTERSALL *and helps put him on frame at right.*) Tom, you put his arms on the sticks there, and, Annie Laurie, you fix his hat at a nice sporty angle. (*The children help with* TATTERSALL, *who is quiet for a moment. As they step back to admire him, he bursts into tears again.* ANNIE LAURIE *dries his tears and then steps aside.*)

ANNIE LAURIE: Sakes alive, he's worse than a leaky barrel in a rainstorm.

BIG DAN'L: He doesn't think he can do what I *know* he can do.

LITTLE DAN'L: What do you know he can do, Uncle Dan'l?

BIG DAN'L: If I were to tell you that, you'd know, too, wouldn't you? There are some things in this world that you have to find out by yourselves.

TOM: That sounds awfully mysterious, Mr. Smith. How do we find out?

ANNIE LAURIE: And when?

BIG DAN'L: Well, now. It's after sunset. It's about time folks began coming to the Harvest Festival. You children go along and find Phineas Phluster. Tell him the Harvest Moon is round and ready. He'll understand.

TOM: I can't stand much more of this mystery. Come on, gang. (*Children exit left.* TATTERSALL *breaks into fresh tears.*)

TATTERSALL: Big Dan'l, old friend, don't make me enter this terrible contest.

BIG DAN'L: Here now, Tattersall, I'm surprised at you. For thirty years you've been my prize scarecrow. Every fall you flap in the wind and chase those pesky crows plumb to the ocean. I never thought you'd be afraid of the rascals.

TATTERSALL (*Puffing out his chest*): Afraid of the crows? Of course I'm not. It's that Professor Pepper. He invents such weird things. Now he's invented some kind of atomic scarecrow that'll be twice as good as I am. You'll see. I won't stand a chance! (*He sags on his frame and begins to cry again.*)

BIG DAN'L: Professor Pepper is a pretty smart fellow, that's for sure. But I don't think even an atomic scarecrow could stand up to you. (*He busies himself arranging* TATTERSALL's *straw and clothes. The children enter left, followed by* PHINEAS PHLUSTER *and* JABEZ JONES, *who carries a sheet, a bag of grain, and an easel with a sign reading: "Tonight Only! The Great Big Shoo!" While* PHINEAS *directs* JABEZ *in setting up the sign down left, the* FARM FOLK *enter in twos and threes and seat themselves on benches left. The children cross right to* BIG DAN'L.)

LITTLE DAN'L: Phineas is here, Uncle Dan'l.

TOM: Everybody else is here, too.

PHINEAS (*Joining* BIG DAN'L *and children*): Howdy, Big Dan'l.

BIG DAN'L: Evening, Phineas. Fine night for the Festival.

ANNIE LAURIE: Oh, tell us! Please tell us what this is all about!

BIG DAN'L: Well, children, you take your seats (*Indicates bench right*), and then suppose we let Phineas Phluster do the talking. He's Master of Ceremonies—or should I say, "Master of Scaremonies."

PHINEAS: Thank you, Big Dan'l. I always appreciate an opportunity to exercise my tonsils. Say—is Professor Pepper here yet?

JABEZ: I saw him coming along by the creek a minute ago. He had something big and white with him. Looked like a ghost.

TATTERSALL: Oh, I knew it! He's bringing along a Spook-crow!

BIG DAN'L: That's enough from you, Tattersall.

PHINEAS: All righty, folks. Since Professor Pepper is expected shortly, we'll commence the proceedings. (*He goes up center.*) Ladies and gentlemen, boys and girls.

TATTERSALL: And scarecrows.

PHINEAS: And scarecrows. Welcome to the Harvest Festival. (*All applaud.*) I reckon you're wondering what we're up to. Well, sir, we have a real ding-dong surprise to-night. Last week, Professor Pepper told me and Big Dan'l here that he'd invented the most modern and efficient scarecrow to be found anywhere in the world. Well, we couldn't let that pass, could we? We told Professor Pepper that *we* had the best scarecrow in the world. That's our Tattersall there. (*More applause as he points to* TATTERSALL.)

TATTERSALL: I wish I were back in my own cornfield.

PHINEAS: And so we decided to hold a Championship Contest. Yes, siree. Right in this very field we are going to hold the Great Big Shoo!

ANNIE LAURIE: Oh, it's a *crow* shoo.

PHINEAS: That's correct, little lady. Two champion scarecrows are going to battle it out for the honor of being Grand Scarecrow of the entire county.

TOM: Mr. Phluster, here comes Professor Pepper. (*Points offstage right*)

ANNIE LAURIE (*Looking off right*): He's bringing something big and scary looking.

LITTLE DAN'L: It's all covered with a white sheet.

PHINEAS: Good. That must be our second contestant. (PROFESSOR PEPPER *enters down right, pushing a sheet-covered robot in front of him.*)

PROFESSOR: Out of the way, please. Out of the way. (*He puts the robot on the platform.*) Good evening, one and all. Am I late?

PHINEAS: Evening, Professor Pepper. No, sir, you are right on the button.

TATTERSALL: The panic button!

PHINEAS: I just finished explaining about the contest, and introducing Tattersall, our native son.

PROFESSOR: Oh, yes, the old-style scarecrow.

TATTERSALL: Old-style!

PROFESSOR: Hah! Wait until you see my Scarecrobot. He's a stainless steel, transistorized model, and he has three thousand printed circuits. Why, he'll put those handmade ragtags out of business.

TATTERSALL: Boo-hoo. I don't even have one printed circuit.

BIG DAN'L: There, there, old fellow. You have a good heart. That's all I care about. Here, I'll have to cover you with a sheet for the time being. (*He drapes a sheet over* TATTERSALL.)

PHINEAS: All righty, folks. We're ready to start the show. Now when I wave this red bandanna, some folks with bells out in the fields yonder will shoo the crows down here. Jabez will scatter grain in front of Tattersall, and he'll time the scarecrow with his stop watch. Then, we'll do the same thing for Professor Pepper's Scarecrobot. The scarecrow who shoos the crows quickest will be the winner. Ready? (*He waves red bandanna; bells ring off- stage and the crows caw and flap up the center aisle.* JABEZ *sprinkles grain in front of* TATTERSALL. *As soon as the crows arrive on stage,* JABEZ *holds his watch up to the light and clicks it.*)

BIG DAN'L: Go, Tattersall, go! (*He whisks the sheet off the scarecrow.*)

ALL (*Ad lib*): Come on, Tattersall! Try! Scare them! (*Etc.*)

TATTERSALL (*Sniffing timidly*): Er . . . er . . . shoo. (*The crows peck at the grain, paying no attention.*)

BIG DAN'L: Please, Tattersall. For the honor of old-fash- ioned scarecrows!

TATTERSALL (*Swelling proudly, then flapping hands wildly and shouting*): Shoo! Get out! Go away! (*The crows squawk and flap their wings, flying off single file across stage, exiting right.* FARM FOLK *and children applaud and cheer.*)

PHINEAS: Jabez Jones will now give us the official time clocked by Tattersall.

JABEZ (*Consulting watch*): That was exactly thirty seconds.

PHINEAS: Splendid. Thirty seconds, ladies and gentlemen. Thirty seconds for Tattersall. Now, Professor, it is your contestant's turn. (JABEZ *scatters grain in front of* PRO- FESSOR PEPPER's *robot, then stands down right, holding watch. Bells ring off right; the crows enter, cawing as before, and stoop to peck corn.*)

PROFESSOR: Behold! Samson the Scarecrobot! (*He whisks the sheet off the robot, who raises his arms slowly, shaking his hands above his head like a prizefighter.*)

ALL (*Awed*): Oh!

PROFESSOR: Now, Samson. Smite them! (SAMSON *advances slowly toward crows. He raises and lowers his arms stiffly, growling loudly. Lights may flash on and off, and a thunder sheet may be sounded offstage. The crows give one horrified caw, and rush off right.*)

JABEZ: Well, I never! That was barely a second. One second! It's fantastic. (FARM FOLK *talk excitedly among themselves.*)

PHINEAS (*Holding up his hand for silence*): One second. (*He takes* SAMSON's *hand and holds it high.*) Ladies and gentlemen, the new world champion. (*Applause*)

TATTERSALL: Boo-hoo. I knew it. I'm outmoded, that's what. A has-been. A relic. (*To* BIG DAN'L) Go ahead. Put me up in the attic with the rest of the junk.

BIG DAN'L: Never! You'll always be my scarecrow. (*The crows, headed by* RAUCOUS, *enter right.*)

TOM: Look. The crows are back.

PHINEAS: Well, upon my soul. It looks like a delegation.

RAUCOUS: We *are* a delegation. I'm the spokescrow. Raucous is the name.

CROAK: Croak—

SHRIEKER: Shrieker—

CAW-CAW: Caw-Caw—

RASP: And Rasp.

RAUCOUS: Listen here, folks. A joke is a joke.

CROAK: But enough is enough.

RAUCOUS: We crows think we have a right to say who'll frighten us, and who won't.

CROAK: We don't want that hunk of tin (*Points to* SAM-SON) in our fields.

TATTERSALL: In *your* fields!

SHRIEKER: He gives us "corndigestion."

CAW-CAW: He's caw-ful, just caw-ful.

RASP: Tattersall here has been our favorite scarecrow for thirty years.

CROAK: He does a topnotch job of scaring us.

SHRIEKER: We wouldn't know it was harvest time without him.

CAW-CAW: We like to buzz him now and again when we fly over him.

CROWS (*Chanting in unison*): We want Tattersall! We want Tattersall!

TATTERSALL: Listen, everybody. Did you hear that? They like me! They want me! (*He takes off his hat and makes a sweeping bow to the crows.*) My public!

ALL (*Ad lib*): Hurray! Bravo! (*Etc.*)

BIG DAN'L: It appears as if a lot of folks want you, Tattersall. (SAMSON *slowly bends his head and drops nuts and bolts on the floor, as he makes a hollow sobbing noise.*)

LITTLE DAN'L: Look, everybody. The Scarecrobot is falling apart.

ANNIE LAURIE (*On her hands and knees*): And look at this. (*She holds up a bolt.*) There are nuts and bolts coming out of his eyes.

TOM: What's the matter with him, Professor Pepper?

PROFESSOR: Matter? Matter? Why, he's crying, of course. He cries nuts and bolts the same as you cry tears. He's had his first failure, and the crows hurt his feelings by calling him a hunk of tin.

LITTLE DAN'L: But I thought robots didn't have any feelings.

PROFESSOR: Oh, you did, did you? Well, let me tell you, Mr. Whippersnapper, I put the softest heart in the world in that Scarecrobot. It's one hundred per cent marshmallow.

ANNIE LAURIE: Oh, the poor thing. I feel so sorry for him. He's out of a job, isn't he?

TOM (*Snapping his fingers*): Wait a minute. Did you say he has three thousand circuits, Professor?

PROFESSOR: Yes, indeed. I devised 'em myself.

TOM (*Going to* PROFESSOR *and whispering in his ear, then aloud*): Do you think Samson can do it?

PROFESSOR: Of course he can.

TOM: And could he shout loud enough?

PROFESSOR: Why, that's kindergarten stuff for Samson.

TOM: That's great. What are we waiting for?

PHINEAS: Say, young feller, don't you think you ought to let us in on the plot?

TOM: Sure, Mr. Phluster. (*To* FARM FOLK) Folks, grab your partners for a square dance!

PHINEAS: Hold your horses, young'un. We don't have a caller yet.

TOM: You do now. Samson, do your stuff! (*Square dance music begins.* SAMSON *claps his hands and calls boomingly.*)

SAMSON:
Grab your spark plug for a do-si-do,
Grease your wheels, and away we go!
(*Square dance forms.* SAMSON *calls the dance.* TATTERSALL, *surrounded by the crows, claps. At the conclusion of the dance, the curtains close.*)

THE END

Spaceship Santa Maria

Characters

TELEVISION COMMENTATOR
SPACE COMMANDER SOLAR SMITH
COMPUTER TECHNICIAN
RADAR MAN
DR. VECTOR
DR. THEOREMBUS
DR. QUANTUS
DR. ALICIA ARCHIVISTA
PRESIDENT INUK
CAPTAIN STARDRIVER
ASTRO-NAVIGATOR MADGE ELLEN STARDRIVER
APPRENTICE SPACEMAN COSMO STARDRIVER
ASTRO-BIOLOGIST PHOEBE STARDRIVER
TWO UNITED NATIONS AIDES
LOUDSPEAKER VOICE

TIME: *Friday, August 3, 2492.*
SETTING: *A blockhouse at the New Palos Rocket Complex, Palos, Spain. Up center is a large television "screen," showing the sky and a cutout rocket in launch position.*
AT RISE: *The* TELEVISION COMMENTATOR *is down center, preparing for broadcast. Up right, the* RADAR MAN *is checking out his equipment, and up left, the* COMPUTER

TECHNICIAN *is threading tape reels.* COMMANDER SMITH
*is up center at a microphone. At the table at center are
seated* DR. QUANTUS *and* DR. ARCHIVISTA, *facing audience.* DR. THEOREMBUS *and* DR. VECTOR *sit at opposite
ends of the table, facing each other.*

COMMENTATOR: Good morning, ladies and gentlemen. The
World-Wide Network of Three Dimensional Television
brings you a special program this morning. Please adjust
your focus dial for three dimensions. This is the blockhouse of the New Palos Rocket Launching Center, on
the coast of Spain. What you are seeing now (*Indicating
television screen*) is the new spaceship, the Santa Maria
the Second, preparing to venture through the dark
reaches of interstellar space.

VOICE (*From loudspeaker*): T-minus ten minutes. Repeat.
Ten minutes to launch time.

COMMENTATOR: That was the latest advisory from the Central Control. In just ten minutes, Santa Maria the Second will lift off from earth at exactly the same hour and
day that the ancient mariner Christopher Columbus set
sail for the New World one thousand years ago, in 1492.
Let me introduce you to the Space Commander in
charge of operations here at New Palos. He will tell
you something about the astronaut who will pilot this
mighty ship. Commander Solar Smith.

COMMANDER SMITH: Thank you. After exhaustive tests of
many deep-space astropilots, we have chosen Captain
Stardriver to make this journey. Not only has Captain
Stardriver piloted atomic-drive ships between our galaxy and Andromeda, but he has a theory which may
benefit mankind tremendously.

COMMENTATOR: Are you at liberty to disclose this theory,
Commander?

COMMANDER SMITH: Certainly. It is no secret to us here

at the base that Captain Stardriver has long been at
work on a plan to find a shorter route to the Golden
Galaxy.

COMMENTATOR: The Golden Galaxy is of course the source
of many precious gems and very rare metals.

COMMANDER SMITH: Correct. Our galaxy is running low
on these precious commodities. If we do not find a new
supply, our whole space program will be in jeopardy.

COMMENTATOR: Thank you, Commander Smith. Now we
are going to turn our attention to this table over here.
(*He goes up center to the table.*) Here is a panel of experts from all fields of science to help explain some of
the details of the launch. Because of the many coinci-
dences between this liftoff and the sailing of Christopher
Columbus back in the dawn of exploration, we will hear
first from Dr. Alicia Archivista, a specialist in ancient
history at the University of Genoa. Dr. Archivista, what
strikes you as most important about this journey?

DR. ARCHIVISTA: I am most impressed with the extraordinary way in which history seems to be repeating itself.
Christopher Columbus set sail from this very town of
Palos, on the same date—the morning of August the
third. And he even had somewhat the same reason for
making his voyage—to find a shorter route to the Spice
Islands which supplied Europe with precious spices. I
shall follow this launch with the utmost interest!

COMMENTATOR: Thank you, Dr. Archivista. Our next expert comes to us from the field of mathematics. This is
Dr. Vector. Tell us, Dr. Vector, do you think this flight
to the end of the cosmos will end in success?

DR. VECTOR: Absolutely. I have seen Captain Stardriver's
equations. They are brilliant and sound.

DR. THEOREMBUS: Piffle!

DR. VECTOR: Ahem! Let me explain to the television audience. Captain Stardriver has been studying the shape

of the universe for many years. He believes that the universe curves upon itself, so that if he starts his voyage from earth, he can sail to the Golden Galaxy, and then by following the curve of the universe, he will come to earth again.

DR. THEOREMBUS: Piffle! Nonsense! The whole idea is an impractical daydream. I am Dr. Theorembus, the foremost cosmic geographer of this century. This notion of a curved universe is completely false. Take it from me. My equations have proved that the universe is shapeless and unbounded. Do you know what will happen to this Captain Stardriver if he dares to trifle with the universe? I will tell you. His ship will fall off the edge of space like a pea off a saucer. It will be swallowed up in nothingness.

DR. ARCHIVISTA (*Laughing*): There, you see? History does repeat itself. This sounds just like the arguments which raged among the learned professors in 1492. Was the world round or flat? It took a brave man to defy the experts and find out for himself—and for humanity.

VOICE (*From loudspeaker*): Attention! Announcing the arrival of the President of the United Nations and his aides at the main building. Announcing the arrival of Captain Stardriver and the crew of the Santa Maria the Second at the rocket gantry. It is now T-minus five minutes. Repeat, five minutes to launch time. (*All applaud and talk excitedly among themselves.*)

COMMENTATOR: Ladies and gentlemen, you just heard Central Control. The President of the United Nations is now coming to the blockhouse for a farewell speech. Captain Stardriver is ascending to the Command Module of the spaceship, and the excitement and tension of the launch grow more intense with each passing moment. Suppose we have a brief description of this remarkable vehicle from Commander Smith.

COMMANDER SMITH: The Santa Maria the Second is the largest, most well-equipped, and swiftest spaceship ever assembled on earth. All the nations of the world contributed over four million dollars each, through a special United Nations tax, to have her built.

DR. ARCHIVISTA: And poor Columbus had to beg and borrow for those three tiny wooden ships!

COMMANDER SMITH: There are certain operations of the spaceship which I am not able to discuss, so let me introduce our chief physicist and fuel expert, Dr. Quantus.

DR. QUANTUS: Thank you, Commander. For her brief trip through the solar system, the spaceship will use ordinary atomic fuel. However—and this will come to the world as a startling revelation—when the spaceship gets beyond the orbit of Pluto, the hull will unlock on one side, and from the skin of the ship, one hundred miles into space, a gigantic aluminum sail will emerge.

ALL (In astonishment; ad lib): A sail! What? On a spaceship? (Etc.)

DR. QUANTUS: Yes, a sail on a spaceship, unbelievable as it may seem. This sail will make use of extremely fast particles of radiation called "photons." So, if I may be just a bit poetic, the Santa Maria the Second will skim through the interstellar void propelled by a photon wind!

DR. ARCHIVISTA: Wonderful, wonderful! One thousand years of progress and our new Columbus is returning to the power of his ancestor—wind and sail!

DR. THEOREMBUS: Photon sail—I say "phony" sail. It won't work. Take it from me, that sail will drag him to a stop. He'll be becalmed for the rest of eternity.

VOICE (From loudspeaker): Attention all personnel. Mr. Inuk, President of the United Nations General Assembly, is entering the blockhouse with his aides. (All stand,

as PRESIDENT INUK, *flanked by* AIDES, *enters.* COM-
MANDER SMITH *and technicians salute.*)

COMMENTATOR: Ladies and gentlemen, President Inuk of
the United Nations and his aides have just entered the
blockhouse in an unprecedented show of world faith in
Captain Stardriver's voyage. The President is dressed in
the colorful costume of the North Polar Federation.

VOICE: Attention all personnel. Captain Stardriver and his
crew are ready in the Command Module.

COMMENTATOR: Keep your eyes on the blockhouse television screen, ladies and gentlemen, as we switch you now
to the Command Module of the Santa Maria the Second. (*The rocket and sky background are removed, to
reveal* CAPTAIN STARDRIVER, MADGE ELLEN, PHOEBE, *and*
COSMO, *holding space helmets, standing in front of
chairs which have wide seat belts.* PHOEBE *has a guitar.*)
Citizens of the world, here are Captain Stardriver and
his crew! (*All remain standing, and applaud long and
loudly.*)

COMMANDER SMITH (*Into microphone*): Blockhouse to
Command Module. Do you read me, Captain Stardriver?

CAPTAIN STARDRIVER: I read you loud and clear, Commander Smith.

COMMENTATOR: Captain Stardriver, I wonder if you would
say just a few words, and introduce us to your crew.

CAPTAIN STARDRIVER: I'd be glad to. I am Captain Stardriver. This is my first mate and wife, Astro-Navigator
Madge Ellen Stardriver, and my children, Astro-Biologist Phoebe Stardriver, and Apprentice Spaceman Cosmo
Stardriver.

COMMENTATOR: I understand that Columbus had a crew
of eighty-eight men. Why do you have a crew of only
four?

MADGE ELLEN: I can explain that. Even though our spaceship is a giant, her payload is still relatively small. We need tremendous room for food storage, air, and fuel. The most efficient way for a crew to function in deep space is for each of us to have several different jobs. For instance, in addition to being an astro-navigator, I am a planet geologist, an electronics engineer, and a computer programmer. And I also make a very fine Martian crab soup.

PHOEBE: I've been planning for voyages in deep space since I was three. All deep-space pilots ship out with their families. Sometimes it takes years to travel between galaxies, and the strain on pilots and the folks back home would be too great if we didn't go together.

COMMENTATOR: Is that a guitar I see strapped to your space suit, Phoebe?

PHOEBE: Sure is. The nights are long and lonely out there between stars. Even with three or four jobs to do, we get very lonesome for earth and our own sun, so we're allowed to bring along a few things to remind us of home.

COMMENTATOR: How about you, Spaceman Cosmo—what are your jobs aboard the ship?

COSMO: Well, I shine up the fuel pipelines, and change the algae tanks. I'm also an expert space medical aide. I have my own kit of radiation pills this year. Actually, I'm just a glorified space cabin boy, but my dad says if I do a good job welding oxygen tanks and patching meteor holes, he'll make me a Second Lieutenant on the trip home.

COMMENTATOR: We'll all root for you, Cosmo. Now, Captain Stardriver, in the few moments that remain before liftoff, will you tell us how far your journey will take you?

CAPTAIN STARDRIVER: We will head the ship straight through the Spiral Nebulae and outward to the bounds of the visible universe. We expect to hit the rim of the universe in ten years. It's about two and a half gigaparsecs.

COMMENTATOR: And how far, in earth miles, is a gigaparsec?

CAPTAIN STARDRIVER: Look at it this way—a gigaparsec is a billion parsecs. A parsec is about three and a quarter light-years, and a light-year is six million million miles. Let's just say that we hope we don't have to walk home!

COMMENTATOR: As you prepare to launch your impressive spaceship, the Santa Maria the Second, can you tell us one more thing? Many astronauts have nicknames for their vessels. Have you a pet name for your ship?

CAPTAIN STARDRIVER: Yes, we have. We call her "The Infinity Express."

VOICE (*From loudspeaker*): Attention all personnel. Ready your equipment, please. It is now T-minus thirty seconds. Repeat, it is now thirty seconds to liftoff!

COMMANDER SMITH (*Into microphone*): Captain Stardriver, helmet your crew, please.

CAPTAIN STARDRIVER: Roger. (*All crew members put on their helmets.*)

COMMANDER SMITH: Fasten your gravity webs.

CAPTAIN STARDRIVER: Roger. (*All sit, buckling the wide belts.*)

VOICE (*From loudspeaker*): Twenty seconds to liftoff. All systems are go.

COMMANDER SMITH: Central Control. Calling Central Control. Switch to the video picture of the rocket. (*Rocket and sky slide onto screen, in front of* CAPTAIN STARDRIVER *and crew.*) Intercom. Repeat: Intercom. Hold lines open for a voice communication from the President of the United Nations.

PRESIDENT INUK (*Into microphone*): Captain Stardriver, we, the citizens of earth and the territorial outposts on the moon and Mars, send you our prayers and good wishes for a successful voyage to the boundary of the finite universe. With this brave quest, you will answer once and for all the many questions which haunt the best scientific minds of the earth. Bon voyage, Captain Stardriver, until we meet again.

VOICE (*From loudspeaker*): Commencing final count. T-minus ten, nine, eight, seven, six, five, four, three, two, one. (*At the count of one, the rocket on the screen begins to rise. All watch screen, shouting and applauding excitedly.*) Liftoff. All systems are still go. It looks like a beautiful launch. (*Sounds of radar and computer are heard, as* RADAR MAN *and* COMPUTER TECHNICIAN *work at their equipment.*)

RADAR MAN: I'm tracking him, sir. We are in voice communication now.

DR. ARCHIVISTA: Ah, if only Columbus had had radio!

COMPUTER TECHNICIAN: Computing his speed, sir. Estimated speed—fifty thousand miles per hour and still accelerating.

RADAR MAN: Still tracking, sir. Radar beam getting fuzzy. He's far out. I've never tracked anything so fast.

COMPUTER TECHNICIAN: Estimated position—intersecting orbit of the planet Pluto.

RADAR MAN: Spaceship is slowing.

ALL: Slowing!

RADAR MAN: Information on radar-scope indicates the great sail has been unfurled.

DR. ARCHIVISTA: He's setting sail across a new Atlantic!

RADAR MAN: Ship is slowing still more. I don't understand.

DR. THEOREMBUS: I told you so. Nobody listens to me. He'll come to a dead stop soon. And then what will he do? Paddle back to earth?

DR. VECTOR: He'll pick up speed. I know he will.

RADAR MAN: The ship has resumed its former speed, sir.

COMMANDER SMITH: Whew! That's good news.

RADAR MAN (*Excitedly*): Acceleration is proceeding in powers of ten. It's gone into such a fantastic speed I can't pick it up with normal radar.

COMMANDER SMITH: Switch to laser beam transmission.

RADAR MAN: Roger. Laser beam activated. (*High-pitched laser sound is heard.*)

COMPUTER MAN: Computer reports spaceship has headed into the Spiral Nebulae.

RADAR MAN (*Excitedly*): Sir . . . sir! I can't follow him with the laser beam. What shall I do?

COMMANDER SMITH: Lock your homing system into a stable beam. This is where we leave Captain Stardriver. He has gone beyond the reach of earthly transmission.

ALL (*Ad lib*): What? Something's gone wrong! What's happened? (*Etc.*)

COMMANDER SMITH: Please, please. There is no cause for alarm. Quite the contrary. We expected that if the ship exceeded the speed of light, we would lose him.

ALL (*Awestruck*): The speed of light!

DR. VECTOR: He's broken the light barrier!

DR. ARCHIVISTA: Just as his ancestors broke the sound barrier!

DR. THEOREMBUS: I'll believe it when I see it. Besides, even if he has broken the light barrier, who knows what dangers may await him!

DR. VECTOR: Who knows what tremendous opportunities await him!

DR. ARCHIVISTA: When will he reappear, Commander Smith?

COMMANDER SMITH: In twenty years, if all goes well. Meanwhile, we have set up a laser beam in space, like a searchlight, to guide him on his way home.

DR. ARCHIVISTA: Ah, a lighthouse for the new Columbus.

RADAR MAN: Commander Smith, I have a transcription of

the voice contact with the spaceship. Perhaps you would
like to hear it.

COMMANDER SMITH: I'm sure we all would. (*All nod, face
front.*) Is it Captain Stardriver's voice?

RADAR MAN: No, it's his daughter. She's singing. Listen—

PHOEBE (*Singing with guitar background to tune of "Over
Yandro"*):
We're bound away, for to stay
A little while,
But we're comin' back,
Though we're infinity away—
Oh, please remember us,
And leave a candle in the sky,
To guide us home,
Far away,
Far away,
Over yonder. . . . (*Softly fading*)
Over yonder. . . .

COMMENTATOR: Ladies and gentlemen, you have just wit-
nessed the unforgettable launching of the pioneer spaceship, the Santa Maria the Second. This ends our three-
dimensional telecast from Palos, Spain, Friday, August
the third, in the year twenty-four hundred and ninety-
two.

DR. ARCHIVISTA: And to think it all began with Columbus
on August the third, fourteen hundred and ninety-two!
(*Curtain*)

THE END

Penny Wise

Characters

PENNY BRIGHT
OLD TIMER (*a penny*) ⎱ *chorus*
EIGHT PENNIES ⎰
NICKEL
DIME

QUARTER
HALF DOLLAR
DOLLAR
SALLY SPENDER
SAVIN' STEVEN

SETTING: *Ten chairs are arranged in a semicircle at one side of stage. Down right is a basket of balloons and, beside it, a telephone on a pole. Signs read,* BALLOONS 5¢, *and* TELEPHONE HERE 10¢. *Down left is a gumball machine with a sign reading,* GUMBALL MACHINE—ONE PENNY.

AT RISE: EIGHT PENNIES *and* OLD TIMER, *all holding tambourines, sit in chairs. Tenth chair is empty. The* PENNIES *chant, one after the other.*

1ST PENNY: One little—
2ND PENNY: Two little—
3RD PENNY: Three little—
FIRST THREE PENNIES (*Together*): Pennies. (*They shake tambourines.*)
4TH PENNY: Four little—
5TH PENNY: Five little—

6TH PENNY: Six little—

FIRST SIX PENNIES (*Together*): Pennies. (*They shake tambourines.*)

7TH PENNY: Seven little—

8TH PENNY: Eight little—

OLD TIMER: Nine little—

ALL: Pennies.

Nine little pennies in the bank. (*They shake tambourines.*)

1ST PENNY: What can you do with nine little pennies?

OLD TIMER: There's nothing you can do with nine little pennies.

2ND PENNY: Where, oh, where is the tenth little penny?

ALL: Put ten little pennies in the bank.

8TH PENNY (*Pointing*):
There's a place, there's a space
For another little penny—

3RD PENNY (*Pointing*):
There's a spot, there's a slot
For another little penny—

7TH PENNY:
Oh, we aren't very many—

4TH PENNY:
Oh, we're hardly even *any*—

ALL:
And we need another penny
In the skinny penny bank.
With a jingle and a jangle
And a bingle and a bangle,
We need another penny
In the skinny penny bank!

(PENNY BRIGHT *enters right, skipping.*)

5TH PENNY (*Pointing*): Look there, my fine copper cousins. Look what just strolled out of the mint.

OLD TIMER: A brand-new, grand-new penny. Sakes alive!

I'd better hurry right down and help him. There's nothing like a new penny for getting into trouble. (PENNY
BRIGHT *"spins" to center.*)

PENNY BRIGHT (*Waving his arms*):
Hey, look at me, folks!
See how I shine?
I'm fresh from the mint, folks—
The whole world is mine!

Watch me go places
And do big things—
I'm a penny with style, folks,
A penny with wings!
Wheee! (*He "spins" about stage.*)

OLD TIMER: A penny with wings, indeed. Only quarters
have wings.

PENNY BRIGHT: Hi, Old Timer! I make a big flash, don't
you think?

OLD TIMER: You're very brash, I think. You need some
good advice, I think. Now, listen. I was minted back in
1880, and I've seen a lot of change. There's a great deal
about the world that you don't know—

PENNY BRIGHT: Don't bother, Old Timer. I'll find out
about the world my own way. Right now, I want to roll
along. I'm headed for far places and big things.

OLD TIMER: Tsk, tsk. That's the trouble with you young
"whipperpennies." A new penny has hardly any "cents."

PENNY BRIGHT: Never mind. Just show me the hot spots
around town. I'm a big spender.

OLD TIMER: That's what you think. (PENNY BRIGHT *goes
to balloon basket, down right, and* OLD TIMER *follows,
leaning on cane.* NICKEL *enters and stands watching.*)

PENNY BRIGHT: See this red balloon. I'll just buy it for
myself. (*He takes the balloon, but* NICKEL *pulls the
string out of his hand.*)

NICKEL: Pardon me, small change. Did you say *you* were going to buy this balloon? Well, I have news for you. Balloons cost five cents, or to put it my way—a nickel. *I'll* take the red balloon. (NICKEL, *with nose in the air, exits right, holding balloon.*)

PENNY BRIGHT (*Putting hands on hips; angrily*): He can't do that to me!

OLD TIMER: Oh, yes, he can. It takes five of us hardworking fellows to measure up to a nickel.

PENNY BRIGHT: Aw, I didn't want an old balloon anyway. (*Going to telephone on pole*) See this telephone? I'm going to call my friends back at the mint. (DIME *enters left, and watches smugly, as* PENNY BRIGHT *jumps up to reach phone and knocks receiver off the hook.*)

DIME (*Hanging up receiver*): Never send a penny to do a dime's work. You can't make a phone call. Only dimes are allowed to do that.

PENNY BRIGHT: Who do you think you are? You're smaller than I am.

DIME: I'm a dime, that's who I am. And small or not, it takes ten of you lowly coppers to make one of me. So long, small change! (*Exits right*)

PENNY BRIGHT (*To* OLD TIMER): Is that true? A little old dusty dime is worth more than a big, shiny penny?

OLD TIMER: I'm afraid so. You see, dimes are made of silver, and silver is worth more than copper.

PENNY BRIGHT: Well, I don't care. I'm still going to go far places and do big things. (SALLY SPENDER *enters, skipping. She faces audience and jingles coins in pocket of her pinafore.*)

SALLY:
There's a hole in my pocket
That money is burning;
To end it and spend it
Is what I am yearning.

Money never lingers—
It slips through my fingers,
(*She tosses coins about the stage.*)
And when it is gone,
I beg and I borrow,
Never minding tomorrow.
(*Turning pocket inside out*)

And I'm broke—oh, so broke—
Most all of the time;
(*She grins at audience.*)
I seem to be short—
Can you spare me a dime?
(*She holds out hand.*)

PENNY BRIGHT (*To* OLD TIMER): Say, this girl looks adventurous. If I shine up to her, maybe she'll take a shine to me.

OLD TIMER: A rolling penny gathers no interest, young one. That girl looks mighty careless. I wouldn't shine up to her.

PENNY BRIGHT (*Waving* OLD TIMER *away*): Aw, get lost, Old Timer. I know my way around the world. (OLD TIMER *shakes his head, and goes back to his seat.*) Yoo-hoo, girl! Girl!

SALLY (*Noticing* PENNY BRIGHT): A penny! (*Going to him*) Somebody has dropped a new penny on the floor. This is my lucky day. (*Taking* PENNY BRIGHT *by the hand*) Come on, penny. (*She leads him down left*)

PENNY BRIGHT: Oh, boy. We're on our way to far places and big things! (SALLY *helps* PENNY BRIGHT *climb into slot of gumball machine; only his head shows above the slot.*) Hey, what *is* this?

SALLY: Oh, I don't care about far places and big things. I'm Sally Spender. Money goes through my fingers like water through a sieve. Now, be a good penny and go down the slot. (*She pushes his head down.* PENNY BRIGHT *goes inside the box and pushes red beach ball through hole in front.* SALLY *picks it up.*) Ah, there's my gumball now. (*She skips off left.*)

PENNY BRIGHT (*Poking head up through the slot*): Help! Help! It's dark down there. It's like a prison down there. I don't want to spend the rest of my life in a gum machine. Help! Get me out of here.

CHORUS (*Shaking tambourines in rhythm*):
Shake, little penny.
Shake, little penny,
Shake, shake, shake about!

Roll, little penny,
Roll, little penny,
Roll, roll, roll, right out!

(PENNY BRIGHT *shakes himself and rolls out of coin return slot at side of carton. He sits cross-legged at center, dejectedly holding chin in hands.*)

PENNY BRIGHT: Now I understand at last! I know what a penny is! (*Wiping his eyes and reciting sadly*)
I could never pay a bill,
I'm petty cash that's almost nil,
Low man on the wampum pole,
Much too small to pay a toll.
I'm short-range, short-change,
And no one pays me heed.
I've a yen to be a sterling chap—
(*Sniffles*) But I'm only—chicken feed!

(SAVIN' STEVEN *enters, with his piggy bank under his arm. He crosses to* PENNY BRIGHT.)

STEVEN: Hey—look at this! A new penny on the floor. Just what I've been looking for. (*He tries to lift up* PENNY BRIGHT.)

PENNY BRIGHT (*Waving him away*): Go away. Let me rest in peace.

STEVEN (*Pulling him up on his feet*): Come on, penny. I have plans for you. Want to go far places and do big things?

PENNY BRIGHT: Far places? Big things? Why, I've been waiting for a fellow like you. When do we start?

STEVEN: Right now. Hop into the bank with the rest of my pennies. We're saving up for a trip to Disneyland. Is that far enough away for you?

PENNY BRIGHT: Absolutely!

STEVEN: And then we're going to save up for a six-gear English racer with a headlight and a siren. Is that big enough for you?

PENNY BRIGHT: Positively!

STEVEN: Good. (*Pointing to empty chair near* PENNIES) Then step right in, penny. Welcome home.

PENNY BRIGHT (*Standing by the empty seat*): Say, there's lots of copper in your hopper!

PENNIES: Well spoken, token.

PENNY BRIGHT: Then, may I join you?

PENNIES: Join, coin!

PENNY BRIGHT: All right. You can bank on me! (*He sits.*)

PENNIES: Bravo, centavo! (*They wave tambourines and shake them. All join in singing, to the tune of "Farmer in the Dell."*)

PENNIES (*Singing*):
Oh, the pennies in the bank,
The pennies in the bank,

OLD TIMER:
Hi ho, the money-o,

PENNIES:
The pennies in the bank.
(NICKEL *enters;* PENNY BRIGHT *rises.*)

PENNY BRIGHT (*Joining hands with* NICKEL):
　The penny takes the nickel—
　The penny takes the nickel—
PENNIES:
　Hi ho, the money-o,
　The penny takes the nickel.
　(DIME *enters.*)
NICKEL (*Taking* DIME's *hand*):
　The nickel takes the dime—
　The nickel takes the dime—
　(*All three dance.*)
PENNIES:
　Hi ho, the money-o,
　The nickel takes the dime.
　(QUARTER *enters.*)
DIME (*Joining hands with* QUARTER):
　The dime takes the quarter—
　The dime takes the quarter—
　(*All four dance.*)
PENNIES:
　Hi ho, the money-o,
　The dime takes the quarter.
　(HALF DOLLAR *enters.*)
QUARTER (*Joining hands with* HALF DOLLAR):
　The quarter takes the half—
　The quarter takes the half—
　(*All five dance.*)
PENNIES:
　Hi ho, the money-o,
　The quarter takes the half.
　(DOLLAR *enters, and others drop hands and clap.*)
DOLLAR:
　The dollar stands alone,
　The dollar stands alone,

ALL:
  Hi ho, the money-o,
  The dollar stands alone!
  (PENNY BRIGHT *takes* DOLLAR'*s hand*.)
PENNY BRIGHT (*To audience*): But remember—
  Rack it up and stack it up,
  And stash your cash away—
  Sunshine's daylight saving time
  Before that rainy day.

  In a row the dollars grow,
  The bankbook says how many,
  But every dollar crisp and green
  Started with a penny!
  (*He bows as the curtain closes.*)

THE END

Scaredy Cat

Characters

TONY REESE
TERRY, *his sister*
MRS. REESE, *his mother*
SHADOW, *the cat*
LINDA ⎱
WALTER ⎰ *trick-or-treaters*

DR. BLUNDER
WILLY LIGHTFINGERS
POCKETS THE SNATCH
POLICE OFFICER

SCENE 1

TIME: *Halloween, in the early evening.*

SETTING: *The Reeses' living room.*

AT RISE: MRS. REESE *is standing at a card table at center, drawing a face on a sheet which covers the table and hangs to the floor.* SHADOW *is under the table, hidden from the audience.* TONY *sits on a sofa up center, and* TERRY, *dressed in a Halloween costume, sits at left.* (NOTE: *The actor playing* SHADOW *imitates kitten's voice in Scene 1, and appears as the giant cat only in Scene 2.*)

TONY: Almost finished, Mom?

MRS. REESE: Almost. All we need now is a ghastly grin for the ghost.

75

SHADOW (*Piteously, from under table*): Mew . . .

TERRY: Oh, Mother, listen to Shadow. You shouldn't have said "ghost."

SHADOW (*Wailing*): Meeeow . . .

TONY: Ah-ah-ah, Terry. You shouldn't have said *that word* either.

TERRY: I'm sorry, Shadow. Poor kitten. She's so sensitive. She just hates Halloween.

SHADOW (*Howling*): *Meow!*

MRS. REESE: My heavens, now we can't even mention Hallow—I mean, October 31st. Never mind, Shadow. I've sent for a veterinarian, and we'll soon find out just what the trouble is. (*The doorbell rings.*)

TONY: I'll answer it, Mom. (*He goes off left and returns with* LINDA, *dressed as a gypsy, and* WALTER, *dressed as a pirate.*) Hey, look, everybody. Look who I found skulking around on our front porch—Captain Kidd and Miss Fortune.

WALTER: Yo-ho-ho and a bottle of rum. Treat me right or I'll make you walk the plank.

TERRY: Don't tell me, let me guess. It's Walter Bryan.

LINDA (*Speaking with an exaggerated accent*): Hello, dollings. I am Zelda ze mysterious. Cross my palm with silver and I tell you strange gypsy fortune!

TONY: Zelda the mysterious, eh. It's more like Linda the ordinary.

WALTER: Oh, well, you can't win them all. Hey, Tony, we heard you have a real spooky black cat. Could we see it, Mrs. Reese?

MRS. REESE: Why, of course you can. But I must warn you, Shadow's not used to people.

TONY: She's hiding under the card table. Have a look. (TONY, WALTER *and* LINDA *bend down and look behind sheet.*)

SHADOW (*Angrily*): Yeow! Sssst! Hisssss! (LINDA *and*

WALTER *draw back and retreat quickly down left.* TONY *pretends to stroke kitten, then straightens up.*)

TONY: My goodness, she *is* upset. Did she scratch you?

WALTER: No, but she looked like she had six heads and five hundred claws.

LINDA: Come on, Walter—before the little beast pounces on us. Goodbye, everybody. (*They start to exit left.*)

TERRY: Wait—we haven't given you a treat yet.

WALTER: Oh, we've already had our "treat". So long. (*They exit.*)

TONY: Well, can you beat that? Walter Bryan went off without his taffy apple. That crazy Shadow! (*Knocking is heard off left.*)

TERRY: More trick-or-treaters, I guess. I'll get it, Mother. (*She exits left.*)

MRS. REESE: Don't blame the cat, Tony. Something awful must have happened to make her behave this way. (TERRY *re-enters with* DR. BLUNDER, *who carries a black bag.*)

TERRY: Guess who this is.

TONY: Don't tell me. Let me guess. Dr. Frankenstein? Where's the monster? You should get two taffy apples for that costume.

DR. BLUNDER: Costume? What costume? (*To* MRS. REESE) Mrs. Reese, are these outrageous children your outrageous children?

MRS. REESE: Oh, my goodness. You must be the veterinarian! Oh, dear. It's been such a topsy-turvy day with all the trick-or-treaters stopping by. Tony, apologize to the doctor at once.

TONY: Jeepers, I'm sorry, Doctor.

DR. BLUNDER: Humph. Did you expect me to bring a horse to identify myself? Dr. Frankenstein, indeed. What could he do? He was only a doctor for monsters. Now you take ·me—Barnstable Blunder. I am an animal doctor and a vegetable doctor, and I sometimes take on a few minerals for a sideline.

TONY: A *vegetable* doctor?

TERRY: How can you doctor vegetables?

DR. BLUNDER: How can you doctor vegetables, they ask me! Didn't you ever hear of hothouse calls? Who do you think sits up nights in the nursery with the sick seedlings, eh? Who's the surgeon that cuts out the cutworms? Who prescribes the right spray when there's an epidemic of sore eyes in the potato patch? Me, Barnstable Blunder, Doctor of Veterinary and Vegetary Medicine, that's who. Now, where's the patient? (TERRY *reaches under table and brings out a basket holding a toy kitten.*)

TERRY (*Handing basket to* DR. BLUNDER): Here, Dr. Blunder. (*He takes basket and squints at it, then holds up kitten's tail.*)

DR. BLUNDER: Humph. You didn't pot this plant right. The roots are dragging.

TERRY: Pot what plant? What roots? That's a tail.

DR. BLUNDER: Wrong. Plants don't have tails. Unless they're cattails. Ha!

MRS. REESE: Dr. Blunder, you don't understand. I called you to treat a sick kitten, not a plant.

DR. BLUNDER: Oh, a *kitten*. An animal, in other words. Why didn't you say so in the first place? All right, kitten, what's the matter with you?

TONY: Well, you see, Shadow is scared all the time. She hides when people come. And you should hear her howl when you mention (*Spelling*) H-A-L-L-O-W-E-E-N.

DR. BLUNDER (*Peering over his glasses at* TONY, *sternly*): Did I ask your opinion? Did I? No. I asked the kitten here what was the matter. Now, be quiet while she tells me. Now, pussycat, tell me all about it. (*Holding basket near his ear.*)

SHADOW (*From under table*): Ow-ow-ow.

DR. BLUNDER: You don't say. And when did this all take place, eh?

SHADOW: Meow-ow-ow.

DR. BLUNDER: Is that so? Last October? Tsk. Tsk. Tell me, what brought on the symptoms?

SHADOW: Row-ow-psst. Spat! Mew-mew-mew.

DR. BLUNDER: Terrible. Awful. Dreadful. Of course you don't feel so happy about October 31st, you poor little kitty cat.

MRS. REESE: Er—what did Shadow tell you?

DR. BLUNDER: Everything. Now we know why this cat does not like October 31st. It seems she was owned by an outrageous boy who dressed her up in a poodle costume. Imagine dressing up a cat like a poodle!

TERRY: Poor Shadow.

DR. BLUNDER: That wasn't all. This miserable boy put the kitty in a large pumpkin, and left it on the doorstep of the local dog catcher, for a joke. It was no joke, I can tell you. Now she is a very nervous cat. Very nervous, indeed.

MRS. REESE: What a shame. Can you help her?

DR. BLUNDER: Can I help her! Of course I can help her. In my bag I have a powerful tranquilizer for nervous cats. It will calm her down. Make a cool cat of her. (*He opens his bag, takes out pill and pretends to pop it into the cat's mouth.*) Swallow, kitty. That's a good feline. See—she's calmer already. Now keep her quiet, in this room, away from the light until morning. I'll stop by in the morning. (*Hands basket to* TERRY)

MRS. REESE: We certainly thank you, Dr. Blunder.

DR. BLUNDER: Not at all. Good night. (*He exits left.*)

ALL: Good night, Doctor.

MRS. REESE (*As* TERRY *strokes kitten*): Perhaps you'd

better put Shadow back under the card table, Terry. We'll leave the sheet over it to keep the light away from her.

TONY: But, Mom, that sheet is my ghost costume. What'll I wear tonight for trick-or-treating?

TERRY: Why don't you go as something really strange and unearthly? (*She puts basket behind sheet.*)

TONY (*As curtains start to close*): What?

TERRY: Yourself! (*She and her mother laugh as* TONY *makes a face. Quick curtain.*)

*   *   *

SCENE 2

BEFORE RISE: DR. BLUNDER, *carrying his bag, enters in front of curtain from left, talking to himself.*

DR. BLUNDER: Let me see, what was my next call? It was either Mrs. Dawson on State Street or Mrs. State on Dawson Street. Ah. I have it! It was Mrs. Lawson on City Avenue. She is worried about her wilted lettuce. Lettuce. For that I need my plant bag. But wait. (*Stops and stares at his bag.*) In my hand I already have my plant bag. How can that be? I just treated an animal. I gave the animal a red tranquilizer. Pink pumpkins! That was no tranquilizer—that was a quick-growth pill! By midnight, that kitten will grow to the size of a panther! Of course, it will shrink by one o'clock, but what damage it can do before then! Horrible! I must call those people quickly. Now what was their name? Rice? Roose? Reese? Purple peppers! I can't remember. I'll have to call every name beginning with R in the telephone book. (*He rushes off right.*)

*   *   *

TIME: *Midnight.*

SETTING: *The same as Scene 1.*

AT RISE: SHADOW *is still under the card table, hidden by the sheet. A clock begins to strike twelve.* WILLY LIGHT-FINGERS *steals onstage from left, carrying a bag over his shoulder.* POCKETS THE SNATCH *enters from right, also carrying a bag.* WILLY *sweeps bric-a-brac from an end table at left of sofa into bag, as* POCKETS *does the same with objects on right end table. On the twelfth chime, they meet at center in front of card table and shake hands.*)

WILLY: Right on the dot, Pockets. Am I smart or am I smart?

POCKETS: You're smart, Willy.

WILLY: I took everything but the light bulbs. Just look at this silver. (*He takes a spoon out of the bag and holds it up.*) Solid as Gibraltar. This is a classy family.

POCKETS: Do you think they'll stay asleep upstairs?

WILLY: Sure they will. I thought of everything. On Halloween everybody expects a little more noise than usual. Nobody will bother to come downstairs tonight. Say, Pockets, am I smart, or am I smart?

POCKETS: You're smart, Willy. But how about dogs? A lot of people keep big watchdogs. (SHADOW, *still hidden by sheet, moves the card table down left.*)

WILLY: Relax. I told you I thought of everything. The only animal in this house is an itsy-bitsy black kitten. Am I real smart, or am I real smart?

POCKETS: You're real smart, Willy. (*Pointing to card table.*) Hey—did you move the table?

WILLY: No. How come it's over there? (*Pointing to center*) It was here a minute ago. (*The table moves across stage to right of sofa.*)

POCKETS: Willy—look at that. It moved! A spooky table.

WILLY: Aw, it's nothing, Pockets. Remote control, that's

all. We activated a switch somewhere. (*Patting him on the back*) You leave the thinking to me. Now, who are you going to leave the thinking to?

POCKETS: You, Willy. (*They sit on sofa, and examine some of the objects in their bags.* SHADOW, *now a giant cat, comes out from under the table, unnoticed by burglars. She yawns and stretches, then goes behind the sofa, and purrs loudly. Her head and paws are visible behind the two on the sofa.*) Do you hear that noise, Willy? It sounds like a subway.

WILLY: Naw. This is the country—no subways around here. It must be a diesel truck. (SHADOW *playfully hits* POCKETS *on the top of his head.*)

POCKETS (*Annoyed*): You don't have to hit me, Willy.

WILLY: Hit you? I never touched you. (SHADOW *thumps* WILLY *on the head.*) Hey, Pockets, cut out the rough stuff.

POCKETS: Who, me? (SHADOW *trots around to the front of the sofa and sits watching the two, head cocked to one side.*)

WILLY (*Not taking in the size of the cat at once*): Look at that. There's the little black kitten I was telling you about.

POCKETS: Yeah. Hi, kitty. What's new on the back fence? (*They do a double-take, then climb on the sofa in terror.*)

BOTH: Little black kitten!

WILLY: Yipes, it's a panther! Sh-sh-shoo. Shoo. Go back to the zoo, panther. (SHADOW *sidles up to the men, purring and rubbing against their feet.*)

POCKETS: Oooh. Oooh. Look at the size of that cat! Willy, you know what?

WILLY: What?

POCKETS: I'm not leaving the thinking to you any more. I don't think you're so smart. (SHADOW *stands up with paws on* POCKETS' *chest, and begins to eat his tie play-fully.*) Help! Help! (*She moves to* WILLY *and yawns in his face.*)

WILLY: Let's go! This is no Halloween joke! (*At the word "Halloween"* SHADOW *growls and retreats under the card table.* POLICE OFFICER, *gun in hand, rushes in from left, and* MRS. REESE, TONY, *and* TERRY, *all in bathrobes, enter from right and stand, thunderstruck, watching the action.*)

OFFICER (*To* WILLY *and* POCKETS, *who are still standing on sofa*): Hands up, you two. (*They raise their hands, but remain on sofa.*) My, what noisy burglars. (*Going up to men*) Well, well, well. Willy Lightfingers and Pockets the Snatch.

MRS. REESE: Good heavens. Police! And men standing on my sofa. Get off my sofa, you big brutes. (*They step off sheepishly.*)

TONY: Boy, oh boy, what a night! Policemen! Robbers! And it's not trick-or-treat. It's the real thing.

TERRY: What is this all about? Will somebody please explain?

WILLY: Explain? Us? You're the ones who ought to explain. (*Pointing to family*) Officer, arrest these people.

OFFICER: What? Willy, have you flipped? Arrest them for what?

WILLY: Illegal ownership of a dangerous panther.

ALL: A panther!

WILLY (*Pointing*): Under that table. He's waiting to spring—

OFFICER: Is he now! (*He smiles at the family*) I'll have a look, if you don't mind. (*He tiptoes to the table, lifts corner of sheet and calls.*) Here, panther, panther. Good old panther. Come out for the nice policeman. (DR. BLUNDER *bursts in from left.*)

DR. BLUNDER (*Shouting*): No, no! Don't reach in there!

TONY: Dr. Blunder! (*The clock strikes one. DR. BLUNDER wipes brow in relief, then stands at right with family.*)

OFFICER (*Bringing out the basket with toy kitten*): Is this the beast that was ready to spring? My, my, Willy, your eyesight isn't what it used to be. But never mind. The prison doctor will fit you out with new specs. Step along now, boys. Step along lively. (*He waves them out, their hands in the air, then pauses before he exits and turns to the family*) Take good care of that panther, eh, folks? (*He hands basket to TERRY and exits with men.*)

MRS. REESE (*Rubbing her eyes*): I really think I must still be asleep!

DR. BLUNDER: I can explain everything.

MRS. REESE: Dr. Blunder, what are you doing here again?

TERRY: It's the middle of the night!

DR. BLUNDER: Never mind the middle of anything. I switched cases—

TONY (*Bewildered*): Cases of what?

DR. BLUNDER: Not cases—medical bags. And the tranquilizer was not a tranquilizer—

MRS. REESE: I don't follow you.

DR. BLUNDER: No, but you should have! I called every name beginning with R in the telephone book! But of course the kitten shrank anyway—

TERRY (*Mystified*): She shrank? She doesn't look any smaller to me.

DR. BLUNDER: No, of course she doesn't. I'll begin at the beginning. No. It's too long. I'll try the middle. Oh! Roaring rutabagas! You wouldn't believe it anyway. I'm going home. I never did like cats anyhow. They move around too much. Give me a nice quiet cucumber any day. Halloween—bah!

TERRY: Dr. Blunder! Shadow didn't howl when you said Halloween.

TONY: Great. You've cured her.

Dr. Blunder (*Taking the basket and speaking to kitten*): Ahem. Halloween! Spook! Ghost! Boooo— (*Looking up, pleased*) Why, you're right. She seems to have much more confidence. There's a real sparkle in her eye. (*Curtain begins to close.*) And a kind of funny smile on her face. Like a cat who swallowed a canary. (*To the audience*) Hm-m-m. You know—I think she's trying to tell us something! (*Quick curtain*)

THE END

The Wayward Witch

WINNIE, *an absent-minded witch*
TWO BLACK CATS
CHILDREN
WITCHES ⎱ *chorus*
WIZARDS ⎰

SETTING: *A living room. A fireplace with pumpkins on the mantel is at center. In front of the fireplace is a stool. A row of chairs extends diagonally from each side of the fireplace.*

AT RISE: WINNIE *is seated on the stool, her broom across her lap, dozing. On either side of the fireplace, asleep, are the* TWO BLACK CATS. WITCHES *and* WIZARDS *are seated on the chairs (the seating arrangement should alternate boys and girls), holding their scripts in books covered with orange and black cardboard. Mysterious music is heard. As the chorus reads,* WINNIE *enacts the scene in pantomime.*

ALL:
  This is the tale of a funny little witch. (WINNIE *holds head in hands, nods in time with chorus.*)
1ST DUET:
  She didn't know what was what—

2ND DUET:
Or who was who—
ALL:
Or even which was which!
3RD DUET:
She couldn't tell time from tide—
4TH DUET:
Or groom from bride—
5TH DUET:
Or March from May—
6TH DUET:
Or sad to say—
ALL:
Night from day!
1ST SOLO:
She was quite nearsighted in one little eye. (WINNIE *pushes her large spectacles over her nose and squints.*)
2ND SOLO:
To make matters worse, her broom wouldn't fly! (WIN-NIE *shakes her broom.*)
WITCHES:
It was nothing short of awful,
It was nothing short of tragic,
But wayward, backward Winnie
Could *not* do magic!
(WINNIE *takes her wand from the mantel and waves it. It disappears. She takes packet of magic powder from mantel, throws it in the air near the fire, and the fire goes out.* NOTE: *See "Special Effects" in Production Notes. The chorus continues to read while* WINNIE *does this.*)
1ST QUARTET:
She couldn't charm a tumble-bug
With candle, book or bell—

2ND QUARTET:
>She couldn't raise the smallest wish
>From a wishing well.

ALL:
>And not for the life of her,
>The ever-loving life of her,
>The mumbling, bumbling life of her
>Could Winnie cast a spell!

WIZARDS: And the other witches said—

WITCHES: Pooh, pooh! We're not on speaking terms with you! (WINNIE *goes back to stool and falls asleep as chorus continues.*)

ALL:
>Now it happened just to happen
>In the dark of the year,
>When the yellow, grinning goblin moon
>Begins to appear,
>That the time for Halloweening came
>One brown October night,
>When all the proper witches were
>In ghastly, ghostly flight—

1ST SOLO:
>Somehow, snoozing by her grate,
>Winnie missed the proper date!
>(CATS *exit with the pumpkins and fire.*)

HALF CHORUS:
>Outside the days flew by like snow
>Until, December, all aglow
>And festive with a thousand joys
>Came bursting with a glorious noise.
>(*"Deck the Halls"* is heard.)

ALL: It woke poor Winnie!

WINNIE:
>Oh, boo! Oh, toadstools! Loathsome fate!
>It's Halloween! I must be late!

(She mounts broom backwards, starts off backwards, straightens herself out and runs offstage.)
HALF CHORUS:
Then off she buzzed, straight to the scene
Of what she *thought* was Halloween,
While down below the white wind swirled
And Christmas winged throughout the world!
("Jingle Bells" is heard. CATS bring on a large cardboard Christmas tree. WINNIE is behind tree, unseen by audience. As CATS place tree beside fireplace, which has a hinged back, WINNIE hides in fireplace. CATS hang stockings on the fireplace, and put a wreath on the mantel. Four CHILDREN enter, dressed in bathrobes, and take places by the fireplace. CATS sit on floor.)
WITCHES:
Then by their mantel, green and gay,
WIZARDS:
Some children waited for Christmas Day.
1ST CHILD:
Listen—did you hear that hoof?
2ND CHILD:
I heard a sleigh upon the roof!
3RD CHILD:
He's coming! Coming! I see a buckle!
4TH CHILD:
I see his boots! I hear his chuckle!
("Jingle Bells" is played in agitated fashion. WINNIE pops out of fireplace and cackles loudly, waving her broom, and stands at center.)
WINNIE:
Gadzooks! It's spooks! Three gruesome cheers
And Happy Halloween, my dears!
(CHILDREN scream loudly and run offstage. WINNIE turns round and round on broom. She disappears into fireplace as CATS exit, carrying off tree.)

ALL:

Oh, what a faux pas! What a goof!
What a monumental spoof!

1ST QUARTET:

Back flew Winnie through the blue-black night
Determined was Winnie to set things right—

2ND QUARTET:

So she zigged over mountains and she zagged over seas,
Till a copper moon flashed and shone through the trees.

ALL:

And she said: "Well, before I was twixt and between
But now, I'll bet my old black hat,
It's really Halloween!"

(CATS *bring on decorated panel which resembles envelope with a large red heart in the center.* WINNIE *walks behind this, out of view of audience. Four* CHILDREN, *dressed in everyday clothes, come on, run up to valentine. "Let Me Call You Sweetheart" is heard.*)

1ST CHILD:

It's tremendous!

2ND CHILD:

Enormous!

3RD CHILD:

It's perfectly fine!

4TH CHILD:

Let's open our marvelous valentine. (*They go to open it and* WINNIE *pops out through heart.*)

WINNIE:

Goblins are blue,
Demons are green,
I wish you a happy
Halloween!

(CHILDREN *scream and run off.* WINNIE *claps hands to her head.* CATS *exit with the valentine.*)

Merciful monsters, I must persevere.

I must find Halloween midnight, this year.

(*She mounts broom backwards again, goes backwards, then rights herself and exits.*)

ALL:

Off flew Winnie through the misty-moisty night,

Determined was Winnie to set things right,

So she zigged down low, and she zagged up high

Till a fat moon glowed in the evening sky.

And she said:

WITCHES:

"Well, before I was twixt and between

But now, I'll bet my blooming broom

It's really Halloween!"

(*"Yankee Doodle" is heard as* CATS *bring on a giant firecracker, on a bunting-draped wagon.* WINNIE *is crouched down inside.* CATS *hold both sides of firecracker during action.* CHILDREN *enter.*)

CHILDREN:

It's wonderful, wonderful Fourth of July,

Let's shoot our rocket up to the sky!

(CHILD *pulls up the fuse with flame attached.* CHILDREN *back away with fingers in ears as* WINNIE *pops up out of firecracker. She waves her hat and cackles.*)

WINNIE:

Happy Halloween with a big, bad boo!

Three cheers for the orange and black and blue!

(CHILDREN *look at her, astonished. Then they stand and pantomime laughter.* WINNIE, *still in firecracker, looks miserable. She pulls out a large black handkerchief and begins to cry loudly.*)

Oh, fee! Oh, fie! Oh, sulphur and pitch!

I'm a muddle-headed, addle-headed fool of a witch!

(*She sinks down in the firecracker.* CHILDREN *come up*

and peer in, then exit as CATS *push the firecracker off-stage. As the chorus chants,* CATS *bring the pumpkins on stage.*)

WIZARDS (*Slowly and sadly*):
Back flew Winnie through the sad, bad night.
This time things never would be right—
So she sagged through the fog and she dragged through
    the bog
To her witch's hut upon the moor
Beside the hollow log . . .
(CATS *return to their original sleeping position.* WINNIE *limps slowly back on stage, sits on stool, shakes head and goes to sleep, snoring softly.*)

ALL:
Now, it happened just to happen
In the dark of the year,
When the yellow, grinning goblin moon
Begins to appear,
That the time for Halloweening came
Again, that mystic night,
And all the proper witches were
In ghastly, ghostly flight.
(*Mysterious music is heard.* CHILDREN, *dressed in witch hats and masks, creep up to* WINNIE *on hands and knees.*)
Some strange and curious persons
Came a-stalking, came a-creeping
Up to the little stool
Where Winnie lay a-sleeping.

CHILDREN (*Jumping up and yelling*): *Boo!* (WINNIE *jumps and squeals. She stands on her stool, waving her broom at the* CHILDREN. *They take off their masks.*)
Winnie, get ready!
It's time for flight

We came to remind you
It's Halloween night!
WINNIE:
Bats and behemoths! I nearly was late again.
Thank you, dear children, for setting me straight again.
Now, I must hurry, I feel the dark power
Of the magical, mystical midnight hour!
(*She mounts her broom as if poised for flight.*)
Goodbye, dear children, remember this, do,
I'll always be witching over you.
We witches have a simple creed:
A fiend in need is a fiend indeed!
(*She cackles and waves to* CHILDREN, *who wave back.*)
CHILDREN: Happy haunting, Winnie!
ALL:
So Winnie flew off to glorious glory, (WINNIE *flies off-stage; the* CHILDREN *follow her.*)
But this is not quite the end of the story.
For we've heard it from a goblin
Who heard a ghost mention
WIZARDS:
That he heard it from a wizard
WITCHES:
At the witches' convention—
ALL:
That half-past springtime
In a house on a hill,
Some children found an Easter basket
On a window sill,
And out of an egg, with a cackling sound,
Came wayward Winnie, with a bounce and a bound.
(WINNIE *hops in across stage, two white bunny ears in her witch hat, and a powder puff tail on her back. She waves to the audience and shouts.*)

WINNIE:
   Perhaps it's odd! Perhaps it's funny!
   But I'm replacing the Easter Bunny!
   Happy Eastereen! (*Curtain*)

THE END

The Runaway Bookmobile

Characters

DRAGGER DUGAN

BOOKWORM BAILEY

BIBLIO, *the library genie*

MEDUSA

QUEEN ELIZABETH

TOM SAWYER

VOICE OF AUNT POLLY

LIBRARIAN

CHORUS

BEFORE RISE: BOOKWORM BAILEY, *carrying several books, enters in front of curtain, walking briskly.* DRAGGER DUGAN, *walking slowly, enters behind him.*

BOOKWORM: Hey, Dragger, come on. Quit draggin' your heels. You're really living up to your nickname today. The bookmobile doesn't park here forever, you know.

DRAGGER: Aw, I dunno, Bookworm. I don't think I want to hang around an old library on a great afternoon like this. And how can you carry a big armload of books like that? I should think it would make you dizzy to read all that, even if you are a bookworm. Me—I don't even have a library card.

BOOKWORM: What's the matter with the library? I think it's a neat place.

DRAGGER: Aw—I dunno. When you go to a library, they always give you the eye and go "shh-h-h!"

BOOKWORM: Well, you're supposed to be reading, not flapping your jaws.

DRAGGER: Anyway, I really wanted to go to the movies today. There's a great picture—all about time machines and monsters and stuff.

BOOKWORM: Come on, Dragger. Just come in for five minutes while I return these books, will you?

DRAGGER: All right, but only for five minutes. All that peace and quiet makes me nervous.

BOOKWORM (*Looking over his books*): Let's see what I have. Hey, that's funny. This book isn't mine.

DRAGGER (*Looking at book curiously*): What is it?

BOOKWORM: *The Runaway Bookmobile.* Let's see if there's a library card inside. (*He looks at book.*) Nope, not a trace of the owner.

The curtains behind the boys open, revealing the interior of the bookmobile. BIBLIO sits at the desk up center with his back to the audience. The CHORUS is seated downstage at one side. The boys continue to look through the book, and do not notice the bookmobile.

BOOKWORM (*Excitedly*): Hey, listen to the spooky way this book begins, Dragger. (*Reading*) "The two unsuspecting boys entered what seemed to be a normal, everyday bookmobile. Little did they suspect that the most astounding adventure of their lives was about to begin."

DRAGGER: Aw, I dunno. I'll bet it doesn't have any monsters in it.

BOOKWORM (*Turning and pointing at bookmobile*): Say, look at that. The librarian has opened the doors already. Let's go in. (*The two boys enter, take off their caps, and approach BIBLIO, who keeps his back to them. BOOKWORM whispers loudly to DRAGGER.*) That's the librarian.

DRAGGER (*Out loud*): How come she has that funny hat on?

BOOKWORM: Shh-h! Pipe down. She'll hear you.

DRAGGER: See, I haven't been here two seconds, and you're already shushing me!

BOOKWORM (*Whispering*): You know something? That doesn't look like our librarian at all. (*Clearing his throat*) Ahem! Ma'am? (BIBLIO *whirls around and shouts loudly.*)

BIBLIO: Aha! Customers!

BOYS: Yipes!

BOOKWORM: You aren't our librarian! Who are you?

BIBLIO (*Bowing*): I am the Quintessence of Bibliography. But you can call me "Biblio" for short.

DRAGGER: Gee whiz. You look like something from outer space.

BIBLIO: That's a very good guess, Dragger Dugan.
I'm from outer space
And inner space—
From everywhere,
And any place—
From Omicron to Ampersand
By way of Never-Neverland.
Where mankind's restless thoughts must flow—
There goes obedient Biblio.

DRAGGER: Wow! A real genie. Are you going to put us in your power and keep us prisoners?

BIBLIO: Not at all, Dragger Dugan, not at all. As a matter of fact, you are one person I do *not* have in my power. As for holding you prisoner—the only kind of prisoners a library can hold are those who are under the spell of the written word. And I sadly fear, Dragger Dugan, that you will not let yourself be enchanted.

DRAGGER: So?

BIBLIO: So, it is my job to try to open that closed mind of

yours and let the sunlight of the printed word trickle in.

CHORUS (*High and mysterious*): Trickle, trickle, trickle, trickle, trickle.

BOYS: What's that?

BIBLIO: Those are my disembodied voices. Every genie has disembodied voices.

BOOKWORM: Golly, are they ghosts?

BIBLIO: Not exactly. Those are the voices of all the books, in all the libraries, in all the world.

CHORUS: Books, books, books, books, books.

BIBLIO: Tell me, boys. What do you think this bookmobile *really* is?

BOOKWORM: It's a kind of library on wheels—isn't it?

BIBLIO: Look sharp! Listen well! Things are never what they seem.

CHORUS:
Things are never what they seem,
Walls and floor may be a dream,
A wink of eye may change this scene,
From bookmobile to *time machine!*

BOYS: A time machine!

BIBLIO: Listen!

CHORUS:
Tic-toc, tic-toc,
Now we stop the cosmic clock
Halfway up from tic—to—toc.

1ST SOLO (*Mysteriously*): What—time—is—it?

CHORUS:
It's Once Upon a Time,
It's way back when—
It's the time of the phoenix, the basilisk, the salamander.
It's tall tale time,
It's time for the old, old legends.

BIBLIO: How would you like to meet a monster, Dragger?

DRAGGER: Sure I would. Boy, maybe libraries aren't so dull after all!

BIBLIO (*Picking up mirrors from desk and handing them to boys*): Here are two mirrors. When the monster comes, look into the mirrors. Do not look at her directly or you will be turned to stone.

DRAGGER: *Her?* You mean this is a girl monster? Aw, I'm not scared of any old girl. I don't need a mirror.

BIBLIO: Quiet! I must summon Medusa, the Gorgon. Come, Medusa. Wake, Medusa. Wake from your black cavern under the aegis of Athena. Come to us out of the swirling mists of Hades, out of the dim distance of the golden age of Greece. (MEDUSA *enters, fluttering her arms. The boys hold mirrors so they can see her over their shoulders.*)

MEDUSA: Who calls me? Who calls me from the pages of the ancient manuscripts of eternity?

DRAGGER: Wow! She sure needs a manicure. Who is *she?*

MEDUSA:
I am Medusa the Terrible, Medusa the Gorgon.
Once, I was a lovely maiden with soft white fingers,
And hair that rippled like moonlight
Over the wine-dark sea.
But then came Athena, Goddess of Olympus most high;
She saw my great beauty, and she was jealous.
In a stroke of vengeance, like lightning,
She wiped the beauty from my face.
She left me as you see me—
A monster with claws of bronze
And fangs, like a swine!
Oh, pity me! Misery me! Woe is me! (*She sobs.*)

DRAGGER: She could use a haircut, too. Ah-h-h. Her hair —it's moving! She has snakes on her head! (*He turns and looks at* MEDUSA.)

BOOKWORM: Don't look, Dragger! (DRAGGER *shudders, and stands rigid.*) Help, Biblio! He's petrified! Look at him!

BIBLIO: Tsk! Tsk! That was naughty of you, Medusa. I shall have to send you back home. (*He holds up his hands and advances toward her.* MEDUSA *covers her face with her arms and backs slowly offstage.*) Back, Gorgon! Back to your cave in antiquity. Back, I say. There, that did it. Now, Bookworm, don't worry. Your friend, Dragger, just needs a good shake, that's all. (BOOKWORM *shakes* DRAGGER, *who shudders again, sighs deeply, and comes back to life.*)

DRAGGER: That was great! She was a first-class monster, even if she was a girl.

BIBLIO: Shall we try another kind of time now, boys?

BOYS: Let's!

BIBLIO: Very well. Suppose we ask our time machine to take us to historical time.

CHORUS:
Tic-toc, tic-toc,
Now we stop the cosmic clock
Halfway down from tic—to—toc.

1ST SOLO: What—time—is—it?

CHORUS: It is the time of Elizabethan England.

2ND SOLO: What time is it, *exactly?*

CHORUS: It is the merry month of May, in fifteen hundred and eighty. (*The voice of* QUEEN ELIZABETH *is heard from offstage.*)

QUEEN ELIZABETH (*Off, shouting*): My lords! My ladies! What ho! Where is my royal court?

BOYS: Who is that?

BIBLIO: How remarkable! Our time machine has captured a very great lady indeed. Buckle on your swords, lads, for here comes Her Majesty, Elizabeth of England.

ELIZABETH (*Striding on majestically*): Odds bodkins. Who

hath summoned me from my quiet abode in the pages of history? Who, I say? I shall have him in the Tower, if he speaketh not!

BIBLIO: Gracious Majesty, 'twas Biblio who summoned you. One of these young bucks does not believe in libraries. (*Points to* DRAGGER)

ELIZABETH: Fie and forsooth. Why, my England keeps its printers busy both night and day turning out folios and quartos for the public. Libraries? In truth, they are magical places. Stand forth, lad, and let me see you. (BIBLIO *pushes* DRAGGER *forward toward her.*) Why, he's a *likely* young fellow. Come now, away with these surly notions about books. Swear to me that you'll no longer be such an ignoramus, and I'll dub you both knights of my court.

DRAGGER (*Bowing*): I swear, Your Majesty.

ELIZABETH: In my court, even the most bold fellows are well read and well spoken. Why, Sir Walter Raleigh himself both reads and writes books. Shall I have him teach you two to fence, and ride to hounds?

DRAGGER: Sir Walter Raleigh! Oh, boy!

ELIZABETH: And my lord, Sir Francis Drake, if it please you, is a most brilliant navigator and seaman. Where did he learn his trade? From the journals of Magellan and Vasco da Gama, I'll warrant. Tell me, would you like to sail as midshipmen aboard *The Golden Hind,* and search for treasure?

DRAGGER: I won't even wait to pack my toothbrush. I'm ready to go right now.

BOOKWORM: Oh, could we go with the Queen, Biblio?

BIBLIO: I'm sorry, boys. Both of you are tied by time and fortune to the twentieth century. And Her Highness must return to the sixteenth century.

ELIZABETH: 'Tis true, alas. 'Twas all too brief a visit, but my England calls me. Farewell. (*She waves a handker-chief as she exits.*) Farewell. Visit me again, in your history books.

DRAGGER: Aw, that's not fair, Biblio. Just when we were starting to have fun. Now she's gone nearly four centuries away.

BIBLIO: Nonsense. You are no further away from merry old England than your nearest history book. Open it, and presto! there you are. Now come along with me to visit a third kind of time.

CHORUS:
Tic-toc, tic-toc,
Now we stop the cosmic clock
Halfway across from tic—to—toc.

1ST SOLO: What—time—is—it?

CHORUS:
It's the twinkling of an eye,
It's time out of mind,
It's imagination, creation,
Daydreaming time.

BIBLIO: It's time to meet somebody who never was. And yet, he's somebody who is just as real as you two boys —in his own way. Let's see if you recognize him. (TOM SAWYER *enters, whistling. He carries a fishing rod.*)

BOOKWORM: I don't know him. Does he look familiar to you, Dragger?

DRAGGER: Nope.

TOM (*Looking them over*): Howdy. You fellers new here?

BOOKWORM: I guess you might say we are.

TOM: Thought so. Want to come fishing with me on the Mississippi?

DRAGGER: Hey, Bookworm. Now, at least we know he lives on the Mississippi.

BOOKWORM: What do you do on the river besides fish?

TOM: My friends and I are building a raft right now.

There's a deserted island, smack dang in the middle of the river. We aim to go exploring it—maybe cook catfish over hot coals for supper. Don't know what we'll find there—maybe river pirates, or even Injuns in war paint and feathers. Come on. Why don't you come with us?

DRAGGER: Wow! A deserted island! I'll come with you right this minute.

BOOKWORM: These friends of yours—are they from your school?

TOM: Nope. My friend Jim, he's grown up, and as for Huckleberry Finn, why, he wouldn't go to school if you paid him a million dollars. No, siree!

BOOKWORM: Huckleberry Finn? Did you say you're a friend of Huckleberry Finn?

TOM: Sure. We're closer than two pickles in a bottle, Huck and me.

AUNT POLLY (*Calling from offstage*): Tom . . . Tom! Where are you, you pestiferous young'un?

TOM: Oh-oh. I have to get humpin'. That's my Aunt Polly. Ever meet my Aunt Polly? She's a head whacker. If she finds me here, she'll take a thimble and whack my head. And that hurts! (*He rubs his head.*)

BOOKWORM: Aunt Polly? Why, I know who you are!

BOYS: You're Tom Sawyer!

TOM: Of course I am. I thought you knew that all the time. Now, listen. I have to go, but you two meet me at moonrise, over by the graveyard. When you see me, hoot real low (*He hoots.*) like an owl. I'll shinny down the drainpipe when Aunt Polly isn't looking. Don't forget—moonrise—or we'll push off without you. So long. (*He exits whistling.*)

DRAGGER (*Starting after him*): Wait, Tom. We have to ask permission.

BOOKWORM: Please, Biblio, let us go with him. Tom

Sawyer had more adventures than you could shake a stick at.

BIBLIO: Let you go with him? Now wouldn't that be a fine kettle of catfish. How can you go trotting off with Tom Sawyer? You'd have to be written right into the book, and I don't think Mr. Mark Twain, the author, had any such characters as Dragger Dugan and Bookworm Bailey in his masterpiece.

DRAGGER: You mean we can't go down the Mississippi with him?

BIBLIO: Oh, you can still keep that appointment with Tom. You'll find him waiting for you at moonrise, right between the covers of a book. Now, boys, I must take you back to your own time.

CHORUS:

Tic-toc, tic-toc,

Now we stop the cosmic clock

Halfway around from tic—to—toc.

1ST SOLO: What—time—is—it?

CHORUS:

It's the right time,

The actual,

The real time,

The factual.

2ND SOLO: What is the authentic, genuine, true and accurate time?

CHORUS: It is (*Insert exact date*).

BIBLIO: Now, boys, you are at your correct chronological stations. I must leave you here, for the sand in my hourglass has run low. My time is "yesterday unlimited" and "tomorrow inexhaustible." I won't say goodbye, for I dwell in the mystical land of everywhere. I'll simply say "au revoir" until we meet between the pages of a book. Look for me wherever you find the enchanted bookshelves of your neighborhood library. (*He exits, waving.*) Au revoir.

CHORUS:

Au revoir, au revoir, au revoir.
Things are never what they seem,
Walls and floor may be a dream,
A wink of eye will make things *real*,
From time machine to *bookmobile!*

(*The* LIBRARIAN *enters. The boys rub their eyes.*)

LIBRARIAN: Hello, boys. You're early, aren't you? Have you been waiting long?

BOOKWORM: Hey! Are my eyes playing tricks? It's our librarian!

DRAGGER: Yes, we've been waiting quite a while. About half of eternity, I think.

LIBRARIAN: Why, it's Dragger Dugan. I never thought I'd see you here. Welcome to the library, Dragger. Here, Bookworm, I'll take those books from you. (*She holds up copy of "The Runaway Bookmobile."*) Well, look at this. You've taken out a very popular book. It's all about a bookmobile that turns into a time machine. It runs away—not in space, but in time. (*Boys clear their throats.*) But of course you must know all about it.

BOYS (*Nodding significantly to each other*): Yes, ma'am!

LIBRARIAN: You know, I've had many boys and girls tell me that this story is written so vividly that they felt as if they were actually living the story themselves. Tell me, did you feel the same way?

BOOKWORM: Yes, ma'am.

DRAGGER: It's so realistic it takes your breath away.

BOOKWORM: Come to think of it, I could use a little fresh air. I feel sort of dizzy. Coming, Dragger?

DRAGGER: Just a minute, Bookworm. If you don't mind, I'd like to browse around the bookshelves. I might even want to take out a library card.

LIBRARIAN: One library card coming up for Dragger Dugan! (*She starts to write out card.*)

BOOKWORM (*Shaking his head*): Now I have seen absotively posilutely *everything!* (LIBRARIAN *hands* DRAGGER *a card and then exits with the boys.*)

CHORUS:
We are books, books, books.
We are books, books, books.

1ST SOLO:
Rare books and rocket books—

2ND SOLO:
Cookbooks and pocket books—

3RD SOLO:
Books of dogs and books of birds—

4TH SOLO:
Books of singing silver words—

5TH SOLO:
Books of jesters, books of sages,
Thousands of stories, all epochs and ages,
With folk of the universe, crowding their pages.

CHORUS:
Brave men and cavemen,
Johnson and Boz,
Ivanhoe and the Wizard of Oz,

6TH SOLO:
Mary Poppins and Peter Pan—

7TH SOLO:
Pippi and Puck,

8TH SOLO:
Oliver Twist,

9TH SOLO:
Roaring Camp's Luck—

10TH SOLO:
Giants and gingerbread,

11TH SOLO:
Elephants and elves,
CHORUS:
Side by side jostle
On library shelves.
12TH SOLO:
What a world you can conquer!
13th SOLO:
What a world to explore!
14TH SOLO:
You can read till the dawnlight.
15TH SOLO:
There'll always be more.
CHORUS:
Oh, come along with us,
Come with us today.
Oh, come along with us
Down library way.
1ST SOLO:
Yes, come along with us—
2ND SOLO:
Come with us—today!
CHORUS (*Slowly*):
Oh, come along with us
Down library way! (*Curtain*)

THE END

The Insatiable Dragon

Characters

LI-PING, *the scholar*
SAN-SU, *the mother*
SOBA, *the cook*
LUM-FU, *the stoneworker*
WANG, *the magician*
CHU-CHU, *his apprentice*
LITTLE DRAGON, *a hand puppet*
BIG DRAGON
BROTHERS AND SISTERS OF THE DRAGON

TIME: *Long ago, before the discovery of fire.*
SETTING: *Outside the house of Wang the magician, in ancient China.*
BEFORE RISE: *A gong sounds. LI-PING, SAN-SU, SOBA, and LUM-FU enter in front of curtain from left. Gong sounds again, and CHU-CHU enters from right. The others rush up to him, shouting angrily.*

CHU-CHU (*Full of self-importance*): Hush. Be quiet. I've never heard such a noisy crowd. What do you want?
LI-PING: Don't be so high and mighty, Chu-Chu. I knew you when you fed the pigs for the farmers. Ever since you became an apprentice to Wang the magician, you have been impossible.

SAN-SU: Please tell the honorable Wang that we wish to see him.

CHU-CHU: It is too early to see my master. (*He yawns.*) Go away. Come back at noon. Don't summon Wang—he'll summon you. (*He yawns again and turns to go.*)

LUM-FU (*Taking hold of* CHU-CHU's *jacket and pulling him around*): Not so fast, Chu-Chu. Wang the magician promised us something.

SOBA: Wang the magician promised us this something over four moons ago. We have been very patient.

LI-PING: Now the sands of our patience have run low. We want our something special today. We can wait no longer.

ALL (*Pushing forward toward* CHU-CHU, *ad lib*): Yes. We won't wait. Let us see Wang. (*Etc.*)

CHU-CHU (*Pushing them away*): Tut, tut, tut. My master is deep in sleep. If you waken him with foolish requests, he will give you something special, oh, yes, indeed! Now, go home. Shoo! (WANG *enters from right and stands behind* CHU-CHU, *glaring at his back, arms folded inside his robe, Mandarin-fashion. The gong sounds again. All bow very low, except* CHU-CHU.) What are you bowing for, you sillies? (WANG *clears his throat.* CHU-CHU *turns and sees him.*) Oh! Master, I didn't see you. (*He kneels down, touching his forehead to the floor.*)

WANG: Rise, please. (*All raise their heads except* CHU-CHU *who continues to bump his forehead on the floor.* WANG *pokes him impatiently.*) Oh, get up, Chu-Chu, and stop overdoing things. Why did you not tell me *immediately* of this important delegation? (CHU-CHU *scrambles to his feet, looking very downcast.*) Pray excuse the bad manners of this most unworthy apprentice.

CHU-CHU: But, master, I thought you were asleep. I thought you would be angry. I thought—I thought—

WANG (*Sighing*): Enough of your thoughts. You have

many thoughts, yet you never think. Now, let us waste no more time. Let us go at once to my chambers.

He claps twice. The gong sounds. The curtains open, revealing the interior of WANG's house. Down center is a table, covered with a cloth that reaches to the floor. On the table is a shallow, brass-colored bowl. Both bowl and table have holes cut in them, placed directly over each other, so that the LITTLE DRAGON puppet may be worked from beneath the table. A second tablecloth is draped over one side of the table. Folding screens with Oriental designs form the backdrop. WANG stands behind the table, with CHU-CHU beside him. LI-PING and SAN-SU stand down right, and LUM-FU and SOBA stand down left.

WANG: It was many moons ago that you came to me for a favor, Li-Ping.

LI-PING: Four moons ago, I asked the clever Wang to bring this humble scholar a dragon. I wished for a dragon who could turn the night into day, so that I might study after the sun went down.

CHU-CHU (*Rudely*): Turn night into day? Impossible!

SAN-SU: Four moons ago, I asked the warm-hearted Wang to bring this unworthy mother a dragon. I wished for a dragon who would bring the sun of June into the house of December so that my children should be warm all winter.

CHU-CHU: Bring summer to winter? Impossible!

LUM-FU: Four moons ago, I asked the wise Wang to bring this undeserving stoneworker a dragon. I wished for a dragon that would melt the hearts of stones, so that they would weep tears of silver.

CHU-CHU: Tears of silver? Impossible!

SOBA: Four moons ago, I asked the mighty Wang to bring this unimportant cook a dragon. I wished for a dragon who would turn my poor meals into feasts fit for an emperor.

CHU-CHU: Oh, ho, ho, ho! No dragon in heaven or earth could do that! Make *his* meals fit for an emperor? Impossible!

WANG: Quiet, you impertinent boy. Listen to me carefully, citizens. Wang the magician has thought earnestly about your requests. Wang has sent flights of pigeons to the heavens with your wishes. And the heavens have been kind. They have sent a dragon.

CHU-CHU: I don't call that being kind. One dragon for four people.

WANG (*Thundering at him*): Silence, cabbage, or I will turn you into a blade of grass and send a cow to eat you! (CHU-CHU *bows his head and cowers.*) One dragon will suffice. Wang has spoken. Now then, I shall summon the dragon. Give me a flint and a lodestone, Lum-Fu.

LUM-FU (*Taking them from pocket and handing them to* WANG): Here, Wang the wise.

WANG (*Pointing to basket at right of table*): Li-Ping, hand me yonder scroll of paper.

LI-PING (*Handing scroll to him*): Here, Wang the clever.

WANG: San-Su, hold the flint above the brass bowl, thus. (SAN-SU *does as she is told.*) Soba, hold the lodestone on the other side, above the brass bowl, so. (SOBA *does as he is directed.*) When I wave—thus (*He makes a magical motion with his hand*)—strike the two pieces sharply together, and the dragon will appear in the bowl.

CHU-CHU: *Sharply,* now.

WANG: I do not need an echo, Chu-Chu. (*Indicating coal basket at left of table*) Go to the basket and fetch a few bits of charcoal to feed the dragon.

CHU-CHU: Charcoal? Oh, but if I were a dragon, I should much prefer a dinner of rice and peppers.

WANG (*Impatiently*): When you are a dragon, you can eat what you wish. Meanwhile, do as you are bid or I will turn you into a black cloud and cause you to rain out over the sea.

CHU-CHU (*Going to coal basket*): Very well, master. (*To the audience*) A dragon who eats charcoal—ugh!

WANG: Prepare yourselves. (*He raises his hands.*) O most excellent dragon, come from the heart of the flint. Come from the inmost center of the lodestone. Come! (*He makes the magical motion.*) Now . . . (SAN-SU *and* LUM-FU *strike flint and lodestone together. Nothing happens.*) Again. (*They strike again. Nothing happens.*)

CHU-CHU: I had a feeling it wouldn't work.

WANG: Again! (*They strike harder. The* LITTLE DRAGON *puppet appears in the bowl.* WANG *drops the paper scroll into the bowl.*)

LITTLE DRAGON: Hssssst!

ALL (*Coming close to the table*): Ah!

DRAGON (*Swaying*): Hsssssst!

ALL: Oh-h-h. (*They bow low.*)

WANG: Quickly, Chu-Chu, give him charcoal. He is hungry. (CHU-CHU *gingerly drops the charcoal into the bowl. Then he recovers his impudence.*)

CHU-CHU: Oh, tut. He is only a little bit of a dragon. What could such a small dragon do to help all these people?

WANG: He is small but mighty.

LI-PING: Ah, see how he glows.

WANG: Just so. He will give you enough light to read through the darkest night.

SAN-SU (*Holding her hand above* DRAGON, *wonderingly*): Ah, feel how warm his breath is.

WANG: Just so. He will warm your house through the bitterest winter.

LUM-FU (*Peering into bowl*): Look—there were some stones at the bottom of the bowl. He has melted them. There are tears of silver!

WANG: Just so. You will have tears of silver for bracelets, and earrings, and crowns. No more stonework for you, Lum-Fu.

SOBA: But what about me? How can the dragon help make feasts fit for an emperor?

WANG: One moment. Chu-Chu, fetch me a bit of raw fish on a green stick.

CHU-CHU: Yes, master. (*He goes off right, returning with a small stick, on which is a bit of fish.*)

WANG: We will hold the fish over the head of the dragon. He will cast a spell over the fish. Watch. (CHU-CHU *holds the fish over the* DRAGON. *The puppet weaves and dances beneath the fish.*)

SOBA (*Sniffing*): Something smells delicious.

WANG: Now, taste it. (SOBA *takes the stick from* CHU-CHU. *He gingerly nibbles the fish, wrinkles up his nose, and cocks his head uncertainly. He takes another nibble, then gobbles the fish.*)

SOBA: Something *tastes* delicious. Heavenly! Fit for an emperor! What *is* this dragon?

WANG: The dragon has a name. He is called "fire."

ALL (*Nodding*): Fire.

CHU-CHU: Oh, I knew *that*. (*Nodding*) Yes, fire. That's right.

WANG: Fire can be given to all of you, but we must have sticks called "torches" so that fire can be carried to your homes. Chu-Chu will stay here to watch the fire, while we find sticks.

CHU-CHU: Yes, master.

WANG: Beware, Chu-Chu. Fire is wily, and like a serpent. There are three things you must *never* do with fire. Do not feed him. Do not let him out of his bowl. And above all, do not let his brothers and sisters into the room. Do you understand?

CHU-CHU: Oh, certainly, I understand, master.

WANG: I hope so. Come with me, all of you. We will go to the pine forest.

ALL (*As the gong sounds*): We will go to the pine forest. (CHU-CHU *bows low as others exit right, then rises impishly with a grin. He goes to the bowl and hovers over the* DRAGON, *who continues to weave and dance slowly.*)

CHU-CHU: Gone at last. The old worrywart. What can be dangerous about such a tiny dragon? Look how weak he is. (*He blows on the* DRAGON, *who weaves and bows more rapidly.*) Why, he bows when I breathe on him. Ah. Now I am the master of the dragon. (*He claps twice and blows harder.*) Bow low, dragon. (*The* DRAGON *bows.*)

DRAGON: Hssssst! Master—

CHU-CHU: The dragon spoke to me. Wonder of wonders. What do you wish, little dragon?

DRAGON: More paper, master, please.

CHU-CHU: More paper? But my master said not to feed you.

DRAGON (*Pathetically*): Do you wish me to starve, master?

CHU-CHU: Oh, no, dragon. If you are hungry, it is only fair to feed you. (*He puts a few scrolls in the bowl.*) There!

DRAGON (*Eating at the scrolls*): Yum! (*He grows bolder.*) Hsst! Master, would you like to see me dance?

CHU-CHU: Oh, yes. Please dance for me.

DRAGON (*Craftily*): You will have to let me out of this bowl. I am very cramped.

CHU-CHU: Let you out of the bowl? Oh, but my master said I must not do that.

DRAGON (*Sighing*): He is an old spoilsport. Doesn't he ever let you have any fun?

CHU-CHU (*Vexed*): No, he doesn't, and that's a fact. Well, I can't see that it would hurt to let you out for a little while. Do you promise you'll get back in the bowl when I tell you it's time?

DRAGON (*Jumping up and down*): Oh, yes. (CHU-CHU *tips the bowl. The puppet withdraws, and out from under the table rolls the* BIG DRAGON. *He stretches and stands, then sways back and forth.*)

CHU-CHU (*Backing away*): Oh, how tall you are. (*Shields his eyes*) How bright you are.

BIG DRAGON: How hungry I am. (*Turns and begins to stuff the cloth which is draped over the table into his robes.*)

CHU-CHU: Here—what are you doing to my master's tablecloth? Stop! That's silk!

BIG DRAGON: Yum! I love silk.

CHU-CHU (*Taking one end of the tablecloth, and pulling*): Give it back! (BIG DRAGON *growls and touches* CHU-CHU *on the tip of his nose.* CHU-CHU *jumps back and rubs his nose.*) Oh, you bit me! Ouch!

BIG DRAGON: Give me my silk dinner. (*He pulls in the rest of the tablecloth.*)

CHU-CHU (*Fanning himself*): Whew, your breath is hot, and you have an evil mist. (*He coughs.*) I'm very tired of you, dragon. It's time to get back into the bowl.

BIG DRAGON (*Insolently*): Never.

CHU-CHU: You promised!

BIG DRAGON: Fire doesn't keep promises. Not when it's hungry. And the more fire eats, the hungrier it gets. Ah, your sleeve looks good. (*He weaves toward* CHU-CHU, *who backs away, terrified.*)

CHU-CHU: Don't you touch me. Go back. Go back, I command you. I am your master.

BIG DRAGON: Ha, ha. Are you indeed? No, little Chu-Chu. The tables are turned. I am *your* master. (*He weaves over the stage*) Why, there are lots of good things to eat here. A feast. Do you know what? I'm going to have a party. (*Calling*) Brothers! Sisters!

CHU-CHU (*On his knees*): No, no. Don't call them, I beg of you. (*The gong sounds several times in rapid succession.* BROTHERS AND SISTERS OF THE DRAGON *weave and dance out from behind the screens.*)

BROTHERS AND SISTERS: Too late! Too late! We're here. (*If desired, they may do a fire dance to appropriate music, as* CHU-CHU *watches in terror.*)

BIG DRAGON: Eat and be merry, Brothers and Sisters. Flicker and burn. Devour and consume.

CHU-CHU: No! No! (*Shouting*) Master! Master! (WANG *rushes in, and puts his hands to his head in dismay, as he sees dancing* BROTHERS AND SISTERS.)

WANG: Stop this! Oh, you foolish boy! What have you done? (*Calling offstage*) Ho! Citizens, bring buckets of water.

BIG DRAGON: Water? Oh-h-h!

BROTHERS AND SISTERS: Water? Oh-h-h! (*They stop dancing and begin to cower as* LI-PING, SAN-SU, SOBA, *and* LUM-FU *rush in, carrying buckets. They pretend to throw water on the dragons, who creep behind the screens, leaving only the* BIG DRAGON *crouching on the floor in front of* WANG. *As the four citizens exit,* LI-PING *hands* WANG *a bucket of water, with which he threatens* BIG DRAGON.)

WANG (*Sternly, as* DRAGON *crawls toward table on all fours*): Go on. Go back where you belong. (BIG DRAGON *crawls under the table. After a moment,* LITTLE DRAGON *puppet appears in the bowl and bows very low.*) That's better. Now, dragon, if you ever disobey again, I shall put you out entirely. Do you hear me? (LITTLE DRAGON *nods. To* CHU-CHU) As for you, you impossible boy, perhaps I had better change you into a snowball and let you melt in the hot sun!

CHU-CHU (*Bowing abjectly, touching his head to the floor*): Oh, no, master.

WANG: No, you are right. I will simply send you back to the farmers.

CHU-CHU (*Wailing*): Please, master, let me stay with you. I'll be good. Oh, I will be good.

WANG: Well, I am a foolish old Wang. I will let you stay. But hereafter, you will have *nothing* to do with fire. Do you understand?

CHU-CHU: Oh, yes, master.

WANG (*Clapping twice*): Enter, citizens. (*The four citizens enter carrying large sticks for torches. They stand beside the table.*) Take a bit of the fire, now. It will serve you well if you are careful, but *only* if you are careful. I would give you a proverb about fire, but I think this disobedient boy with the blister on his nose can give you a better lesson.

CHU-CHU (*Very subdued*): Oh, yes, I can. Fire is a good servant—but a bad master. (*He wags a finger at the* DRAGON. DRAGON *draws back.*)

OTHERS (*As they dip torches in the bowl*): Fire is a good servant—but a bad master. (*All turn to audience and bow. The* DRAGON *bows, too, as the curtains close.*)

THE END

Meet the Pilgrims!

Characters

REMEMBER ALLERTON
MARY ALLERTON
HUMILITY COOPER   } *Pilgrim girls*
ELIZABETH TILLEY

LOVE BREWSTER
WRESTLING BREWSTER
FRANCIS BILLINGTON   } *Pilgrim boys*
SAMUEL FULLER, II
RESOLVED WHITE

TOWAMI, *an Indian boy*

BEFORE RISE: LOVE BREWSTER *leads a line of Pilgrim boys and girls across stage in front of curtain. They are arranged by height.*

GIRLS (*Curtsying and addressing audience*): Good day to ye, young mistresses.

BOYS (*Bowing and addressing audience*): Good day to ye, young masters.

LOVE BREWSTER (*To audience*): Good day to ye all. Look at us closely. (*All Pilgrim children turn slowly.*) Do you know who we are? Can you tell where we come from?

GIRLS: We are the Pilgrim maids—

BOYS: We are the Pilgrim lads—

MARY: We are the company of saints—

FRANCIS: And strangers—

ALL: From Plymouth Colony,
Territory of New England,
Continent of America.

LOVE: Our names were written in the logbook of the *Mayflower*. I am Love Brewster.

MARY (*Curtsying*): Mary Allerton.

FRANCIS (*Bowing*): Francis Billington.

REMEMBER (*Curtsying*): Remember Allerton.

SAMUEL (*Bowing*): Samuel Fuller, the second.

ELIZABETH (*Curtsying*): Elizabeth Tilley.

RESOLVED (*Bowing*): Resolved White.

HUMILITY (*Curtsying*): Humility Cooper.

WRESTLING (*Bowing*): Wrestling Brewster.

LOVE: There is yet one more important person.

MARY: His name was not in the logbook of the *Mayflower*.

LOVE: He was here before any of us.

ALL: Where is he? (*They scan the audience with hands on brows.*)

LOVE: He's late! We will continue. Perhaps he will come soon.

MARY: If it please you, why are we here?

REMEMBER: I'll tell you. More than three hundred and forty years have passed since that historic November in Plymouth—

SAMUEL: And American boys and girls have eaten many a Thanksgiving dinner since then.

REMEMBER: Every year for more than three hundred and forty years they have been remembering us—

ALL: The boys and girls of Plymouth Colony.

ELIZABETH: Now it is our turn. We wish to send all of you an invitation.

RESOLVED: It is an invitation to The First Thanksgiving.

LOVE: Aye, come and sit with us at *our* table.

MARY: Haven't you wondered what it was like that very first Thanksgiving?

REMEMBER: We remember it well. We'll show you. Please come.

ALL: Please come!

TOWAMI (*Running down center aisle*): Wait! Wait! Wait for your Indian friend. Wait for Towami.

ALL: 'Tis Towami at last. Hurry!

LOVE: Aye, hurry, Towami. 'Twould not be a proper Thanksgiving without the Indians. Now, hold your breath everyone. We will pull back the curtain of time. (TOWAMI *jumps on stage*) Are ye ready, one and all?

ALL: We are ready, one and all.

LOVE: Back, back, back we go, to the year 1621.

Curtains open slowly on outdoor autumn scene in a clearing in Plymouth, Massachusetts, November, 1621. Bright foliage at back and sides encloses clearing. There is a rude table with benches at left side of stage, laden with platters of turkey, fish, pies, pastries, etc. At one side a fire is laid, with a tripod crane holding a large pot.

REMEMBER: I remember! It was a warm and hazy day. The clouds were like white wool.

SAMUEL: I remember, too. The leaves were brown and gold. They crackled when we walked upon them.

TOWAMI: It was Indian summer. The corn was ripe. The apples were red and gold.

ELIZABETH: We were having a harvest feast. . . .

BOYS:
What did the girls do? What did the girls do?
What did they do that first Thanksgiving day?

GIRLS:
We rubbed, and scrubbed, and polished, and scoured
And stirred, and basted, and stuffed, and served.

MARY (*Leading the girls to table left, where platters of food are waiting; to the audience*): Would you like a sniff of our Thanksgiving feast? Just a sniff now. No more.

REMEMBER: Remember? We had turkeys as fat as mountains. (*Holds up platter of turkey*) And roast ducks, and fat brown geese.

HUMILITY (*Going down center and holding up bowl*): And gravy. A whole ocean of gravy.

BOYS: Yum-yum!

ELIZABETH (*Going down center, calling like a vendor*): Fish . . . fresh fish. . . . Boiled cod, and baked scrod. Steamed clams, fried eels, pickled oysters, and salted herring. . . . Fish . . . fresh fish. . . .

BOYS: Delicious!

MARY (*Leading the line of girls down center as they hold their platters and bowls up*): Pies, pies, pastries and pies. . . . Tuppence, thruppence for pastries and pies. I have blueberry, blackberry, pumpkin and apple. And for a special treat there is a huge, sweet Indian pudding, with rich, dark molasses and raisins.

FRANCIS (*Stealing up behind her*): Just one little raisin. She'll never know—

MARY (*Catching him*): Help! A pudding thief! (*The other girls put down their bowls, form a circle around FRANCIS, banging on trays with wooden spoons.*)

GIRLS: A pudding thief! A pudding thief!

FRANCIS: Please, Mary Allerton, I did take but one raisin.

MARY: One raisin indeed. You took a piece the size of your great head.

GIRLS: Shame! Shame!

ELIZABETH: Put him in the stocks! Feed him fishtails.

REMEMBER: Throw him in the bay and let him ride the sharks.

HUMILITY: Ah now, Mary Allerton. 'Tis harvest time. The poor boy was hungry. Give him another chance.

FRANCIS: Thank you, Humility Cooper. You are very gentle.

MARY: Very well. We shall be merciful. But go about your business, Francis Billington, you troublemaker.

FRANCIS: I'll go. I'll go. (*He goes up right, and sits, indolently watching the boys work.*)

GIRLS:
Now what did the boys do, the boys do, the boys do?
What did the boys do, that first Thanksgiving day?

BOYS:
We chopped, we sawed, we sanded, we nailed. (*They pantomime the action.*)

WRESTLING: We made snares for the rabbits—

TOWAMI (*Proudly*): *I* taught them how.

RESOLVED: We pounded the mud for eels—

TOWAMI: *I* taught them how.

SAMUEL: We cut the tasseled ears of corn.

TOWAMI: *I* taught them how.

LOVE: We cleaned muskets for the soldiers. We raised houses for our fathers. We found firewood for our mothers. We stood in the tops of trees and watched for ships from England.

WRESTLING: No wonder we were always hungry!

LOVE: Come on, lads. Let's bring the tables and benches under the trees. (*Girls exit.*)

WRESTLING (*Sniffing*): Hot turkey. I speak for the drumstick.

LOVE: Hurry. The sooner the tables are up, the sooner we'll eat. (*He spots* FRANCIS.) Here, Billington. Why aren't you working, too?

FRANCIS: I do not feel like working. 'Tis pleasant under the trees. I'll watch you, and give you advice. (*The boys exchange glances and form a circle around* FRANCIS.)

LOVE: Listen to him, lads. He does not feel like working.

BOYS (*Clucking*): He does not feel like working.

LOVE: See here, Billington. Do you feel like eating?

FRANCIS: Oh, yes. I am hungry clear down to my toes.

LOVE: Ah, I see. But surely you know Governor Carver's famous law?

FRANCIS: Which law?

LOVE: This one: The lad who doth not work—

BOYS: Doth not eat.

LOVE: So you just sit there. We will eat the hot roast corn . . .

WRESTLING: And the juicy turkey . . .

SAMUEL: And the sweet, rich blueberry pies . . .

RESOLVED: And the steaming gravy.

FRANCIS (*Groaning*): Oh, no! I give up. I shall obey the law. What work is there for me?

LOVE: Come with us.

RESOLVED: You can carry a nice, hard, heavy oaken bench! (*All the boys except* LOVE *exit right.*)

LOVE (*Going downstage; to audience, sighing*): As ye can see, we were not all *saints!* (*He exits.* MARY *and* RE-MEMBER *re-enter, carrying a large white cloth, which they shake out as* LOVE *and* WRESTLING *bring in a table and benches which they set down at right side of stage.* LOVE *also brings in parchment scroll, which he puts on table.* HUMILITY *and* ELIZABETH *bring a platter of turkey and a large metal pitcher to table. They bring carving set, wooden bowls and spoons to the table. The other boys enter, carrying benches, and set them up at table.* NOTE: *If desired, appropriate Thanksgiving music may accompany the setting of the table. When table is set,* LOVE *claps his hands for attention.*) Hear me now, children. The setting of the children's table is complete. Mary Allerton and I shall take the end places, since we are oldest among ye. Towami shall sit at the right, in the place of honor. Let each lad sit next to a maid. (*They take places quietly and remain standing.*)

MARY (*As all stand in place at the table, hands folded solemnly*): Here we are, this good November day, we who remain of the company of children of the *Mayflower,* from tall Love Brewster to small Resolved White, no bigger than a mouse. Let us hear what Elder Brewster has to say to us.

LOVE (*Using his spoon like a gavel, pounding three times*): Give me your attention, children of Plymouth Colony. Somehow, we came through the bitter winter and the starving spring to this day of bountiful harvest. I say, "Thanks be" for all our blessings. Who will join me?

HUMILITY: I, sir! I say thanks be, for this warm sunshine.

WRESTLING: Thanks be that none of us were taken with the smallpox!

ELIZABETH: Thanks be that our fathers and mothers were spared to be with us.

SAMUEL: Thanks be that our good ship, the *Mayflower,* stood the storm winds, and stayed here until spring.

MARY: Thanks be for every ear of corn that stands upon this table. Surely each one is a miracle!

RESOLVED: Thanks be that the bears didn't eat me!

LOVE: Francis Billington—?

FRANCIS (*Sticks his lip out stubbornly*): I do not have to be thankful for anything. I am not one of you Pilgrim saints.

RESOLVED (*Indignantly*): You don't have to be a saint to be grateful. You just have to be human!

FRANCIS (*Thinking a moment*): Oh, all right. . . . Thanks be for the turkey and gravy!

RESOLVED: Amen!

REMEMBER: I remember the King's soldiers in England. I remember how they took us prisoners and kept us in a hateful jail. Thanks be for this free land, where we do as we please.

TOWAMI: Towami speak, too. Towami also make a "thanks be." Thanks be to great spirit for rabbits in the tall grass. For deer in the forest. For fish in the sea.

LOVE: And I say, thanks be for Towami and all the men of Chief Massasoit's tribe. We would not be at this table today without their help.

ALL: Amen!

LOVE (*Unrolling a parchment*): This is a parchment that Elder Bradford gave to me. I must read it to all the children of the Plymouth Colony. Listen well. (*Reading*) "It is not with us, as with other men, whom small things can discourage, or small discontentments cause to wish themselves at home again. Our fathers were Englishmen, which came over this great ocean, and were ready to perish in this wilderness. But they cried unto the Lord, and he heard their voice, and looked on their adversity. Let them therefore praise the Lord, because he is good and his mercies endure forever." .

ALL: Amen!

LOVE: And now saints and strangers, Pilgrims and Indians, let the feast of Thanksgiving begin. (*He holds carving knife over the turkey.* MARY *picks up the pitcher. The boys and girls sit down.*)

ALL (*To audience*): Let Thanksgiving begin! (*Curtain falls.*)

THE END

The Christmas Revel

Characters

TOWN CRIER
TOM ⎫
JOAN ⎪
HARRY ⎬ *village children*
JILL ⎪
BETSY ⎪
NAN ⎭
OTHER BOYS AND GIRLS
WILL
KATHERINE DE MONFORT
WALTER DE MONFORT
LADY JOYCE LUCY
LORD THOMAS LUCY (*Lord of Misrule*)
MAID
FOOTMAN
MAYOR
TITANIA (*Queen Elizabeth*)

SCENE 1

TIME: *Christmas afternoon, 1578.*
SETTING: *A village square in Warwickshire, England. If desired, the scene may be played before the curtain.*

At Rise: Tom, Joan, Harry, Jill, Betsy, Nan, *and* Other Boys and Girls *enter, singing to the tune of "Greensleeves."*

Children (*Singing*):
Oh, once upon a time, in England
Lord and commoner mingled so;
On Christmas Eve with yule log blazing
And candles all aglow.
Green, green were the holly branches,
Green, green the mistletoe,
Green, green the pine and laurel
Once in the long ago . . .

Town Crier (*Entering*): Hear ye! Hear ye, good citizens of Warwickshire! His Lordship, Sir Thomas Lucy, of the Manor Charlecote, announces a Christmas revel!

Children: Merry Christmas, town crier!

Town Crier: Merry Christmas, children! Have you heard the news? A Christmas revel is held at Charlecote this very evening.

Joan: Oh, that's nothing to us, crier. That's for ladies with their noses in the air, and for gentlemen in fine ruffs and doublets.

Town Crier: Not so. Not so at all, Miss Snippet. 'Tis for all the people of this village and especially for the children.

Children (*Ad lib; happily*): The children? A revel? For us? (*Etc.*)

Betsy (*Shyly*): Do you say it is for all of us?

Nan: Even for me?

Town Crier: Especially for you. This is a special revel—not like any before it. (*He motions them to draw near.*) Hear me well. Her Ladyship is having a doll contest.

Jill: Dolls? What sort of dolls?

Town Crier: All sorts of dolls. Rag dolls, wooden dolls,

china dolls and paper dolls. For the best doll brought to the revel, there will be a prize.

CHILDREN: A prize, a prize!

JOAN: And pray, what is it?

TOWN CRIER: A bag of gold sovereigns, that's what.

CHILDREN (*Ad lib; excitedly*): Gold pieces! Prizes! Sovereigns? (*Etc.*)

TOM: Forsooth, this is a contest for girls.

HARRY: His Lordship should have a contest for the boys.

TOWN CRIER: He has. Indeed, fellow, he has. Are there any lads here who are well spoken and have a courtly manner?

BOYS (*Ad lib*): Me! Me! I have! (*Etc.*)

HARRY: Here, town crier. I am Harry of the Duck Farm. The whole town knows how courteous and quick-witted I am.

TOM: No, town crier, take me. I am called Tom. (*Striking a pose*) I speak pure pear-shaped tones.

BOYS (*Interrupting each other*): Take me . . . take me . . . (*Etc.*)

TOWN CRIER (*Holding up his hand for quiet*): Wait upon my words, lads. Each of ye who wishes to enter will be the champion of a doll put in the contest by a girl.

TOM: I must speak for a *doll?*

TOWN CRIER: You must.

TOM: Oh, fie! I withdraw.

TOWN CRIER: There's another bag of gold in it, boy—

TOM: I'll do it!

BOYS (*Ad lib*): And I. And I! Me, too! (*Etc.*)

TOWN CRIER: Good villagers, I must tell my news in other places. Come one and all with your dolls and champions, or not, as you please, to the great hall at Charlecote this evening when dusk falls.

BETSY: Must we bring anything—gifts or tokens?

TOWN CRIER: Only your merriest heart, child. And now farewell. (*He bows and exits, calling*) Hear ye, hear ye!

CHILDREN: Farewell! Farewell!

GIRL: Let us be off to find our dolls and champions.

BOY: Aye. Come! We must practice our speeches. (OTHER BOYS AND GIRLS *exit.* TOM, JOAN, HARRY, JILL, BETSY, *and* NAN *gather in a group at center.*)

JOAN: A doll contest. Fancy that! I shall enter it, for I have a fine doll made for me by my grandmother. 'Tis a muslin moppet, embroidered in scarlet, with two buttons for eyes. She is dressed in a linen frock with wool tassels.*

TOM: Very fine. Tell me, do you have a champion in mind?

HARRY: Here now, she looked plainly at me, didn't you, Joan?

JILL: Come, Harry of the Duck Farm. I'll have you for my champion. My doll is made of smooth cedar wood, all painted like a courtier, and dressed in leather with a pair of buckled boots. It has arms and legs that move. What say you to that?

HARRY: Why, that's a sporting kind of doll, Jill! I'll champion that one. Wait until you hear how I beat the air with my silver words.

TOM: Ho, ho. You'll quack like your ducks, Harry. Listen to me, Joan. I've been to school for a whole month. I've already learned a poem. (WILL, *a boy of fourteen, enters left, carrying a box.*)

HARRY (*As* WILL *steps forward*): I know you. You live at Stratford, don't you, fellow? Your name is on my tongue. . . . Will, that's it, isn't it?

WILL: That's what I am called, true enough.

---

* Other dolls may be substituted throughout play, if appropriate changes in descriptions are made.

TOM: Yes, I've seen you in the town, too. Your father's a glover— What's the last name? Ah, I have it. Tremblestaff. Will Tremblestaff.

HARRY: No, you dolt, 'tis Quiverlance. Will Quiverlance.

WILL: 'Tis neither, but I'll not tell you at all. Then when you think of it, you'll remember me better.

JOAN (*Impatiently*): Come along, Tom, we've work to do. Let us be off. (*She takes his arm, and they exit.*)

JILL: There—you see, Harry. They've nipped in already to get ahead of us. Now come along, and mind you, we'll take the shortcut home. (*She takes his coat sleeve and pulls him after her as she exits.* WILL *looks after them, puzzled. He shakes his head.*)

BETSY: We could be part of that contest, Nan!

NAN: But we've no doll, Betsy.

BETSY: We have that strange little figure Father gave us —the Italian doll.

NAN: The one with strings attached, the marionette? Is she a doll?

BETSY: She's like a doll, and surely no other girl will have a doll that walks and sits and moves her head.

NAN: But where will we find a champion? We know not one lad who would help us.

WILL (*Crossing over to the girls*): I beg your pardon, ladies, pray—

NAN: Why, he addresses us as if we were ladies of the court. My name is Nan, if it please Your Lordship.

BETSY: Fine ladies we are, dressed in rags. I am Betsy Osborne. We're orphans, the two of us. We live with Old Granny.

WILL: No! I mistook you for ladies of the court of Raggle Taggle. Now, if it please you, tell me the way to Charlecote Hall. I must deliver a box of gloves to Her Ladyship.

BETSY: 'Tis up the hill and down the hill and left through a grove of willows.

WILL: Well told, Lady Betsy. Thank you. (*Hesitating*) Will you be entering a doll in the contest at the Christmas revel?

NAN: We could, we surely could.

BETSY: But we can't.

WILL: What kind of riddle is this—"We could, we could, but we can't—"?

NAN: We have a doll. Our father was a sea captain but he was lost in a shipwreck. Once he went on a trip to Naples and brought us back a curious doll with strings upon it. It moves and dances when you pluck the strings.

BETSY: But we know no boy who would be a champion for us.

WILL: I think you are mistaken. You do know a boy who would champion the doll. Now think—

NAN (*Putting her hands to her head*): I'm thinking.

BETSY (*Shaking her head sadly*): We know of no one.

NAN: Tell us, who might he be?

WILL: Do you see no one in front of your nose?

NAN: You.

WILL: Well, then—and what am I?

NAN: A boy.

BETSY: *You* would be our champion? But you scarcely know us.

WILL: It would give me great pleasure to be champion to the noble ladies of the Raggle Taggle Court.

BETSY: I do not know what to say—

WILL: Then I'll write your speech. Say, "Thank you, generous sir. I accept your gracious offer."

NAN: Wait, wait! (*To* BETSY) We do not know what kind of champion this lad will be! Why, he might swallow his words or forget himself.

BETSY: Shush, Nan. He seems nimble enough with words. What would you have him do—brag and boast like Tom or Harry?

WILL: What say you, ladies?

BETSY: I say, "Thank you, generous sir—"

NAN: "I accept your gracious offer."

WILL: Good! I'm at your service, good my ladies. Now— here's the plot. Let me come with you to see the doll and work her strings. I'll plan my speech on the way to Charlecote, using the doll as an audience to practice on. Then, I'll leave her on the mantel at Charlecote Hall, ready and waiting for me this evening when I enter the lists as her champion. Is it agreed?

BETSY *and* NAN (*Jubilantly*): Agreed!

BETSY: Let us be off.

NAN: This way, noble Will. This way— (*They exit triumphantly, followed by* WILL, *as the curtain falls.*)

*   *   *

SCENE 2

TIME: *Later that afternoon.*

SETTING: *The Great Hall at Charlecote.*

AT RISE: *A* FOOTMAN *is standing on a ladder hanging holly about the room.* LADY JOYCE LUCY *rushes about the room, with her* MAID *following her.*

LADY JOYCE (*Perturbed, to* MAID): Oh, why did that town crier have to come near here? Now my niece, Katherine de Monfort, will insist on entering the doll contest!

MAID: But it is a contest open to everyone, my lady.

LADY JOYCE: It really should be only for the children of the village, and that headstrong girl will spoil it for them by entering her doll. No doubt her cousin Walter, who is here, is behind this. He is insufferable!

KATHERINE (*From offstage*): Aunt Joyce, Aunt Joyce!

LADY JOYCE (*Sighing*): Alas, I'm sure she heard the town crier's announcement, and now there will be no way to stop her.

MAID: Perhaps His Lordship will be able to help you.

LADY JOYCE: You're right. He's the only one strong enough to handle her. Come, let us go find him this moment. (LADY JOYCE *and* MAID *go to exit right and reach door just as* KATHERINE *bursts in, followed by* WALTER.)

KATHERINE: Aunt, why did you not tell me of the doll contest? (*Pushes past* LADY JOYCE *and* MAID, *with* WALTER *close behind her.*)

LADY JOYCE (*Moving back to center; feigning innocence*): Contest? Oh, the *doll* contest. It must have slipped my mind, my dear Katherine.

WALTER (*Pompously*): You forgot us, Aunt, your own flesh and blood? Surely this revel is not intended simply for the common village children. Are we to pine and languish for lack of amusement?

LADY JOYCE: Come, come! Surely you and Katherine have no need of contests. You shall both sit among the revelers.

KATHERINE (*Stamping her foot angrily*): But I *want* to enter the contest, and indeed I *shall* enter. I have a fair china doll with eyes that open and close. She must win the prize. She *must*, I say!

WALTER: And gentle Katherine has chosen me to be her champion. I have already written a speech of presentation. 'Tis full of clever conceits, and pretty phrases. We must win, Aunt.

LADY JOYCE: What shall I do? Of course, you would win. That is not the point, children. 'Twould not be fair for my own noble flesh and blood to enter and win a contest for village children. Oh, where is your Uncle Thomas? He must help me with this matter.

KATHERINE (*Sneakily*): Uncle Thomas is so stern a man, Aunt. He is not kind and generous as you are.

WALTER (*Flatteringly*): I shall mention you in the speech, dear Aunt. I shall make you a benefactress.

LADY JOYCE: No, no, no. 'Tis a matter of principle. 'Twould not be fair at all. I must say nay.

KATHERINE (*Angrily*): Do not say nay, Aunt. Do not! (*She pretends to hold her breath.*)

LADY JOYCE: Now then, Katherine, pray hold your temper. You are becoming red in the face.

WALTER (*Smugly*): See what you have done, Aunt. Katherine will hold her breath until she swoons. I have seen her do it many times.

LADY JOYCE (*Shaking* KATHERINE): Katherine. Ho, niece —dear niece. Pray, stop. Stop!

WALTER: You should not have crossed her wishes, Aunt. She will hold her breath until she turns blue! (*A knock at door right is heard.*)

LADY JOYCE (*To* MAID): Go! Answer the door whilst I call His Lordship. (MAID *crosses to the door, admitting* WILL, *who carries a marionette and a box.* KATHERINE *continues to puff out her cheeks.* LADY JOYCE *crosses left and calls*) My lord! My lord! Come hither.

MAID (*Crossing to center with* WILL): 'Tis the lad from the glover's at Stratford, my lady.

LADY JOYCE: Oh, interruptions, interruptions! Fie. . . . What shall I do? Go, girl. Fetch His Lordship this instant. (MAID *exits left.* LADY JOYCE *takes a fan, fans herself violently.*)

WILL (*Examining* KATHERINE *curiously*): Has she the mumps, fellow?

WALTER (*Stiffening*): I'll thank you not to call me "fellow." I am the Viscount Walter de Monfort. This is my noble cousin, Katherine.

WILL (*Laughing*): Your noble cousin Katherine has uncommonly plump cheeks. Does she store nuts in them, like a squirrel?

LADY JOYCE (*Fanning* KATHERINE): 'Tis not a laughing matter, boy. The girl will make herself ill. She is holding her breath, and I fear she will turn blue.

WILL: Oh, well—if 'tis a cure Your Ladyship needs, why I know a certain remedy.

WALTER: Indeed? The likes of you—?

LADY JOYCE: Oh, I would be so grateful if you could help her.

WILL (*Standing to one side of* KATHERINE, *arms extended and fingers pointed*): I have a small sister at home. She likes to hold her breath when things do not go her way. This is how I cure her. (*He tickles* KATHERINE *so suddenly that she lets out all her breath, and giggles. Then furious, she turns on* WILL.)

KATHERINE: Oh! Churl! Varlet!

WILL (*Amused*): Are you trying to guess my name? Try again.

KATHERINE: A plague upon you, villain. (LORD THOMAS *enters left.*)

LORD THOMAS: Here now, what's the noise?

LADY JOYCE: My lord, 'tis Katherine. I have said she must not enter a doll in the contest, and she will not listen.

LORD THOMAS: She will listen to me. Now, then, Katherine. We will have no more of this nonsense. Do you hear me?

KATHERINE: Aye, sir.

LORD THOMAS: And you, Walter?

WALTER (*Hastily*): Oh, I had no part in this, sir. 'Twas all Katherine's imagining.

LORD THOMAS: Both of you shall leave your aunt in peace. It is my wish that you shall observe the revel, but you shall take no part in it.

BOTH: Yes, Uncle.

LORD THOMAS: Off with you, then. (*They exit left.*)

LADY JOYCE (*To* WILL): Well, fellow. We've had no time for you. What have you in the box?

WILL: Gloves you ordered from my father, Your Ladyship. (*He gives her box.*)

LADY JOYCE: This is the boy who cured Katherine when she held her breath.

LORD THOMAS: Did you, lad? I must reward you well.

WILL: Your Lordship, I ask but one small boon. I am champion of this doll. (*He holds out the marionette.*) May I but leave her upon your mantel for her owners?

LADY JOYCE (*Taking the doll*): A strange little minikin. Leave her, boy. No one shall harm her. (*She puts the doll on the mantel.*)

WILL (*Bowing*): Farewell, Your Ladyship.

LADY JOYCE: Farewell, boy. (*He exits right.*) An odd boy, indeed. He did not want a reward. I did not think to ask his name.

LORD THOMAS: Never mind. The sun is going down. We must costume ourselves for the revel. I will put on the robes of the Lord of Misrule, and you, madam, must be certain that all is well with our special guest and her ladies.

LADY JOYCE: I'll go at once and see to her. Will it not be a wonderful surprise? Why, they'll talk of the excitement of Charlecote for years to come. (*They exit left. After a moment* KATHERINE *and* WALTER *re-enter stealthily.*)

KATHERINE (*Beckoning* WALTER *to come to center*): Hssst, Walter. Come here now.

WALTER: Oh, Katherine—pray, let us stay out of trouble. No more schemes and plots, please, Katherine.

KATHERINE: Pasty face! (*She pokes him in the back.*) Is that a spine I see, or a wet noodle? Where's your courage, Walter? Let me tell you this: We *shall* enter the contest!

WALTER: What, after Uncle has forbidden us to enter?

KATHERINE: We must. Something strange is afoot. This afternoon I saw gilded carriages arriving at the east wing of this very hall. Ladies and gentlemen in velvet cloaks went through the door, and someone all wrapped in furs and satin robes arrived, and they bowed to her. Mark my words, someone high and mighty from London is here. I mean to see her.

WALTER: How?

KATHERINE: I have a plan. (WALTER *groans.*) We shall not enter the contest as Katherine and Walter de Monfort. We shall don rags and tatters, and wear masks.

WALTER (*Turning up his nose*): Rags and tatters indeed!

KATHERINE: Aye. I shall be Plain Kate, the forester's daughter, and you shall be Dirty Walt of the Peat Bog.

WALTER: Dirty Walt of the Peat Bog! Oh, no, Katherine, you go too far.

KATHERINE: Too far for a pretty speech and a bag of gold?

WALTER: Well—

KATHERINE: 'Tis settled then. (*She catches sight of the doll on the mantel.*) Ho—what's this? (*Takes down the doll to look it over*)

WALTER: A doll, methinks.

KATHERINE: Toad brain! I can see it is a doll. But who left it here? Look—it moves when I lift the strings.

WALTER: Gadzooks. The hands wave as if the little thing were alive.

KATHERINE: Look! I'll make her dance a tarantella. (*She moves the doll faster, tangling the strings.*) Oh, help! The strings are tangled.

WALTER: Oh, fie! What have you done? (*He takes small knife from his scabbard*) Here's my jeweled dagger. I'll cut the strings loose. (*Cuts strings*)

KATHERINE: Oh, you cabbage. You've cut the strings that move her. Now see— (*She holds up the doll. Most of the strings hang limply down.*) 'Twill not dance any more. What have you done?

WALTER: What have *you* done? 'Twas you who took the doll and tangled the strings. Let us go quickly hence. I feel a calamity coming.

KATHERINE: So do I. (*She replaces the doll and walks close to* WALTER, *staring intently*) Swear to me, Walter, never to tell a living soul of this, or I shall send the bony Witch of Endor to ride upon your back when the moon is full.

WALTER (*Trembling*): I s-s-swear.

KATHERINE: Good. Let's be gone. (*They exit, as the curtain falls.*)

*   *   *

SCENE 3*

BEFORE RISE: *There is a brief musical interlude.*

TIME: *Christmas night.*

SETTING: *Same as Scene 2. Benches are placed about the room, and there is a dais set beside the fireplace.*

AT RISE: *Village children are seated on the benches, the girls holding their dolls.* OTHER BOYS AND GIRLS *sit on the floor.* NAN *and* BETSY'S *marionette is on the mantel.* LADY JOYCE, MAYOR, TITANIA, *who wears a mask, and* LORD THOMAS, *who is dressed as the* LORD OF MISRULE, *sit on dais.* TITANIA *holds basket containing two bags of gold sovereigns.* WALTER *and* KATHERINE, *who sit behind village children, wear masks and peasant costumes.* KATHERINE *holds a china doll.*

LORD OF MISRULE (*Capering down center*): A Merry Christmas to you, one and all!

---

* If desired, additional Christmas program material may be added to the following scene.

ALL: Merry Christmas, my Lord of Misrule.

LORD OF MISRULE: Welcome to this house. Today we shall have none of pomp and rank, but lord and servant, highborn and commoner, shall eat, drink, and play together as if all were born to the same parents. We shall tease out Christmas from his hiding place with songs and merriment. I do proclaim that frowns and tears shall be banished, and solemn words shall hide in the cellar with the cobwebs. Come one, come all, give us a cheer to shake the welkin! For now we bring in the monarch of the forest, the mighty yule log. (*All cheer, as* FOOTMAN *and* TOWN CRIER *enter with yule log, which they carry to center.*)

Ho, children, sit upon the yule log and wish us good luck in the coming year. (*Several children sit on the log and sing a short carol.*)

Well done, my cheery songsters. (*He takes firebrand from fireplace and holds it up.*) Roll the yule log into the fireplace. (FOOTMAN *and* CRIER *do so.*) Here's a firebrand I hold from last year's log, to light our way to Christmas. (*He "lights" the fire, as all applaud.* NOTE: *A red light may be used to simulate fire.*) Now, before we go to the groaning board, is there not something we have forgotten to attend to?

CHILDREN: The contest—the contest—

LORD OF MISRULE: Oh, to be sure, the contest. We shall have dolls of all kinds and descriptions this very evening. And to present them, we shall have young lads, like the gladiators of old, to fight for their puppets, not with swords, but with words. Now, let us hear the champions exclaim, proclaim and declaim for their ladies fair of wax or wool. Will the first champion rise and make his presentation. . . . (JOAN *hands her doll to* TOM, *who takes it and hesitantly comes forward.*)

JOAN (*In a loud whisper*): Bow! (TOM, *confused, curtsies.*)

No—that was a curtsy. Bow! (TOM *bows so low he is in danger of toppling, and* JOAN *rushes to help him regain his balance, prodding.*) Speak!

TOM (*Opening his mouth, and shutting it several times*): My lord. My ladies. My lord. My ladies.

JOAN (*Angrily*): Go on!

TOM: I have before me in this hand a-a-a—

JOAN: Doll, dolt.

TOM: A doll dolt. That's it—a doll.

ALL (*Good-naturedly*): Hurray!

TOM (*To* JOAN): I said what it was, can I go now?

JOAN: No. Tell them about it.

TOM: I have before me in this hand a doll, made of the finest—ah—

JOAN: Muslin.

TOM: Muslin. This same doll has garments woven of the softest—ah—

JOAN: Linen.

TOM: Linen. This same doll has a face. (*He holds the back of the doll toward the children. They laugh, and* TOM *quickly turns doll around.*) And the face is embeedered—

CHILDREN: What?

TOM: Embordered—

CHILDREN: What?

JOAN: *Embroidered*—

TOM: That's what it is. (*He takes a deep breath.*) That's all, so please you. (*He sits down, cringing as* JOAN *shakes her finger at him*)

HARRY (*Guffawing*): Did you hear that? And he's been to school a month!

LORD OF MISRULE: Next champion! (*Before* HARRY *can object,* JILL *thrusts her doll into his hands and pushes him forward. He looks around and gulps.*) What is your name, lad?

HARRY: 'Tis Harry of the Doll Farm. No, 'tis Doll of the Harry Farm. Oh, fie! 'Tis Harry Farm of the Duck Doll. Oh!

LORD OF MISRULE: And what do you wish, Harry?

HARRY (*Miserably*): I wish I were dead.

JILL: Speak, Harry.

HARRY (*He clears his throat and speaks in falsetto*): Ladies and gentlemen. (*Looks around; now in normal voice*) And others. (*Children laugh.* HARRY *continues in singsong.*) Please to cast your eyes upon this fine wooden duh—duh—

JILL: Doll, Harry.

HARRY: I have it—duck. See how the joints of this duck move with hardly any—squeaking. And look how 'tis all dressed in leather that has hardly any cracks. If you should want for yourself a duck that will last you a lifetime, buy yourself a duck like this . . . like this . . . like this . . .

JILL: Finish, Harry.

HARRY (*Desperately*): How do I finish? (*He thinks, then suddenly says*) Ah . . . ah . . . amen! (*He sighs with relief and sits down, as* JILL *snatches doll.*)

LORD OF MISRULE: Well and religiously spoken, Harry Duck. And now, have we another champion? (KATHERINE *hands her doll to* WALTER.)

WALTER (*Stepping forward with confidence*): Here, sire.

LORD OF MISRULE: Ah, a masked stranger. Give your name to us, stranger, that we may be acquainted with you.

WALTER: 'Tis Dirty Walt of the Peat Bog, sire. I speak for Kate, the forester's daughter.

LORD OF MISRULE: Speak, then.

WALTER (*Bowing in courtly fashion and speaking fluently*): My lords, my ladies, children of the village, and servants of the house. (*He holds up a china baby doll beautifully dressed in christening clothes.*) I shall champion the cause of this china doll, made by a craftsman in London. See her bisque head, as smooth and milky as that daughter of an oyster, the pearl. (*He makes doll open and shut her eyes.*) Behold how she is like a real child —with eyes so cunningly emplaced in their orbits that they open and close to a lullaby. The clothes are fashioned of the most downy silk, spun by Minerva, and dyed by the nymphs who guard the rainbow. Surely, there is no other doll in England made like this. Therefore, I beg you, lay the wreath of victory upon the doll of Kate, the forester's daughter. (*He bows right and left, and smiles smugly, and takes his place beside* KATHERINE.)

LORD OF MISRULE: Well spoken, lad. And now, have we concluded with our champions?

BETSY: No, Your Lordship. There is yet another.

WILL (*Coming forward and taking marionette from mantel*): 'Tis I, Your Lordship, come to champion the doll of Betsy and Nan Osborne.

LORD OF MISRULE: Champion away, then.

WILL (*Holding the doll behind his back*): Good Christmas revelers, I champion a doll of such talents that it would stagger the mind. Fancy this: a doll that can sit and stand, walk and dance, clap and wave.

CHILDREN (*Excitedly*): Show us!

WILL: At a motion of my hand, this doll will merrily nod, or gravely shake her head.

CHILDREN: Let us see her.

WILL: Since you one and all desire the sight of this prodigy —here she is! (*He brings the marionette out from behind his back and tries to move the strings, but the doll will not work.*)

CHILDREN (*Murmuring; ad lib*): He said it would move. His doll is broken. I wanted to see it move. (*Etc.*)

WILL: Why—what is this? She moved this afternoon. (BETSY *runs to* WILL.)

BETSY: What will we do now?

NAN (*Beginning to cry*): All is lost, lackaday!

WILL (*Putting the doll aside*): Poor useless bauble. (*He puts his finger to his head, thoughtfully.*) Ladies and gentlemen, did I not tell you of a marvelous creation that could walk and dance?

CHILDREN (*Ad lib*): Yes! Where is it? Forsooth, you did, lad. (*Etc.*)

WILL (*Pulling* NAN *along with him*): That manikin was but a wooden fraud. I have the true creation here. (NAN *catches on and plays along.*) See here—the stringless marvel, a living doll, a miraculous mite. (*He holds* NAN's *hand out to the audience.*) Examine, I beg you, this well-made bit of skin and bone. Do you see a seam anywhere? Is there mayhap a rough peg, or a nail in this elbow? (*Holds her hair out*) Look at this hair. Why 'twould take a wigmaker a hundred years to make strands like that. Now watch you well. (*To* NAN) Close your eyes, doll. (*She does so, and continues to follow instructions.*) Open your eyes, doll. Wink. Walk, doll. Faster. (*She runs around the stage.*) Dance. (*She dances back to him.*) There. Do you see? An obedient slave.

NAN (*Pertly*): I am *not* an obedient slave!

WILL: Aha, a *talking* doll. The pigwidgeon even talks back to her master. Is there another doll in all the universe like this? Here is the empress of all minikins, a warm-blooded dandiprat, winsome of smile and saucy of mind. If it please you, judges, award the prize to this bantam original, of which dolls are but fanciful shadows, this immortal . . . mortal *child*. (*He bows,* NAN *curtsies, and there is much applause as they return to their seats.*)

LORD OF MISRULE (*Rising*): Come, judges, let us put our

heads together and see which doll and which champion shall win the prize of gold. Strike up a song, children. (*Children sing short carol, as* LADY JOYCE, MAYOR, *and* TITANIA *rise and confer with* LORD OF MISRULE. *As carol ends, all but* LORD OF MISRULE *take their seats.*) 'Tis done. Our most mysterious and sovereign fairy queen will present the prizes this evening. But first, how many of you clamor to know the identity of the person behind the mask? Who can she be, this most mysterious Titania?

CHILDREN (*Ad lib*): Tell us! Who can she be? Who is the fairy queen? (*Etc.*)

LORD OF MISRULE: If it please you, gracious magical majesty, divest yourself of that concealing mask, and reveal yourself to us now. Stand, good citizens. (*All stand as* TITANIA *slowly takes off her mask.*)

CHILDREN (*In surprise and awe, ad lib*): Queen Elizabeth! England's fair queen! Your Majesty! (*Etc.*) (*Ladies all curtsy, and men bow.*)

QUEEN ELIZABETH: A most merry Christmas to you, good subjects. I am indeed your queen, come to join you in this frolic. In this basket I have two bags of golden sovereigns, one for the champion whose speech most charmed and impressed us, and one for his remarkable doll. One champion, one doll stood out above all the rest. (*Pause*) Which were they?

CHILDREN: Tell us!

QUEEN ELIZABETH: The champion is . . . is . . . why, by my troth, we know not his name.

TOM (*Rising*): My name is Tom, Your Highness.

HARRY (*Rising*): Harry of the Duck Farm, Your Majesty.

WALTER (*Rising*): Dunderheads! (*Boys sit.*) Her Majesty would have none of your stammers. (*He smiles pompously.*) My name is—er—Walt of the Peat Bog, Your Highness.

QUEEN ELIZABETH: Sturdy lads, and true, all of you. But

this champion came last. (WALTER *sits*.) He had so quick
a wit, and so silver a tongue, that we all voted without
hesitation to award him the prize.

BETSY: The last champion? Oh, Will, 'tis you.

NAN: We've won, Will, we've won!

QUEEN ELIZABETH: Stand forth, lad, and receive your prize
— (WILL *comes forward with* NAN *and* BETSY. *He kneels,
and they curtsy*.) Rise, champion of the doll and receive
these golden sovereigns from thy Sovereign. And tell me,
what is thy name?

TOM: I remember! I remember, Your Majesty. 'Tis William.

QUEEN ELIZABETH: William what—

TOM: William What! That's it. William What!

HARRY: No, Your Highness. 'Tis a strange name. William
—William—Shivertimbers!

QUEEN ELIZABETH: Take then, thy tribute, William Shivertimbers. (*She hands him the bag*.) And take thou, thy
tribute, Nan Osborne. (*She gives other bag of sovereigns
to* NAN.)

WILL, NAN *and* BETSY (*Bowing*): Thank you, Your Majesty.

KATHERINE (*Pushing her mask to her forehead and rising*):
'Tis not fair!

LADY JOYCE: Forsooth! 'Tis Katherine! (WALTER *pulls*
KATHERINE'*s mask down, and pulls her to the seat again.
She pulls her mask back up*.)

KATHERINE: 'Tis not fair, I say. He won by trickery, the
scurvy knave.

LORD OF MISRULE: Hold your tongue, Kate. (*He pulls off
their masks*. WALTER *tries to hide behind* KATHERINE.)

KATHERINE (*Loudly*): He won by trickery and trumpery,
I say. He had no doll.

LORD OF MISRULE: He had a doll ere you arrived on the
scene, I'll warrant. What say you to that, Walter?

WALTER (*Fearfully*): I only meant to free the doll that Katherine tangled. I didn't mean to cut it apart, truly.

LORD OF MISRULE: Shame, shame on you both. As for trickery, what think you of two scamps who disobey their uncle and try to win a contest clad in tatters and masks? Eh, Katherine? Is that not deceit? Is that not trickery? (*He collars them and takes them down left.*) Away with you now. To the kitchen with you. You shall do no more harm to Will Shivertimbers.

QUEEN ELIZABETH: Will Shivertimbers. Marry, 'tis a strange name.

WILL: 'Tis not my true name, Your Majesty. They have not remembered aright. My name is William, indeed. But my surname is Shakespeare. Therefore I am your obedient servant, William Shakespeare.

KATHERINE (*Tossing her head*): Shakespeare. William Shakespeare, forsooth! A lowborn rascal, I call him. Tell me this—in a hundred years who will remember "William Shakespeare"? (WALTER *and* KATHERINE *start left, then pause at door.*)

QUEEN ELIZABETH: *I* will remember you, lad. And so shall all of us. For, by my troth, I do believe you have a keen and rich imagination. One day, when you are grown to be a man, I'll look for you in London. Mayhap you'll be an actor, or write books. When I am at court, someone will present you to me, as a fellow of rare talent. I'll look into those deep gray eyes and say—"Ah yes, I know this Shakespeare. Now, where have I met him before?" And then I shall think of this revel, this merry Christmas revel at Charlecote, and I will say to myself, "Ah, yes. I met young William Shakespeare once . . . upon . . . a . . . time . . ." (*All hold positions as children sing.*)

CHILDREN (*Singing*):
Oh, once upon a time, in England

Lord and commoner mingled so;
On Christmas eve with yule log blazing
And candles all aglow.
Green, green were the holly branches,
Green, green the mistletoe,
Green, green the pine and laurel
Once in the long ago . . .
(*Curtain starts to close as children repeat last line.*)
Once . . . in . . . the . . . long . . . ago. (*Curtain*)

THE END

Star Bright

Characters

ZODIAC, *Keeper of the Sky*
KING CONIFER
COMETTA ⎱
GLOBULO ⎟
POLARIS ⎟
VESPER ⎬ *stars*
METEORUS ⎟
ASTRA ⎭
THREE SAILORS
CHILDREN OF ALL NATIONS

TIME: *Christmas Eve.*
SETTING: *The midnight sky. Six pedestals are arranged in a semicircle upstage.*
AT RISE: ZODIAC, *Keeper of the Sky, is pinning stars to the backdrop. He does not see* KING CONIFER *crouching behind cloud bank down left.* ZODIAC *goes down center, polishing a star on his sleeve.*

ZODIAC: Another Christmas Eve. Almost midnight. Here, star. Let's polish you up a bit. Every star must look his best tonight. (*He waves at the stars.*) Glitter! Sparkle! Glow! (*Crossing left to cloud bank*) Now what is this—

a cloud? (*Waving it away*) Shoo! Scat, you pesky cloud. I didn't order any clouds for Christmas Eve. (KING CONIFER *slowly rises from behind cloud bank and stands on a stool hidden behind it.*)

KING CONIFER (*Stretching*): Ah-h-h. At last I have reached the sky.

ZODIAC (*In astonishment*): Why, it's a tree. A tree in my sky? Here now, tree. What are you doing up here?

KING CONIFER: Growing, friend Zodiac, Keeper of the Sky. (*He stretches again.*) There . . . now I am the tallest pine tree in the world. The children of the earth have adopted me. I am to be their Christmas tree. They call me "King Conifer the Tall."

ZODIAC: Pleased to meet you, King Conifer the Tall. It isn't often a tree comes my way. How may I help you?

KING CONIFER: I have a small favor to ask you. Soon boys and girls from the four corners of the earth will be coming to decorate me. I would like to surprise them with a real live star for my tip-top branch. Have you a star to spare?

ZODIAC: I have millions of them. All shapes and sizes. Help yourself, King Conifer. Take your pick.

KING CONIFER: Ah, not so fast. This must be no ordinary star. This must be a worthy star, to shine for all the children in the world.

ZODIAC (*Scratching his head*): A worthy star? I've heard of shooting stars, and double stars, dwarf stars and nova stars, but what in heaven's name is a *worthy* star? Here, I'll whistle up my choicest stars and let you decide.

KING CONIFER: Wait. I hope you will agree to one condition. I must give your stars a test.

ZODIAC: A test, indeed. My, my. Trees are certainly fussy creatures. However I see no reason why the stars should not agree to a test. (*He blows a whistle. As he summons them,* COMETTA, GLOBULO, POLARIS, VESPER, *and* ME-

TEORUS *enter from up right, and stand in place on their pedestals*)
Hither, thither, swiftly fly
To Zodiac in the midnight sky,
Come, Cometta, Globulo bright,
Meteorus, Polaris, Vesper white.
Come, the honored star to be
Upon the tallest Christmas tree.

ALL: We come. We come. We come. (ASTRA *enters, out of breath, from up left.*)

ASTRA: Please, sir, is there room for another star? May I try my luck? Please? (*On her knees*)

COMETTA (*Looking down her nose at* ASTRA): Pooh. You are a very common star.

GLOBULO: Pooh. You are a very dim star.

POLARIS: Pooh. You are a very unimportant star.

ALL: Pooh. You are the smallest star in the sky.

ASTRA: Oh, but I want to be the star on the Christmas tree. I do, I do. More than anything in the universe.

ZODIAC: All right. All right, little Astra. (*Indicating empty pedestal*) Anything to stop this bickering. Stars shouldn't bicker on Christmas Eve. Now listen well, all of you. King Conifer, the Christmas tree, is going to give you some sort of test. If you pass it, you will be The Right Honorable Star of the Christmas Tree.

ALL (*Except* ASTRA, *who hangs her head modestly*): The Right Honorable Star of the Christmas Tree! (*Each points to himself*) Me!

VESPER: Is this a test for the star who shines the longest? Then I will win, for I shine all through the night and from dawn to dusk.

METEORUS: Now, Vesper. This is probably a test for falling stars. You stars sit in your places like big lumps. But I, Meteorus, glide through the sky from pole to pole.

COMETTA (*Preening*): Well, I don't like to brag, but if this

is a test for beauty, then the rest of you had better find
a cloud to hide behind. There is nothing in the universe
more beautiful than a comet.

POLARIS (*Haughtily*): Beauty has nothing to do with it,
vain comet. This is a test for importance, I am sure. And
who is more important than the Pole Star? Why, the
earth itself tips toward me, and great admirals of the
sea ask my advice for latitude and longitude.

GLOBULO: You are all wrong. This must be a test for
power. And who is more powerful than Globulo, the
brightest star cluster in the sky? I can outgleam, out-
glint and outglitter any galaxy from here to infinity.

KING CONIFER: To be sure. To be sure. But are you worthy
stars? That is the question. (*He brings out a scroll.*) Are
you ready?

ALL: We are ready.

KING CONIFER: Then let the test begin. Attention, stars—

ZODIAC (*Interrupting him*): Stop a moment. Something is
happening down there on earth. (THREE SAILORS *enter
slowly. They are paddling wearily, and shading their
eyes as they look to the distance.* ZODIAC *points to them.*)
A mighty storm has blown them off their course. Listen.
I hear them calling to the heavens.

SAILORS: Help us. Save us.

1ST SAILOR: Our ship is gone. We have only a small raft.

2ND SAILOR: The night is black and cold.

3RD SAILOR: Land . . . where is land?

SAILORS: Send us a star. Send us a star to guide us home.
(*They paddle in place, as* KING CONIFER *turns to stars.*)

KING CONIFER: Is there a star here who will help those
sailors? Vesper, you are the most faithful star in the sky.

VESPER: Oh, that's true. But just now I can't leave my
place. Why, I might miss the test and then I would
never be the Christmas star.

METEORUS: And I would gladly help them, but you know

what happens to falling stars when they get too near the sea—pfft! A black cinder!

COMETTA: Well, you certainly can't ask a comet to go and shine for common sailors. I'm too pretty and delicate for such rough work.

POLARIS (*Haughtily*): Cometta is right. We are extraordinary stars. Why should we put ourselves out for ordinary seamen?

KING CONIFER: Globulo, great beacon of the sky, will you help?

GLOBULO: Er . . . ahem . . . well, I am very, very busy just now. Perhaps after the test is over, I will shine for them. Yes, I'll definitely help—after the test.

ASTRA: Oh, but it may be too late then. The sailors may be dashed against the rocks. A whirlpool may sweep them down to the bottom of the sea. Oh, how dreadful. I will go. I will shine for them.

ALL (*Astonished*): You, little Astra?

COMETTA: Foolish firefly! Then you will miss everything. You'll never become the Christmas tree star.

ASTRA: I know. But those poor men will not have a Christmas again, not ever at all, if I do not shine for them.

METEORUS: But if you go too far, you may drown in the sea, and never live in the sky again.

ASTRA: I must take that chance.

POLARIS: You are a very dim star, Astra. Perhaps the sailors will not see you, however hard you shine. Your deed will be all in vain, all in vain.

ASTRA: Even so, I will try. I will do my best.

SAILORS (*Coming a little right of center*): Light. Send us a light. (ASTRA *goes to center, extends her arms. Spotlight shines on her.* SAILORS *look up at her.*)

1ST SAILOR: Look—a star has broken through the clouds.

2ND SAILOR: I know that star. She lives in the western sky.

3RD SAILOR: She's telling us to steer that way. (*He points offstage down right.*) Paddle, boys, paddle for your very lives. (SAILORS *stroke hard.*)

1ST SAILOR: Look over there. A dim blue shape.

2ND SAILOR: An island. It's an island!

SAILORS (*Jubilantly*): Land ho! (*Voices fade as they exit down right*) Land ho! (*Spotlight off* ASTRA. *She returns to her pedestal.*)

KING CONIFER: Well done, O smallest star of the heavens. Well done.

COMETTA: Never mind her. Tell us about the test. We simply cannot wait any longer. What is the test about?

KING CONIFER: It is over.

ALL: Over?

POLARIS: I suppose you simply looked at us and listened to our words of wisdom. How simple. How clever.

GLOBULO: Who is to be the Christmas tree star?

ALL: Who? Who?

KING CONIFER (*Stepping down from his stool and addressing each star*): Cometta, you have a veil like a rainbow of mist. You are the most beautiful thing in all the universe. (COMETTA *smiles knowingly.*) Globulo, you have the power of a thousand thousand suns. (*He swells proudly.*) And you, Polaris, are the sage of the skies. (POLARIS *nods wisely.*) Vesper, you never fail the heavens. (VESPER *curtsies.*) And Meteorus, you are a splendid sight as you streak across the ether like a fiery leopard. (METEORUS *swaggers.*) However—

ALL (*Puzzled*): However?

KING CONIFER: However, none of you is the star I want to honor my topmost branch. (*All ad-lib dismay*) Oh, as far as the sky goes, you are remarkable stars. But when it comes down to earth—you are cold and distant. You do not care about people. A Christmas star, above all things, must care about people. So therefore—(*He bows to* ASTRA, *takes her by the hand and leads her down center. Spotlight shines on* ASTRA *and* KING CONIFER.) I take the smallest star of all to be The Right Honorable Christmas Star!

ASTRA (*Dancing on her toes*): Oh, thank you, King Conifer.

COMETTA: Just a minute. She didn't pass any test!

KING CONIFER: Ah, but she did. Do you remember those three shipwrecked sailors? That was the test. A test to see how much you really care about the people of the earth who look to you stars for comfort and guidance.

ALL (*Disappointed*): Oh!

ZODIAC (*Crisply*): That's enough of that. Stars should be good sports. I hope you have learned your lesson. Now, shine all of you. Sparkle as you have never sparkled before. (*Bells sound from offstage.*)

KING CONIFER: The Christmas bells are ringing. (ZODIAC *brings stool to center.* KING CONIFER *stands upon it, with* ASTRA *posed in front of him, as the* CHILDREN OF ALL NATIONS *enter to group around the tree.*) The children of the world are here. Sing, children, sing. Make the sky ring!

ZODIAC: And you stars up there. Join in the chorus! (*He blows his whistle, and* CHILDREN *and the stars join in carols. Finale is "O Christmas Tree."* CHILDREN *and stars join hands.* KING CONIFER *steps down from his stool and helps* ASTRA *to step up on it. Spotlight shines on* ASTRA *as the curtains close.*)

THE END

Mother Goose's Christmas Surprise

Characters

MISS MUFFET	DR. FOSTER
BOY BLUE	OLD WOMAN WHO LIVED IN A SHOE
BO-PEEP	TWEEDLE-DUM
HUMPTY DUMPTY	TWEEDLE-DEE
MARY CONTRARY	MOTHER GOOSE
MOTHER HUBBARD	SANTA CLAUS
DOG TRAY	

TIME: *Christmas Day.*

SETTING: *Mother Goose's living room. If desired, there may be a large panel downstage painted to resemble a book and titled, "The Christmas Surprise Party, by M. Goose." Behind panel are chairs arranged in a semicircle.*

AT RISE: *Characters from Mother Goose are seated in semicircle, with* MISS MUFFET *sitting at far right.* TWEEDLE-DEE *and* TWEEDLE-DUM *leave their places at the feet of* OLD WOMAN WHO LIVED IN A SHOE *and open panel, which may then be taken offstage.* TWEEDLE-DEE *and* TWEEDLE-DUM *re-enter and resume their places.*

MISS MUFFET (*Looking around fearfully*): We've been here for nearly an hour, and Mother Goose has not

come yet. Why has she asked us to her home? Oh, dear!
I hope she hasn't invited any spiders!

BO-PEEP (*Nudging* BOY BLUE, *who wakes up and rubs his
eyes*): Wake up, Boy Blue. It isn't polite to snooze in
company. Have you seen my sheep?

BOY BLUE (*Yawning*): I think they're in the meadow. At
least they were before I started my last nap. (*Looking
around*) Isn't Mother Goose here yet? Say, Humpty
Dumpty, did Mother Goose tell you what this is all
about?

HUMPTY DUMPTY (*Swaying left*): She didn't tell me the
rhyme. (*Swaying right*) And she didn't tell me the reason. Maybe she was afraid I'd get things all scrambled!
(*He pitches forward, and* MARY CONTRARY *catches him.*)

MARY CONTRARY (*Angrily*): Stop that, Humpty Dumpty.
Do you want Mother Goose to come in and find you're
a little cracked?

HUMPTY DUMPTY: Ha, ha! Then the yolk will be on me!

MOTHER HUBBARD: Dearie me, I do hope Mother Goose
is planning to have refreshments. When I opened my
cupboard this morning, there wasn't a crumb to be seen.

DOG TRAY (*Putting up his paws as if begging*): Arf!

DR. FOSTER: I hope there'll be some entertainment at this
party. Achoo! Excuse me. I seem to have caught cold
from that last puddle in Gloucester.

OLD WOMAN: And I hope there'll be room for all of us.
I had to leave the other four and twenty children home
in the shoe. I only brought my twins—

TWEEDLE-DEE: Tweedle-Dee, that's me.

TWEEDLE-DUM: Tweedle-Dum, I'm his chum. (*Bells jingle
offstage.*)

MARY CONTRARY: Bells are jingling. (*Bells jingle louder.*)

BOY BLUE: Coming closer—

OLD WOMAN: And closer— (*Bells jingle still louder.*)

ALL: And *closer.* (MOTHER GOOSE *sails in from down left*

on a broom gaily trimmed in Christmas style, with bells on the handle and red and green streamers. She wears a tall green hat, red cloak, red dress, and green apron.)

MOTHER GOOSE (*Riding around stage*): Merry Christmas! Surprise, my dears. Surprise!

DR. FOSTER: Why, what a turnabout! We've never had our very own Christmas party in Mother Goose Land.

MOTHER GOOSE: Then it's high time we had one today.

MARY CONTRARY: Mother Goose, what have you done to yourself? Where is your traditional black hat and cape?

MOTHER GOOSE: It's high time for another tradition. The red and green of Christmas. Come now, everybody perk up. Laugh. Be happy. We're going to have a Merry Christmas. (*All laugh and cheer.*)

HUMPTY DUMPTY: We'll all come out of our shells.

BOY BLUE: I'm wide awake.

MOTHER GOOSE: That's the spirit. Now, Tweedle-Dee and Tweedle-Dum, I want you to bring in the big, tall, green surprise which is just behind the door. (*She points left.* TWEEDLE-DEE *and* TWEEDLE-DUM *bow and exit left.*)

ALL: A big, tall, green surprise?

HUMPTY DUMPTY: I know. It's a pickle!

ALL (*As* TWEEDLE-DEE *and* TWEEDLE-DUM *bring on a Christmas tree*): A big, tall, green Christmas tree!

MOTHER HUBBARD: Dearie me, there's nothing on that tree. It's as bare as my cupboard.

MOTHER GOOSE: We'll soon remedy that. Now, anyone can have a tree with tinsel and electric lights. But only *we* can have a Mother Goose Land tree. Now, how shall we decorate this tree to make it our very own? (*All look at each other and shake their heads.*)

DR. FOSTER: We didn't bring a thing to decorate a tree.

MISS MUFFET (*Reaching into her pocket*): Wait. I have an idea. (*Rising*) Perhaps it's not so gay as tinsel, but it is rather pretty. Spider webs. I have lots of those. They look almost like white lace. (*She takes lacy doilies or snowflake ornaments from her pocket and hangs them on bottom tier of the tree.* NOTE: *As each character decorates the tree, he hangs his ornament a little higher than the last, then resumes his seat.*)

BOY BLUE: My horn. It's like a Christmas trumpet. (*Hanging horn on tree*) I'll put it here, where the light will shine on it.

BO-PEEP (*Rising*): Look. My crook. With this red ribbon wound around it, it looks like a candy cane. (*She hangs crook on Christmas tree.*)

HUMPTY DUMPTY (*Rising*): I have just the thing for a Christmas tree—Easter eggs.

MARY CONTRARY: Easter eggs? Pooh. They'll be out of place.

HUMPTY DUMPTY: Not these eggs. (*Taking eggs from pocket*) They are gold and silver and sparkly. They'll look like Christmas balls. (*He hangs eggs on tree.*)

MARY CONTRARY: Well, I don't like to brag, but I have exactly what this tree needs.

HUMPTY DUMPTY: I don't think the tree needs cockle-shells.

MARY CONTRARY (*Rising*): No, silly—silver bells from my garden. (*She takes bells from her pocket and hangs them on tree.*)

MOTHER HUBBARD: Dearie me, what shall I do? I haven't a thing in my reticule. I don't want to be the only one without a decoration.

DOG TRAY (*Putting paws to his head, as if pointing to his clown cap of red and green*): Arf!

MOTHER HUBBARD: The clown cap! The very ornament. When it is hung upside down, it will look like a Christmas basket. (*DOG TRAY hangs cap on tree, with help of MOTHER HUBBARD.*)

DR. FOSTER: Achoo! Now what can I contribute? (*He

looks through his bag.) Ah, apothecary bottles. Red cherry cough syrup, and green mint liver tonic. (*Going to tree and hanging bottles*) Just right for this upper branch where the light shines through.

MOTHER GOOSE: Why, the tree is almost decorated! There is only one small place at the very top. Old Woman, what have you for our tree?

OLD WOMAN: Nary a thing, Mother Goose. With six and twenty young ones, it's all I can do to find porridge, never mind Christmas baubles.

TWEEDLE-DEE *and* TWEEDLE-DUM: We have something. We have something.

MOTHER GOOSE: Speak up, Tweedle-Dee and Tweedle-Dum.

TWEEDLE-DEE *and* TWEEDLE-DUM: Call Twinkle. Call Twinkle.

MOTHER GOOSE: To be sure. Twinkle, the little star. Why, she would be the perfect ornament for the top of our tree. But she is very shy. All of you must help to coax her from the sky.

ALL (*Softly*):
Twinkle, twinkle, little star,
Come out, come out, where e'er you are.
High above the world so free,
Come and crown our Christmas tree. (*A large, sparkling star is raised to top of tree.* NOTE: *There may be a boy standing behind Christmas tree to do this.*)

MOTHER GOOSE: There! A perfect tree. See what you can do with a little imagination? And now, I have the best surprise of all, my dears. Someone is coming to join us.

ALL: Someone?

MOTHER GOOSE: Someone round, and red, and jolly.

BO-PEEP: Someone round, and red, and jolly?

MOTHER GOOSE: His first name is Santa—

HUMPTY DUMPTY: I know. Santa Tomato!

MOTHER GOOSE: Oh, Humpty Dumpty, wrong again. Rise, one and all, and greet Santa Claus. (*All rise as* SANTA CLAUS *enters with a large bag, from down right. He goes to stand at right of Christmas tree.*)

SANTA CLAUS: Ho, ho, ho! Merry Christmas!

ALL: Merry Christmas, Santa Claus. (*They resume seats.*)

SANTA CLAUS: I suppose you are all wondering what Santa Claus is doing in Mother Goose Land. After all, doesn't Santa Claus usually bring the people of Mother Goose Land to the children of the world? Don't you usually bring fun and entertainment to boys and girls of every country? Well, this Christmas, the children have asked me to come and visit you, and bring you their good wishes and some very special gifts. And speaking of gifts — (*He opens his bag*) here they are! (TWEEDLE-DEE *and* TWEEDLE-DUM *distribute the gifts as* SANTA *reads the tags.*) First of all, a gift for Miss Muffet, from all the children who have read about her troubles with spiders. (*Takes gift from bag*) Here it is. A can of super-duper spider spray.

MISS MUFFET: Thank you, Santa Claus. Will that spider be surprised when he comes creeping down to my tuffet next time!

SANTA CLAUS: And now, Boy Blue. (*Taking gift from bag*) Boy Blue, the boys and girls have sent you a double-siren, four-bell alarm clock to keep you out of trouble with the cows in the corn.

BOY BLUE: Oh, boy! Thanks a lot. (*Yawning*) Oops. I'd better set the alarm right now.

SANTA CLAUS (*Taking out gift*): Little Bo-peep, here is an extra-long leather leash with five collars for that pesky flock of sheep. Now don't lose the leash, will you?

BO-PEEP: Oh, I won't, Santa, cross my crook.

SANTA CLAUS (*Taking out gift*): Humpty Dumpty, this is

for you. A giant economy size bottle of extra-strong, mend-all glue. Now you won't have to keep bothering the King's horses and men.

HUMPTY DUMPTY: Just what I always wanted! Thanks, Santa. You're a good egg!

SANTA CLAUS: Mary, you are next. . . . Now, Mary, I hear from the children that you have been quite contrary again this year.

MARY: Who, me?

SANTA CLAUS: Well, perhaps you're just tired from all that gardening. (*Taking out gift*) Here's something to cheer you up—a book with a thousand jokes.

MARY: A joke book? (*She opens book and starts to read to herself. She giggles, then breaks out laughing and can't stop. HUMPTY DUMPTY finally pats her on the back, and she stops in the middle of a laugh.*)

SANTA CLAUS: And now for you, Dr. Foster. The children gave a lot of thought to your gift. Since you are always falling into puddles (*Taking out gift*), here is a pair of double strength water wings, and a hundred handkerchiefs.

DR. FOSTER: I can't thank you enough. Kerchoo!

SANTA CLAUS: Old Mother Hubbard, the boys and girls are very concerned about your empty cupboard. (*Taking out gift*) Here is a gift certificate for a ten-cubic-foot freezer, and (*Taking out another gift*) for Old Dog Tray, a never-ending supply of dog biscuits.

MOTHER HUBBARD: Oh, dearie me, thank you, kind sir.

DOG TRAY (*Giving his paw to SANTA and "shaking hands"*): Arf!

SANTA CLAUS: Now let me see. (*Reaches down into his bag*) One more present, for the Old Woman Who Lives in a Shoe. (*To OLD WOMAN*) It must be very crowded in that shoe, isn't it?

OLD WOMAN: Oh, it is, Santa Claus. The shoe is only a one-story sandal, and the children are all cramped down in the toe.

SANTA CLAUS: Then you'll appreciate this. (*Taking out gift*) I hereby present you with a deed to a six-story boot with plenty of room in the toe, and a split-level heel!

OLD WOMAN: A six-story boot! Now we'll have to change our rhyme. (*Reciting*)
There was an old woman who lived in a boot—

TWEEDLE-DEE:
And this, all her twenty-six children did suit!

TWEEDLE-DUM:
She gave them roast turkey with a stuffing of bread—

OLD WOMAN, TWEEDLE-DEE *and* TWEEDLE-DUM (*Together*):
And each lucky child had a room and a bed!

MOTHER GOOSE: Now let's all join in a Christmas song. Come, everybody. (*She starts to sing, to tune of verse from "Jingle Bells," and others each sing a line.*)
We've had our share of fun—

HUMPTY DUMPTY:
The feast has just begun—

MISS MUFFET:
We've decked our tree this year,

SANTA CLAUS:
And Santa Claus is here.

BOY BLUE:
We couldn't believe our eyes—

BO-PEEP:
What a marvelous surprise!—

MOTHER HUBBARD:
Our tall, green Christmas spruce—

ALL:
Oh, thank you, Mother Goose! (*All continue singing, now to tune of "Jingle Bells" chorus.*)

Christmastime, Christmastime,
Holly in the snow,
Mother Goose Land people, all
A-caroling shall go . . .
Dog Tray:
Arf, arf, arf!
Santa Claus:
Ho, ho, ho!
All:
Listen well, and look
At Christmas sights and Christmas sounds
(Tweedle-Dee and Tweedle-Dum *exit quickly and return with panel representing book*)
Before we close the book.
(*All repeat last line, singing slowly and softly as* Tweedle-Dee and Tweedle-Dum *close book.*)
Before . . . we . . . close . . . the . . . book.
(*Curtain*)

THE END

A Clean Sweep

Characters

OLD YEAR SWEEPS, *3 boys and 3 girls*
NEW YEAR SWEEPS, *3 boys and 3 girls*
MISERABLE MONDAY ⎫
TERRIBLE TUESDAY ⎬ *bad days*
WOEFUL WEDNESDAY ⎭
VALENTINE'S DAY, *a girl*
EASTER, *a boy*
FOURTH OF JULY, *a girl*
HALLOWEEN, *a boy*
CHRISTMAS, *a girl*
THE NEW YEAR, *a boy*
MAYBE ⎫
TOMORROW ⎬ *good days*
SOMEDAY ⎭

SETTING: *The stage is empty except for a backdrop with the numbers of the old year pinned up. There are twelve chairs arranged in a row upstage. On every other seat is a* NEW YEAR SWEEP, *holding pose, with broom.*
AT RISE: *Six* OLD YEAR SWEEPS, *arranged boy-girl fashion, stand in a line across stage holding brooms in front of them.*

164

OLD YEAR SWEEPS:
Sweep! Sweep!
Any old years?
Any old years?
Any old years to sweep away?
GIRLS (*Taking one step forward*): Any secondhand months?
1ST GIRL: Any cast-off Aprils?
2ND GIRL: Any outgrown Mays?
3RD GIRL: Any out-at-the-elbow Junes?
GIRLS (*Sweeping*):
We'll sweep them up,
And sweep them out,
Off the floor, (*Going faster*)
Up the flue,
Out the door,
Down the street,
And clear out of this world—
Into eternity . . .
BOYS (*Stepping forward as* GIRLS *step back*):
Any old weeks?
Any old weeks?
Any old weeks to sweep away?
1ST BOY:
Any lost weeks,
When it rained and rained and *rained*?
2ND BOY:
Any rag-tag and bobtail weeks,
When everything went wrong—
3RD BOY: And nothing went right?
BOYS (*Sweeping*):
We'll sweep them up,
And sweep them out,
Off the floor,

Up the flue,
Out the door,
Down the street,
And clear out of this world—
Into eternity . . .

OLD YEAR SWEEPS (*Together*): Give us your old days. Give us your three hundred and sixty-five scattered days, battered days, tattered days. (*The three* BAD DAYS *enter like villains, from down right.*)

BAD DAYS: You called us? Heh, heh, heh . . .

MISERABLE MONDAY: The bottom of the morning to you. I'm Miserable Monday. Surely you remember me. I'm the day your teacher gave you a test you didn't expect, and all your lunch money fell out of a hole in your pocket. Oh, we had some bad times together.

TERRIBLE TUESDAY: Don't forget me—Terrible Tuesday. I was the day you missed the last bus and had to walk two miles home.

WOEFUL WEDNESDAY: But you voted me, Woeful Wednesday, the worst twenty-four hours of the whole year. Your best friend moved away. You received a bill for three overdue library books, and you came down with measles on your own birthday. Some fun, eh?

BAD DAYS (*Gloating, as they join hands and dance in a circle*): Three bad days. Three bad days. Three bad days.

3RD GIRL: Begone, bad days!

3RD BOY: Your time has run out.

OLD YEAR SWEEPS (*Together*):
You are over and done with.
Ready . . . aim . . . sweep!
(OLD YEAR SWEEPS *chase the* BAD DAYS *off left and line up again.*) But there were better days, too. Days to keep in your memory . . .

1ST GIRL: For instance—February 14th . . . (VALENTINE'S DAY *enters right, scattering petals from a flower basket.*

NOTE: *The performer may do a short dance to appropriate music.*)

VALENTINE'S DAY:

Forget-me-nots, and true love knots,
Lace borders without end . . .
I brought you hearts,
And cherry tarts,

OLD YEAR SWEEPS:

And a very special friend . . .
(VALENTINE'S DAY *curtsies and goes to stand at one side of stage as* EASTER, *dressed as a bunny, hops in left carrying basket of Easter eggs.* NOTE: *The rabbit may do a dance, if desired.*)

EASTER (*Singing to tune of "Pop! Goes the Weasel"*):

All around the calendar,
Springtime's green and sunny,
The trees are in bloom and the bees go zoom, and—

OLD YEAR SWEEPS:

Hop, goes the bunny.
(EASTER *takes place beside* VALENTINE'S DAY *at one side of stage. "Yankee Doodle" is heard, as* FOURTH OF JULY *enters, wearing cheerleader's costume of red, white, and blue, and carrying pompons.*)

FOURTH OF JULY (*As if leading cheer*):

Bing! Bam! Sizzle, fizzle, boom!
Don't shoot rockets,
In the living room.
Bong! Biff! Sizzle, boom, bah!

OLD YEAR SWEEPS:

July Fourth! July Fourth!
Rah, rah, rah!
(FOURTH OF JULY *goes to side of stage, and holds pose as she kneels down on one knee, holding out pompons. Eerie chords are heard as* HALLOWEEN *creeps on, left, wearing a mask over his face.*)

HALLOWEEN: Boo! (*He lowers mask.*)

OLD YEAR SWEEPS: Boo *who*—?

HALLOWEEN (*Raising mask to cover his face again*): A witch. (*Lowering mask*)

OLD YEAR SWEEPS:
Which witch?
We won't snitch.

HALLOWEEN (*Making a horrible face*):
Woooo! Aren't you scared?
Aren't you shaking and quaking
With fear?

OLD YEAR SWEEPS:
Who, us?
We're prepared.
You're a leftover spook
From last year!

(HALLOWEEN *puts up mask and stands beside* FOURTH OF JULY. CHRISTMAS *enters from down right, carrying small Christmas tree decorated with snowflakes, candles, and bells, as* OLD YEAR SWEEPS *sing to tune of "O Christmas Tree".*)
O Christmastime, O Christmastime,
What gifts are you a-bringing?

CHRISTMAS (*Singing*):
First flakes of snow,
And candle-glow,
And happy bells, a-ringing . . .

OLD YEAR SWEEPS:
Listen! The old year's on his way out. (*1st chime is heard.*)
Listen! The new year's on his way in. (*2nd chime is heard. The holidays, joining hands, quietly exit down left, as* OLD YEAR SWEEPS *begin to sweep again.*)
Any old years? (*3rd chime*)
Any old years? (*4th chime*)

Any old years to sweep away?
(*5th chime; boy sweeps go upstage and take down old numbers from backdrop.*)
We'll sweep them up, (*6th chime*)
And sweep them out, (*7th chime*)
Off the floor, (*8th chime*)
Up the flue, (*9th chime*)
Out the door, (*10th chime*)
Down the street, (*11th chime*)
And clear out of this world—(*12th chime*)
Into eternity.
(OLD YEAR SWEEPS *step back toward empty seats.*)
Going . . . going . . . gone!
(*On the word "gone",* OLD YEAR SWEEPS *sit, and* NEW YEAR SWEEPS *rise and march downstage, lining up boy-girl, boy-girl.*)
NEW YEAR SWEEPS (*Sweeping briskly*):
Sweep! Sweep!
Any new years?
Any new years?
Any new years to sweep in?
1ST GIRL: Any fresh green Aprils?
2ND GIRL: Any brand-new Mays?
3RD GIRL: Any bright Junes, hot-off-the-calendar?
GIRLS (*Together*):
We'll sweep them in,
We'll sweep them in,
We'll pass the howdy hat,
We'll roll the carpet down the steps,
We'll spread the welcome mat!
BOYS (*Together*):
Because it's a new era,
A promised time,
A grab bag year,
And the curtain's going up!

1ST BOY: There might be a blue moon—
BOYS (*Together*): This year.
2ND BOY: There might be a month of Sundays—
BOYS (*Together*): This year.
3RD BOY: Who knows? Mañana might really come—
BOYS (*Together*): This year. (*As "Camptown Races" is heard,* GOOD DAYS *dance in from down right, shaking tambourines like pitchmen.*)
GOOD DAYS: You called us? You say you're tired of the same old days, going round in a circle? You say it's time for a change? Well, tell you what we're gonna do—
MAYBE (*Shaking his tambourine*): Howdy. We're strangers here, newcomers—*x*, the unknowns. We don't have a fancy tent, or a big emporium. But I'll tell you what we do have, ladies and gentlemen—
GOOD DAYS (*Together*): We have hope!
MAYBE: That's it—hope. You don't know what's coming in this spic-and-spandy new year—right? So you need a little help from me. At your service—*Maybe,* that's me. You know me—Maybe. Maybe this year we'll have more sunshine. Maybe this year we'll go to the moon. And the best maybe of all—Maybe this year the world will finally settle down and live a little. I'm the spirit behind the wishbone, and the wishing star, and the wishing well. And speaking of wishing wells—I wish you very well. (*Shakes tambourine*)
TOMORROW: Hurry, hurry, hurry—right this way to Tomorrow. That's me—Tomorrow. I'm the pot of gold at the end of the rainbow. No matter how bad things were yesterday, or today—tomorrow will be better. That's a promise. And promises are what Tomorrow delivers. You say you stubbed your toe yesterday, and today you broke your shoe buckle? Well, my friend, tomorrow you'll dance like a king in golden slippers. (*Shakes tambourine*)

SOMEDAY: High hopes. Get your high hopes here. It doesn't cost one red cent to hope. It'll all come true *someday.* That's me—Someday. I'm the day the chickens come home to roost, and your ship comes in. Your parents know me. Aren't they always promising you that you can go to the North Pole, and wear the crown jewels, and eat a gallon of ice cream—someday? (*Strikes his tambourine*)

NEW YEAR SWEEPS: Good show! Welcome aboard! (*The* GOOD DAYS *kneel down left with tambourines on knees.*)

3RD GIRL: It's time—!

NEW YEAR SWEEPS: What time?

3RD GIRL: Sweeping time! (NEW YEAR *enters, carrying large book with blank pages and the year on the front as a title, as "Auld Lang Syne" is heard.* NEW YEAR SWEEPS *move their brooms in time to the music, and the* OLD YEAR SWEEPS *march down to join them in the finale.*)

ALL SWEEPS:
Come on in.
Right this way.
Step lively—
There's a whole world waiting.

NEW YEAR (*Waving top hat*): Hello, world. Here I am, your brand-new year! Wet behind the ears, and raring to go. Oh, you've seen years come and go, but there's never been one like me. (*Holding out book*) I've brought you three hundred and sixty-five clean white pages—

ALL: What's the story this year?

NEW YEAR: The story? Why, it hasn't even begun to be written yet. And you know what? You are going to write it. It's all up to you.

ALL (*Pointing to the audience*):
It's up to you,
It's up to you,

The story of the year is up to you.

(NEW YEAR SWEEPS *step forward.*)

1ST GIRL: Resolved: I will use my eyes this year to see more than just television and comic books.

2ND GIRL: There will be rainbows this year—

3RD GIRL: And sunrises and sunsets and falling leaves and dancing firelight.

1ST BOY: Resolved: I will use my ears this year for more than just a place to park my hat.

2ND BOY: There will be new bird songs, and new wind songs, and a new sound of surf on the sea . . .

3RD BOY: There will be train whistles, and fog horns, and jet planes screaming like eagles among the stars . . .

ALL: Resolved: This year will be better—

NEW YEAR: Good—better—best. The best one yet! (*Throws confetti*) Happy New Year!

ALL: Good—better—best. The best one yet! (*All throw confetti*) Happy New Year! ("*Auld Lang Syne*" *is played as the curtains close.*)

THE END

The Marvelous Time Machine

Characters

FATHER TIME
TIC TOC, *a brownie*
NECESSITY JONAS, *a Colonial boy*
GRANDFATHER JONAS, *his grandfather*
PRISCILLA, *his sister*
MOTHER JONAS, *his mother*
NED JONAS, *his 20th-century cousin*
PATSY, *Ned's sister*
MRS. JONAS, *Ned's mother*
GRAMPS JONAS, *Ned's grandfather*

BEFORE RISE: FATHER TIME *is seated at a small desk, placed at left in front of curtain. On the desk is a sign reading, "Office of Father Time." Beside the desk is a stool. As lights come up, he is writing on a long scroll with a quill pen.*

FATHER TIME: Now, let me see—we'll need four rainy Tuesdays—twenty sunny Sundays, and a whole week of snow in February. (TIC TOC *enters, carrying a stack of large envelopes.*) Ah, here comes my helper. Ho, Tic Toc! Are those holidays ready to be put in the proper places in our calendar?

TIC TOC: They certainly are, Father Time! (*He puts envelopes on desk.*)

FATHER TIME: Did you check each one to be certain it was in its right place on the calendar? It would be a terrible thing to have the Fourth of July fireworks come exploding through the Thanksgiving turkey!

TIC TOC: I was as careful as I could be! But, tell me, Father Time, did a mix-up like that ever happen to you?

FATHER TIME: Yes, Tic Toc. (*Indicates stool*) Sit down here a moment and rest. Once upon a millennium, we had the most surprising mix-up in all the galaxy. It was started by two boys. These boys were cousins, as a matter of fact. These cousins lived two hundred years apart, and yet they actually met each other!

TIC TOC: How could such a thing happen?

FATHER TIME: Listen, little Tic Toc, and I'll tell you all about the marvelous Time Machine. (*Curtains open.*)

*   *   *

SETTING: *The main room of a Colonial New England cottage is at right. At left is the living room of a modern American home.*

AT RISE: *Only the Colonial cottage is lighted, and the Colonial family hold poses:* PRISCILLA *is sweeping,* MOTHER JONAS *stirs a pot in the fireplace, and* GRANDFATHER *is seated nearby.* NECESSITY *is down center, working on a huge clock-like machine.*

FATHER TIME: It all began back in Colonial New England. The first cousin, whose name was Necessity Jonas, was a true Yankee through and through! There just wasn't any gadget that Necessity couldn't whittle or carve. (*The scene comes to life.*)

GRANDFATHER: By the great hornspoon, Necessity, that's a mighty handsome piece of clockwork. (*To* MOTHER)

What do you think of this son of yours, Martha? Doesn't he beat all for being clever with his hands?

MOTHER: He's clever at making shavings for Priscilla and me to sweep up.

PRISCILLA: It would be a horse of a different color if he were making something practical, like that cradle for my doll he promised six months ago—but that! (*Indicates machine with broom*) Why, I dare say even he doesn't know what that gadget is!

NECESSITY: I really do know what it is. It's something important, but I wouldn't tell you—not if you were Benjamin Franklin! (*Goes back to his tinkering.* PRISCILLA *sweeps with her nose in the air.*)

GRANDFATHER: Now, now, Necessity, you have to abide the womenfolk. After all, they fill your stomach with good bear meat and beans. Maybe it would be best if we helped pick up these shavings before your father comes home.

MOTHER: That's a very good idea. Come along, Priscilla, help me with the mince pies. (MOTHER *and* PRISCILLA *exit.*)

NECESSITY: Grandfather, I'm going to tell you what my secret invention really is. (*Beckons* GRANDFATHER *to machine*) I've always been burning to see what's going to happen in two hundred years. So, do you know what it is I've made?

GRANDFATHER: What is it?

NECESSITY: You won't tell a solitary soul—on your solemn honor?

GRANDFATHER (*Hand on heart, solemnly*): I so promise, Necessity.

NECESSITY: I'm making a machine that will let me travel through time, just as people travel over the ground now. This machine will take me two hundred years ahead, so I can really see what's going to happen! I'm making a

Time Machine! (*They hold pose as lights go down, curtains close. Lights go up on* FATHER TIME *and* TIC TOC.)

TIC TOC: Don't stop there! Did Necessity Jonas really get to see the future?

FATHER TIME: Well, Tic Toc, that's the strangest part of the whole tale! Necessity couldn't get to the future with his machine alone. He needed the help of the science of electronics, and of course there was no science of electronics when Necessity was inventing. But, by the strangest coincidence, at just the very same instant in eternity, his future cousin, Ned Jonas, living in the middle of the twentieth century, was studying all about electricity. Ned was just as bright with his mind as Necessity was with his hands. There just wasn't anything that Ned Jonas couldn't do with electricity. (*Curtains open.*)

* * *

AT RISE: *Only the modern living room is lighted.* MRS. JONAS *and* PATSY *are setting a dinette table.* NED *is sitting on a stool down center, fitting tubes and wires into a large machine.*

NED (*Attaching a coil of wire*): O.K., I'm ready to make another test. Plug in the machine, will you, Patsy?

PATSY (*Horrified*): I'd just as soon touch a king cobra as plug in that machine of yours, Ned.

NED: All right, you scaredy cat. I'll get Gramps to help me. (*Calling*) Hey, Gramps, could you help me, please?

GRAMPS (*From offstage*): All right, Ned.

MRS. JONAS: Goodness, Ned, you've been working so hard. Can't you give us some hint about what you're making?

NED: It's a secret invention, Mom. I can't tell you until it really works. (GRAMPS *enters.*)

MRS. JONAS: Come, Patsy. Help me with the dinner while Ned works on his thingamabob. (*She and* PATSY *exit.*)

NED: Gramps, they just don't appreciate me.

GRAMPS: There, there, Ned. Don't you know a genius is never appreciated by his family?

NED: You appreciate me, Gramps. You always tell me stories about when the Jonases first came to America and about my great-great-great-grandcousin, Necessity. I sure wish I'd lived in those days, when things were really exciting.

GRAMPS: It might have been exciting, Ned, but it wouldn't have been very comfortable.

NED: I'll bet it was wonderful. Gramps, I'm going to tell you what I'm doing. Only, will you promise not to tell anyone?

GRAMPS (*Hand on heart*): On my solemn honor, I promise.

NED: Gramps, I'm making something that nobody in the world has ever made. It's a machine that will take me straight back to the time when Necessity was my age. I'm going to go back two hundred years, to the days when there were bears and Indians and exciting people to meet. Yes, sir, Gramps, I'm making a Time Machine! (*They hold pose with* GRAMPS' *hand on* NED's *shoulder as lights go out and curtains close. Lights come up on* FATHER TIME *and* TIC TOC.)

TIC TOC: Don't stop there, Father Time. What happened to Ned and Necessity?

FATHER TIME: My little friend, nothing in all the assorted nebulae of the grand conglomerated cosmos was ever like what happened to those two young fellows. Each of the boys in his own century worked on his Time Machine until one night Ned had finished the last electrical coil, and Necessity had whittled the last wooden cog. (*Curtains open.*)

*　　*　　*

AT RISE: *Both sides of the stage are lighted.* NED *and* NECESSITY *are both working on their machines.*

NECESSITY: Let's see—this cog'll fit on the third gear from the left— (*He fits it.*) There! Just right. (*Excited*) Now I'll move the century hand and get ready to go. 1900— (*Moves hand*) should I leave it there? No! Just for fun I'll add fifty years or so, then five for luck and some to grow on. And there I am! (*Insert year*)—that looks like a good year!

NED: Almost finished. I'll just hook this amplifier over here, step up the frequency and plug in some juice. I'll have to guess at the exact time. Wish I had a good dial. Let's see—the 1750's ought to be about right. (*He adjusts a small gauge.*)

NECESSITY: Well, here I go! (*He winds the crank. It makes a creaky sound, coughs and dies.*) Shucks! There's not enough power here. Wish I had Ben Franklin to help me. He's a wizard of an inventor. (*He sits on the stool, and tinkers with the handle.*)

NED: Now for the plug. (*Pretends to plug in the cord*) Now, the juice! (*He turns on a switch.*) Hot dog! It's warming up!

NECESSITY (*Turning handle of his machine*): It's turning! It's turning! My machine works! (*Suddenly there is loud sound from thunder sheet. Gong sounds rapidly. Lights flash on and off, then stage goes dark. When the lights come up on NECESSITY's side, NED is on his hands and knees in NECESSITY's cottage. NECESSITY, frightened, peers out from behind a chair. He has musket pointed at NED.*)

NED (*Rubbing eyes*): Where am I? (*He looks around, bewildered.*)

NECESSITY: Who are you?

NED (*Rubbing head*): I think I'm Ned Jonas—anyhow, that's who I was a minute ago.

NECESSITY: You are a Jonas, too? You must be some kin to me, then. I'm sure glad you are kin. I thought you might be an Indian. I almost shot you! (*Puts musket down*) I'm Necessity Jonas.

NED: Necessity Jonas! Then my machine really does work! Am I glad to meet you! (*Puts out hand.* NECESSITY *looks at him blankly.*) I'm your cousin Ned from the twentieth century!

NECESSITY: Twentieth century! Well, if that doesn't beat all. Here I built a Time Machine to carry me to the twentieth century, and instead, the fool machine brought somebody to me!

NED (*Laughing*): No, Necessity, your machine didn't bring me here. I came by my own machine.

NECESSITY: This beats anything since the flood! Cousin Ned, I'm mighty proud to meet you. (*They shake hands solemnly.*) I don't know as how we have much to be hospitable with, but you'd be welcome to some bear meat and beans.

NED: Bear meat? Real bear meat? I'd like to try that!

NECESSITY (*Going to the kettle and ladling into a wooden dish*): Eat hearty, cousin Ned. There's always more. (*Hands dish to* NED)

NED: I've always wanted to eat real bear meat! (*He tries a little, grimaces and chokes a little, then gulps it down*) Necessity, how does your mother cook this?

NECESSITY: Do you like it? My mother is the best cook in the colonies. She puts in a little lard, some bear grease, some molasses and wild onions, and a bunch of sassafras.

NED (*Gulping again*): Do you have some water?

NECESSITY (*Getting a dipperful from the barrel by the table*): Help yourself. (NED *swallows some and chokes.*) Oh, pshaw, cousin Ned! I plumb forgot to tell you. Our spring worked itself down to some rock that had iron and sulphur deposits. It tastes mighty bad, but you get used to it.

NED (*Uncomfortably*): I guess you have to. Say, Necessity, could you turn up the oil burner? It's getting cold.

NECESSITY: What's an oil burner, cousin Ned?

NED: You know—the furnace. (NECESSITY *looks blank*.) I forgot you don't have central heating yet.

NECESSITY: I'm sorry that you're cold, cousin Ned, but I can't put more logs on the fire because the smoke might bring Indians.

NED (*Delighted*): Indians? Are there real Indians here?

NECESSITY: They're real all right. Too real.

NED (*Going to window*): How would you know if there were Indians out there?

NECESSITY: They always prowl around when the moon is rising.

NED: It's rising now—

NECESSITY: And they signal each other with a bird call— like this— (*He whistles. There is an answering whistle from offstage. Boys gasp and stare at each other.* NED *backs away from the window*.) Mohawks! (*He picks up musket, grabs* NED *by the arm*.) Get down on the floor. (*They crouch down on the floor*.)

NED: Necessity, I'm scared. It's exciting when you read about these things, but it's awful when it's your own scalp!

NECESSITY: Don't you worry, cousin Ned. We had three cabins burned out from under us by Mohawks, but we still have our own scalps. (*War whoops are heard from offstage, soft at first, then louder*.) Cousin Ned! We're surrounded. There are more Mohawks than I thought there were!

NED: What'll we do?

NECESSITY: There's nothing we can do but pray they'll think the cabin is empty. If they come in, it's all over!

NED: Oh, why did I leave home! (*War whoops grow very loud, then stop suddenly*.) What does that mean?

NECESSITY (*Standing and pointing musket toward door*): It means they're going to attack.

NED (*Getting up*): What will my mother think when I don't show up for breakfast? I'd give my whole Time Machine just to see my family again! (*Shouting*) That's it! The Time Machine! (*Loud yells are heard.*) Come on!

NECESSITY: Where to? We can't get out of the cabin.

NED: We'll go to my century. My machine is still plugged in, and maybe with the help of yours, we can get away. Grab hold of the handle there, and I'll hang on to you. Crank! Hurry! (*War whoops and banging grow louder as boys crank* NECESSITY'*s machine. Thunder is heard and lights flash. Noise stops and stage is dark for a moment. Then lights come up on* NED'*s side.* NED *is on his hands and knees in the middle of his living room, and* NECESSITY *is sprawled nearby on his stomach. His musket is near* NED'*s machine.*) It worked! It worked. (*He flops into an armchair.*) Am I glad to see this room! (NECESSITY *rises, and he slowly takes in the room, his face showing his amazement.*)

NECESSITY: So this is the twentieth century! It's like a dream! I never in all my born days could have imagined anything like this. (*He looks at the table lamp curiously*) Look at that. Where did you get such a big candle, cousin Ned? It glows like the sun!

NED: That's just an electric light, Necessity. There's nothing special about it.

NECESSITY: It hurts my eyes to look at it for long. (*He blows on it. He takes a bigger puff, as* NED *stands laughing.* NECESSITY *takes an enormous breath and blows with all his might, then stands scratching his head.*)

NED: You have to turn the switch, like this. (NED *switches light on and off as* NECESSITY *backs away.*) Here, you try it.

NECESSITY: No, thank you. It's fearsome to see a candle go off and on with nothing to light it.

NED (*Going to the window*): Come here to the window. (NECESSITY *follows.*) I'll show you the street. We have lots of—what would you call them—horseless wagons.

NECESSITY: That's something I want to see! (*They look out. An auto horn is heard.* NECESSITY *shrieks and buries his head under sofa cushion.*)

NED (*Uncovering* NECESSITY'*s head*): Necessity! What's the matter?

NECESSITY: Go get my musket! (*He points to the musket.*) Shoot it!

NED: Shoot what?

NECESSITY: I saw it out that window with my own two eyes! A monster! It was like a big beetle on wheels with two eyes as shiny as moons. It came rushing by and it roared at us. Lock the door!

NED (*Rocking with laughter*): That was a horseless wagon. The eyes were headlights and the roaring you heard was the horn. We call them automobiles. We have millions of them.

NECESSITY: Millions! I couldn't stand the sight!

NED: Calm down, Necessity. You're shaking like a leaf. Let me think. What will make you quiet down? I know. I'll bring in another twentieth century invention. It's kind of—of—a magic broom. (*He exits.*)

NECESSITY: A magic broom. There can't be anything too fearful about a magic broom. (NED *brings in a tank vacuum cleaner. The hose trails on the floor.* NECESSITY *backs toward the Time Machine in fright*)

NED: We call this a vacuum cleaner. I'll plug it in and you can watch it clean. (NED *turns his back to* NECESSITY *and plugs in the cleaner.* NECESSITY *picks up his musket.* NED *keeps his back to* NECESSITY.)

NECESSITY: Cousin Ned, don't you move now. There's a big snake on the floor there. I'll try to get it. (*Points the musket at the vacuum cleaner*)

NED (*Paying no attention*): Snake? How could there be a snake in an apartment house?

NECESSITY: Just let me get a bead on him. Stay still now. (*He raises the musket.* NED *turns machine on, picks up the hose and puts it on his sleeve.*)

NED: See the suction in the cleaner? It can pick up this cloth and—

NECESSITY (*Screaming*): It's on your sleeve. It's eating your arm! I'll save you, cousin Ned!

NED (*Looking up, startled*): Necessity! Put down the musket! Don't shoot! (*Thunder is heard and lights flash.*) You're too close to the machine. You'll go back! Come here!

NECESSITY: I'll save you! (*He backs into the Time Machine as he shoots at the vacuum cleaner. There is a loud gunshot. Stage goes dark. The curtains close. Lights come up on* FATHER TIME *and* TIC TOC.)

TIC TOC: Don't stop there, Father Time! Did Necessity go back to his own time, after all?

FATHER TIME: Indeed he did, Tic Toc, and he was so happy to get there! (NECESSITY *steps from behind curtain and stands far right.*)

NECESSITY: All that traveling broke my Time Machine, but I'm happy it did. I wouldn't go back to the twentieth century for all the tea in China! Poor cousin Ned. What a lot of dangers he has to face! Monster autymobiles! Magic brooms and giant snakes! I'll take Indians any day of the week! At least I killed that snake for him! (*He holds pose.*)

TIC TOC: But what happened to Ned Jonas, Father Time?

FATHER TIME: Well, sir, Ned's marvelous contraption also

blew a fuse. But I think he was awfully glad to be back in his own time, too! (NED *enters through curtain and stands left, next to* FATHER TIME *and* TIC TOC.)

NED: Whew! It's good to be back home. Gramps was right. There's no time like your own time. It was interesting to be back in Colonial days—but I don't think I care much for bear meat. I have only one problem now. How am I going to explain to Mother about the bullet hole in her very best vacuum cleaner? (*He holds pose.*)

FATHER TIME: There you have it, Tic Toc. That's the story of the grand and glorious Time Machine. Now we'd better get back to those holidays, or there'll be a whole year without any fun. And wouldn't the people down there on earth complain then! We'd never hear the end of it from eternity to eternity! (*They hold pose, with* FATHER TIME *at desk,* TIC TOC *sitting on stool. Lights dim and go out*)

THE END

Young Abe's Destiny

Characters

CLEM
ALLEN
LAURA ⎬ *children*
NELL
ABE
DR. FATE
FORTUNATO, *a mime*

TIME: *The afternoon of February 12, in the early 1800's.*

SETTING: *A clearing beside a cabin in Spencer County, Indiana.*

AT RISE: LAURA *is standing down right, behind a bare tree, blowing on her hands and keeping watch off right. NELL sits on a flat rock down left, shivering. CLEM keeps watch off left, and ALLEN stands at center, slapping his arms to keep warm.*

ALLEN: Is Abe coming, Clem? I'm freezing.

CLEM: Don't see him yet, Allen. Maybe he won't come this way today.

LAURA: Yes, he will. He always stops to read on the big rock.

NELL: Even when it's as cold as this?

LAURA: He sure does, Nell. He claims the sun on the rock gives him half an hour more reading time until sundown.

CLEM (*Pointing off left*): Hssst! He's coming. His nose is in a book, same as usual.

ALLEN: Don't let him see you. Get back of the rail fence. Quick. (*They run back of rail fence up right and stoop down. ABE enters left, hatless, completely absorbed in a book he is reading. ALLEN lifts his head over the fence. The others cautiously do the same. ALLEN slowly creeps toward rock, the others following on hands and knees. NELL starts to giggle. The others shush her.*)

ABE (*Lifting his head*): What was that? Sounded like a turkey gobbling. (*NELL covers her mouth with her hand, smothering another giggle. All scramble behind rock. ABE lifts his hand to scratch his head, then quickly seizes ALLEN by his collar.*) Aha! I have you—a big, fat turkey with a wool muffler.

ALL (*Springing up from behind rock*): Happy birthday, Abe!

ALLEN: Happy birthday, nose-in-the-book. We meant to surprise you.

ABE: Happy birthday? Who, me?

CLEM: Well, we don't mean your grandpa.

ABE: Pshaw. I'd plumb forgotten about it.

LAURA: Oh, you! How could you forget your own birthday? Look—Nell and I baked you a currant cake. (*She brings out covered basket from behind rock.*)

NELL: With a plum right spang in the middle of it.

CLEM (*Reaching in his pocket*): I wanted to get you an axe with a double-steel edge, but my wishes were bigger'n my wallet. So here's something to help you with that whittling you're always doing. (*Hands ABE pocketknife.*)

ABE (*Examining it; smiling*): I'm much obliged, Clem.

And I'm just grateful you didn't get me that axe. I'd only have to split more kindling. Now I can cut you a willow whistle.

CLEM (*Grinning*): Sure. That's why I bought you the pocketknife.

ALLEN: It's my turn now. (*Gets book from behind rock*) Here, you old book-eating lizard. Here's another book for you to digest.

ABE: A book. *Aesop's Fables.* I swan! Thank you, all. I'm mighty obliged to you. Why, it pays a fellow to get born in this county. (*He opens book and pretends to be absorbed in reading.*)

NELL: I declare. He's off again.

LAURA: Studying, always studying. What's in those books, anyhow? Farmers don't need book learning.

ABE: Well, now. That's a real good question. Matter of fact, I don't just exactly know why I study so much. It appears to me that there is more to this world than Spencer County, and I just have the kind of bumptious curiosity that makes me want to find out about it.

LAURA: Brrr. I'm getting cold standing here. Let's move along to my cabin. My ma has a roaring fire and some brown sugar for a taffy pull. (*An owl hoots three times off left.*)

NELL: Listen to that. An owl hooted three times before sundown.

CLEM: You know what that means.

ALLEN: This is going to be a day when something strange and magical will happen. (*Jingling of bells is heard from behind the tree at right.*)

NELL: What was that?

ALLEN: Bells. I told you there was going to be m-m-magic. (*All huddle together, except* ABE *who stands with hands on hips, grinning at them.* FORTUNATO *jumps out from*

behind tree, a knapsack on his back. He crouches, smil-
ing and shaking rattle with bells on it. Children jump
back, afraid. Dr. Fate *steps out.*)

Dr. Fate: Here, Fortunato—you've frightened them. You
made your entrance too quickly. (Fortunato *hangs his*
head and bites his finger foolishly)

Laura: Oh, spooks!

Nell: I'm a-feared!

Clem: Come on, let's go. (*All except* Abe *start toward left.*)

Allen: I knew that owl was hooting something bad.

Abe: Wait a bit. These aren't spooks. These are stage
folks, dressed up for a show. Am I right?

Dr. Fate (*Eying him up and down*): Clever boy. You have
guessed it. Allow me to introduce myself. I am Dr. Des-
tinius Fate, and this is my mime, Fortunato. (Fortunato *makes a low bow and falls. Children laugh.* Fortunato *goes to the rock left, and they group around,*
while Dr. Fate *stands on rock.* Fortunato *puts down*
knapsack.)

Allen: I saw a stage once. 'Twas on a wagon. Are you in
the stage show business for sure?

Dr. Fate: Are we in the stage show business, Fortunato?
(Fortunato *nods vigorously.*) We are. Fate and Fortunato, thespians, magicians, and practitioners of the old
soft-shoe. (Fortunato *does a buck and wing.*) We leave
you gasping in the aisles with our comedy. (Fortunato
rocks with laughter.) We tear at your heartstrings with
our tragedy. (Fortunato *kneels, wrings his hands, and*
weeps.) We tickle your eye with sleight-of-hand tricks.
(Fortunato *produces a deck of cards from his sleeve*
and fans himself.) We read minds. (Fortunato *holds*
his head and stares at Abe.) We cast horoscopes. (Fortunato *gazes at sky.*) And sometimes, if pressed with
generous applause, we sing in the style of the Italian

opera. (FORTUNATO *opens his mouth wide and panto-mimes singing.*)

ABE (*Clapping*): First-rate! Thumping good, I'd say. This is a fine way to celebrate my birthday. (*Others applaud.*)

DR. FATE: A birthday! Why, birthdays are our specialty.

ALLEN: But I want to know what two actors are doing out here in the backwoods of Indiana.

DR. FATE (*Embarrassed*): Er—funny you should ask that. It appears that despite road maps and star fixings, we are—lost! (FORTUNATO *puts his hand to his eyes and looks around as if confused.*) Tell me—is this the road to Washington?

ALL: Washington! (*They laugh.*)

ALLEN: Say, Dr. Fate, you're really comical. Why, the road to Washington is nigh three hundred miles from here. (*All laugh again.* FORTUNATO *takes a brass ring from knapsack and begins to swing it in a circle.*)

DR. FATE: Salamagundi! Our compass was positive this was the road to Washington. (FORTUNATO *nods.*)

ABE: That's a mighty strange compass—

DR. FATE: We're mighty strange fellows. Fortunato, do you have the time? (FORTUNATO *takes a gigantic watch from pocket. He shakes it, holds it to his ear, then shows it to* DR. FATE, *who examines it solemnly.*) Dear, dear, it's almost 1860. (*The children hoot and clap.*)

NELL: *1860?* That's years and years away.

DR. FATE: Only years and years away? Tsk, tsk. Then we must hurry. We must find him right now.

ALL (*Ad lib*): Who? Find who? (*Etc.*)

DR. FATE: Why, the President of the United States! (*They laugh heartily at this.*)

ALLEN: Oh, he's a caution! You won't find any Presidents here, Dr. Fate.

CLEM: This is Indiana. We're all ploughboys and railsplitters.

ABE: Hold on now. There's no law says an Indianian can't get himself elected. He just has to hornswoggle those Easterners into voting for him. Do you have any voting spells in that knapsack?

DR. FATE: Good point, lad, good point. Take those words down, Fortunato. (FORTUNATO *pretends to open a huge book and make a large scrawl as if writing with a quill pen.*)

ABE (*Good-humoredly*): Just what I was afraid of. My words are empty—full of air. (*All laugh.*)

DR. FATE: Listen here now, my fine children. How do you know that one of you couldn't be President?

ALL: One of *us?*

DR. FATE: I'll tell you what. You've been a good, hearty audience. Now, how about giving yourselves a chance to be actors? We'll have an audition for the role of President.

NELL: Audition? Is that like subtraction?

DR. FATE: No, child. An audition is what stage folks have when they try out for a part in a play. The one who fits the part best, gets it. (ABE *turns away thoughtfully as others crowd eagerly around* DR. FATE.)

ALLEN: This is a dandy show. Even beats the circus. All right. I'll have a crack at this or-dition. What must I do?

DR. FATE (*Stepping down from rock*): Step up here, boy. Fortunato, give him the hat and mantle of office. (FORTUNATO *takes tall silk hat and black shawl from knapsack and puts them on* ALLEN.)

CLEM (*As* ALLEN *steps up on rock*): Pass a law, President. Pass a law that says we'll have Sundays seven days a week.

ABE: Speech! Speech!

DR. FATE: Every actor must have a script to try out with— isn't that right, Fortunato? (FORTUNATO *nods.*) Supposing you repeat after me, loudly and clearly, the oath of office of the President of the United States. "I do solemnly swear . . ."

ALLEN: "I do solemnly . . ." (CLEM *points at him, laughing. He breaks into shouts of laughter, taking off the hat and shawl.*) Shucks, I can't be solemn. (*He steps down.*)

ABE: You just laughed yourself right out of your first term.

CLEM: Me next. I want to be next. I can do it. I know I can.

DR. FATE: Step up. (CLEM *steps up on rock.* FORTUNATO *puts hat and shawl on him.*) Repeat after me. "I do solemnly swear . . ."

CLEM: "I do solemnly . . ." (*The hat falls off.* CLEM *is astonished.*) Wind blew my hat off! Ahem. "I do solemnly . . ." (*The shawl slips off.*) Pshaw!

ABE: No—shawl! It appears this President has trouble getting himself together.

CLEM (*Stepping down*): Now, how do you figure that? I couldn't keep that costume on—not for anything. (*He hands hat and shawl to* FORTUNATO.)

DR. FATE: Next? (*There is silence.* ABE *turns to audience and stands very still.*) How about you, birthday boy?

ABE (*Uncertainly*): Not me. Never me.

CLEM: Aw, go on. You'll be the funniest President yet.

ALLEN: Sure, you're as good at speechifying as the schoolmaster.

DR. FATE: Time for only one more. (FORTUNATO *beckons* ABE, *holding out shawl.* ABE *reluctantly steps up on rock.* FORTUNATO *puts hat on his head.*) "I do solemnly swear . . ." (*Lights may dim, and a spotlight may shine on* ABE, *as the others hold their poses.* "Hail to the Chief" *may be played slowly as* ABE *speaks.*)

ABE (*Reciting without help from* DR. FATE): "I do solemnly swear that I will faithfully execute the Office of President of the United States, and will to the best of my ability, preserve, protect and defend the Constitution of the United States." (*A muffled drum is heard as others stare at* ABE.)

LAURA: Why—he looks so tall and so serious.

NELL: And grander—like the whole state of Indiana couldn't hold him.

CLEM: I know he's my friend, and yet he's like a stranger to me, so sad, somehow.

ALLEN: He knows those words. He knows them by heart. He never stumbled once. (*The drums stop. The lights come up and the spell is broken.* ABE *clears his throat.*)

ABE: Ahem. Friends, Indianians, countrymen—and any stray squirrels, bluejays and 'possums. There's a barrel of cider back of the barn for all you folks who voted for me. And for those who voted twice, there's a doughnut besides. (*All cheer.* CLEM *and* ALLEN *pull him off rock and whack him on the back.* FORTUNATO *puts the shawl and hat in knapsack.*)

ALLEN: You had me scared a minute there. I thought you were going straight down that road to Washington.

CLEM (*Relieved*): Shucks, it's good to see you laughing again. It was all a joke, wasn't it?

ABE: It's a joke all right—me, President! (*He shivers.*)

LAURA: What's the matter?

ABE: I just had goosebumps thinking about it.

LAURA: Why, you're getting cold. And the sun's going down fast. Let's go on to my house for that taffy pull.

DR. FATE: One minute. You must sign my register before you go. (FORTUNATO *opens imaginary book and hands imaginary pen to* ABE, *who smiles and signs with a flourish.*)

ABE: There you go. Oh, and good luck finding that road to Washington.

DR. FATE: Oh, we'll find it. Never fear.

ALLEN (*Impatiently*): Come on, I'm starving.

CLEM: Let's go. Last one there is a horned toad. (*He and* ALLEN *run off left.* ABE *turns to* DR. FATE.)

ABE: Thanks for the show. I enjoyed that show a heap. (DR. FATE *nods.*)

LAURA: Oh, come on now. Nell, you take one side of this slowpoke and I'll take the other! (NELL *picks up basket, and grabs arm,* LAURA *takes the other arm and they force* ABE *to go along between them.*)

ABE (*Grinning*): Now this is what I call traveling in style. (*They exit left.* FORTUNATO *and* DR. FATE *look off after them.*)

DR. FATE: What do you think, my old friend Fortunato— is he, or is he not *the one?* (FORTUNATO *slowly nods several times.*) Open the book. I want to read his name. (FORTUNATO *opens the imaginary book slowly. Muffled drums play under* DR. FATE's *last speech*) Abraham Lincoln. (*Looking up*) Well, young Mr. Lincoln, you may think this was just a passing show. You may even forget us by tomorrow. But sometime—somewhere, around another bend, another day you will meet Fate again, on the road to Washington. (*They walk off right slowly as "The Battle Hymn of the Republic" is played and the curtains close.*)

THE END

The "T" Party

Characters

LADY THERESA TIDDLIWINKS   THUMBELINA
COUNTESS TABITHA TRUFFLES   TOM THUMB
MAID   TINKER BELL
FOOTMAN   TOBY TYLER
TITANIA   MYSTERY GUEST
TINY TIM

SETTING: *A garden.*
AT RISE: LADY TIDDLIWINKS *is walking rapidly back and forth downstage.*

LADY TIDDLIWINKS: Well! Well! I might go so far as to say, well, well, well! Where is she? The Countess Tabitha Truffles was to be here at two o'clock promptly. (*Takes large watch from her purse, looks at it, and hastily puts it back.*) It is now one minute after two. Why can't she be on time! (*There is a sound of knocking.* LADY TIDDLIWINKS *claps her hands in delight and rings a little bell on tea table at center. The* FOOTMAN *enters right. He goes to large tree, left, which has a door in the trunk, and opens door.* COUNTESS TRUFFLES *enters.*)
FOOTMAN: Announcing Her Grace, the Countess Tabitha

Truffles! (*He bows and exits right. Ladies reach into their purses and put on their lorgnettes, after which they utter little shrieks of recognition and curtsy to each other.*)

LADY TIDDLIWINKS: My dear Countess Tabitha Truffles! I am simply delighted to see you again!

COUNTESS TRUFFLES: I am overwhelmed, Lady Theresa Tiddliwinks!

LADY TIDDLIWINKS: Whatever kept you? You were a whole minute late! (*They seat themselves at opposite sides of tea table.*)

COUNTESS TRUFFLES (*Sighing*): I had such a distressing time on my way here. One of the wheels rolled off the coach. And as the coachman was about to repair it, bandits came down from the hills and made off with my jewels. The coachman ran off, heaven knows where, and I had to walk simply miles and miles to get here at all.

LADY TIDDLIWINKS: Oh, is that all? But, enough of this chitchat. I must tell you my idea for a perfectly splendid party. As you know, I have always felt that some letters in the alphabet have a much better life than others.

COUNTESS TRUFFLES: Ah, how well I know! That prosperous letter E, for example. It's such a favorite in the English language. Why, it's growing quite fat from being used so much.

LADY TIDDLIWINKS: Precisely. But some other letters, poor dears, have practically no space in the dictionary. They are quite underprivileged.

COUNTESS TRUFFLES (*Wiping eyes*): Poor little things!

LADY TIDDLIWINKS: So, it was my notion that we should give a lawn party for the benefit of some deserving, underworked letter, and it just so happens I have the perfect one.

COUNTESS TRUFFLES: I can't imagine. Which letter is it?

LADY TIDDLIWINKS: It should be our favorite letter. Think

now, dear Countess. Your initials . . . and my initials.

COUNTESS TRUFFLES (*Thinking*): My initials . . . and your initials. Tabitha Truffles and Theresa Tiddliwinks. . . . Ah, I have it! T! The letter T. Why, our lawn party will really be a "T" Party!

LADY TIDDLIWINKS: Exactly. Now . . . we must settle, first of all, whom we shall invite.

COUNTESS TRUFFLES: Well, I've always fancied that nice Bo-peep, and perhaps little Alice in Wonderland—

LADY TIDDLIWINKS: No! No! You are not using your head. These must be persons who names begin with a T.

COUNTESS TRUFFLES: Oh, yes, yes. Well then, how about Titania, the Queen of the Fairies, for a start?

LADY TIDDLIWINKS: I'll write that down. (*She takes a quill and paper and writes.*) Then, we must have a gentleman, to balance things. Let me think. Ah! Tiny Tim, to be sure.

COUNTESS TRUFFLES: Thumbelina is a very picturesque little lady.

LADY TIDDLIWINKS: And tit for tat, we add another gentleman, Tom Thumb!

COUNTESS TRUFFLES: Since we are inviting fairies, how about Tinker Bell?

LADY TIDDLIWINKS: Very well, but I do think we should have a solid, down-to-earth human for our sixth guest. Ah! The perfect addition—Toby Tyler.

COUNTESS TRUFFLES: A tiptop list. Shall I help you write the invitations?

LADY TIDDLIWINKS: Oh, no. We'll do something more appropriate. (*She rings bell. The* MAID *enters right, bringing a cardboard telephone. She curtsies, leaves it on table and exits.*)

COUNTESS TRUFFLES (*Pointing to telephone*): Of course, the very thing. We'll use the telephone, since it starts with T.

LADY TIDDLIWINKS: On the other hand, since we have much more planning to do, I shall give the chore of telephoning to the Footman. (*She rings bell, and* FOOTMAN *shuffles in and takes list, bowing.*)

FOOTMAN: I beg pardon, Your Ladyship, but I notice there is no date or time upon this list.

LADY TIDDLIWINKS: Tush! Put down—let me see—put down Tuesday for the date.

FOOTMAN: But, that's today.

LADY TIDDLIWINKS: The sooner the better. Now, as for the time of the party, why, two-twenty, of course.

FOOTMAN (*Shaking his head*): But, Your Ladyship, it is two-fifteen now!

LADY TIDDLIWINKS: As I said, the sooner the better. Be off with you now.

FOOTMAN: Very well, Your Ladyship. I'll— I'll—

LADY TIDDLIWINKS: We know. You'll *try*. (FOOTMAN *exits.*)

COUNTESS TRUFFLES: Dear, dear me! How will we ever put things in order before the guests arrive? What shall we serve them?

LADY TIDDLIWINKS (*Airily*): We'll have the menu in a trice! (*She rings bell.* MAID *enters with a large tray which she sets on the table.* LADY TIDDLIWINKS *holds up each item of food.*) First we'll have a pot of teasel tea. Next, tabasco tarts with tomatoes. Then, a tureen of tasty turbot, followed by tamales and toast. For dessert, tufts of treacly taffy.

COUNTESS TRUFFLES: Oh, what a tremendous treat! (*There is a sound of knocking off left.* LADY TIDDLIWINKS *rings bell.* FOOTMAN *enters right and goes to door.*)

FOOTMAN: Tarantara! Tarantara!

LADY TIDDLIWINKS: Our guests have arrived. (*She and* COUNTESS TRUFFLES *put on their lorgnettes and form a receiving line, greeting guests.* TITANIA *enters.*) Ah, so good to see you, Queen Titania. What a splendid gown you are wearing.

TITANIA: Thank you, Lady Theresa. It is tufted taffeta with tinsel tassels! (TINY TIM *enters.*)

COUNTESS TRUFFLES: And here is Tiny Tim. What have you been doing since last we met?

TINY TIM: I've been taking tabs and tittles of tin and toggles to tidy tinkers. (TOM THUMB *and* THUMBELINA *enter together.*)

COUNTESS TRUFFLES: Thrilling!

LADY TIDDLIWINKS: And you, Thumbelina and Tom Thumb, how are you?

THUMBELINA: Topsy-turvy!

TOM THUMB: Tolerable . . . tolerable . . . (TINKER BELL *dances in.*)

COUNTESS TRUFFLES: Ah, Tinker Bell. I hope you will entertain us later.

TINKER BELL: I will tootle a troubadour's trumpet, tinkle a tambourine, and toddle a tantalizing tarantella for you. (TOBY TYLER *strolls in.*)

LADY TIDDLIWINKS: Thank you, indeed. Why Toby, Toby Tyler, how you have grown. How are things under the Big Top?

TOBY TYLER: Together we troupers toil and tour the towns treating tiny tots to tumbling and timpani!

COUNTESS TRUFFLES: Titillating! (*All take their seats. * FOOTMAN *stands at attention beside tree.* LADY TIDDLIWINKS *and* COUNTESS TRUFFLES *seat themselves at tea table, taking fans from their purses.*)

LADY TIDDLIWINKS: Dear friends, we are gathered here to honor an unsung hero of the alphabet, the letter T. To start the proceedings, I propose that we tackle a talky task. Shall we try tongue twisters?

ALL: Yes! (*They applaud.*)

LADY TIDDLIWINKS: I'll begin. You repeat it after me. Anyone who twists his tongue shall have to turn a "tumble-sault" or tell twenty tall tales. Now: Twelve twisted thistles thrive in thorny thrumming thickets . . .

ALL: Twelve twisted thistles thrive in thorny thrumming thickets . . . (*There is a knock at the door.*)

FOOTMAN: Tarantara, tarantara!

COUNTESS TRUFFLES: Who can that be? Were you expecting anyone else?

LADY TIDDLIWINKS: Not so much as a titmouse! (FOOTMAN *opens door with a flourish.* MYSTERY GUEST *enters, wearing a half mask, and hands his card to* FOOTMAN.)

FOOTMAN: Why, this card's a blank. Now whom shall I say is calling? Er . . . er . . . Announcing, a Mystery Guest! (MYSTERY GUEST *bows low. The company rises, ladies curtsying, and gentlemen bowing in return.* LADY TIDDLIWINKS *and* COUNTESS TRUFFLES *exchange glances and fan themselves rapidly.*)

LADY TIDDLIWINKS (*Looking through her lorgnette*): I do not believe that you are on my list!

MYSTERY GUEST: Perhaps not, dear lady. And yet, no list is complete without me!

TOM THUMB: I say, this is jolly fun. Are you a king, incognito?

MYSTERY GUEST: I am not a king, sir, but I *am* in "cognito."

THUMBELINA: Oh, let me have a turn at guessing. Have you something to do with small people?

MYSTERY GUEST: I make all tall, and I have naught to do with small. On the other hand, what would little things be without me?

TITANIA: What a puzzle! Mysterious being, have you an address?

MYSTERY GUEST: You will find me at the twentieth place, Alphabet Row.

TOBY TYLER: That sounds familiar, somehow. You know, his name is right on the tip of my tongue.

MYSTERY GUEST: And a very good place for my name, if I do say so!

COUNTESS TRUFFLES: I'm afraid I must give up. My head has begun to throb.

LADY TIDDLIWINKS: Tommyrot! Why, this is becoming more intriguing by the minute. Do continue, Mystery Guest.

MYSTERY GUEST: I shall give you one more clue. (*He slowly extends his arms to form the letter T.*)

COUNTESS TRUFFLES: Are you one of the four and twenty blackbirds baked in a pie?

LADY TIDDLIWINKS: No! Don't you see? Look at him, everybody!

ALL: It's T! It's the letter T! (MYSTERY GUEST *removes mask, revealing a large T marked on his forehead*)

MYSTERY GUEST: Thank you. I am indeed your obedient servant, the letter T. Although I was not invited to this party, still, as you know, there is no party without a T. I came to express my deep appreciation for your kindness, Lady Tiddliwinks and Countess Truffles. Never has a humble letter been so honored.

LADY TIDDLIWINKS: Oh, tut! It was a trifle.

MYSTERY GUEST: In return for your thoughtfulness, please allow me to become your protector and talisman.

COUNTESS TRUFFLES: But what can a mere letter do for us noble ladies?

MYSTERY GUEST: Ah! But the letter T is truly a magician of the alphabet. What other letter can change *here* to *there*? What other letter is always in the middle of "everything"?

TINKER BELL: By the mere presence of the letter T there is an end to fight, and fright, and blackest night!

MYSTERY GUEST: Thunder cannot begin without me.

Theaters cannot start until I am there. I can promise
you that I will be with you always, through thick and
thin!

LADY TIDDLIWINKS: We accept your thoughtful testimo-
nial.

COUNTESS TRUFFLES: We take you as our topnotch talisman!

FOOTMAN: Tarantara! Tarantara!

ALL: Tarantara! Tarantara! (*Boys fling their hats into the
air, and girls applaud. The ladies fan themselves.*)

LADY TIDDLIWINKS:

Give a thunderclap tremendous for the trusty letter T.

Forever may the tocsin toll for timeless, tiptop T!

(*Curtain*)

THE END

Cupivac

Characters

HOBNOB ⎫
MIXIE ⎬ *pixies*
MINGLER ⎭
DR. MENTOR
CUTT ⎫ *technicians*
DRYE ⎭
CUPIVAC (*offstage voice*)
DANIEL CUPID
ROBIN HOOD

MARY POPPINS
CLEOPATRA
SCROOGE
SLEEPING BEAUTY
RIP VAN WINKLE
STEPMOTHER
TWO STEPSISTERS
PAGES
TROLLS

SETTING: *Cloud Nine. A long table is up center with a sign, "Department of Romance."*

AT RISE: HOBNOB, MIXIE *and* MINGLER *are sitting at the table, each with a telephone in front of him. The telephone in front of* HOBNOB *rings.*

HOBNOB (*Answering telephone*): Good morning, Cloud Nine, Department of Romance. Love Makes the World Go 'Round. May I help you? (*Pause*) Daniel Cupid? I am sorry, Mr. Cupid is not here. He's on safari. (*Pause*) What? You want to arrange an accidental meeting? I'll connect you with the Dropped Handkerchief division. (*He jiggles the phone and listens as* MIXIE's *phone rings.*)

MIXIE (*Picking up phone*): Good morning. This is Cloud Nine. Love Makes the World Go 'Round. May I help you? (*Pause*) I am sorry, Mr. Cupid is not here. You want a love potion to put in *what?* In a chocolate malted? Well, that's a bit unusual, but give me your name and address. (*He listens and writes as* MINGLER'*s phone rings.*)

MINGLER (*Answering phone*): Hello. Love Makes the World Go 'Round. May I help you? (*Pause*) A what? (*He puts his hand over the phone and speaks to* HOB-NOB.) It's somebody called Dr. Mentor. He wants to know if he can install a computer today.

HOBNOB: A computer? On Cloud Nine? (*Sarcastically*) Oh, fine!

MINGLER (*Into phone*): He says, "Oh, fine." (*He hangs up.*)

HOBNOB: Wait—don't hang up. We don't want a computer here.

MINGLER: Ooops. I'm sorry. It looks as if we're going to get one. See, they're here already. (*He points off left as* CUTT *and* DRYE, *one on each side of a large computer, bring it in and set it on the floor, down right. The pixies go down right and watch curiously as* CUTT *plugs the computer in and* DRYE *adjusts the knobs.* DR. MEN-TOR *enters from left and flips open an order book, addressing* HOBNOB.)

MENTOR: One computer. Sign please.

HOBNOB: We don't want a computer. There has been a mistake.

MINGLER: This is the Department of Romance.

MENTOR: Exactly.

MIXIE: What do you mean "exactly"? Nothing is exact in this department. It's all rainbows and violins here.

CUTT: Pooh-pooh. Rainbows. Rainbows don't compute.

DRYE: Fiddle-faddle. Violins. Violins don't compute either.

MENTOR: Stand aside, pixies. There is going to be a new

era on Cloud Nine. This is Cupivac, my own invention, the greatest computer ever built. Cupivac will take all the guesswork out of boy-meets-girl.

Cutt: Cupivac will add your aspirations, subtract your sins—

Drye: Multiply your virtues and divide your dynamics—

Mentor: Cross-file you, reshuffle you, index you, and finally find you a mate—a perfect, permanent, scientific, balanced mate.

Mingler: Ugh! It sounds like a breakfast food. Go away. We don't need it.

Mentor: My dear fellow—it's done. We have paired the whole world, including every single and every double character in the world of myth and legend.

Hobnob: The world of myth and legend! That's our world! How dare you?

Mentor: Tut, tut. It's all for the better. Now your favorite fairy tale characters will live not happily ever after, but—

Cutt and Drye: *Logically* ever after. Computers make the world go 'round!

Pixies: Oh, how disgusting.

Mentor: Now, would you like to see a sample of my programming?

Pixies: No!

Mentor: I'm glad you said that. Cutt, hand me the purple perforated punch programs, please.

Cutt: Purple perforated punch programs coming right up. (Cutt *takes purple slotted cards from pocket and holds them fanwise like playing cards.*)

Mentor: Drye, select a card, any card, at random.

Drye: One random card, coming right up. (*He riffles through the cards.*) Alpha-Beta-Gamma-Nu. Out goes y-o-u. This one. (*Hands card to* Mentor)

MENTOR: Ah, Robin Hood.

PIXIES: Not Robin Hood!

HOBNOB: You can't mean Robin Hood. He already has a girl—Maid Marian.

MENTOR: A very poor selection. We will find a better mate for him. Cutt, put the purple perforated punch program in the in-put put-out. (CUTT *inserts the card in a slot in computer. There is a gulping sound from the machine.*) Drye, activate the rheostats. (DRYE *turns handle. There is a beeping sound. A chime plays a fanfare, and a rasping voice sounds over a megaphone from computer.*)

CUPIVAC: Card number 1882498: Robin Hood. (ROBIN HOOD *enters from behind machine right.*)

ROBIN HOOD: Forsooth, good lads. What merry adventure have we here? Who calls Robin from the greenwood?

MIXIE: Run, Robin. Run for your life.

MENTOR: Quiet, pixie. Now, Drye, push the button. Compute a perfect match for Robin Hood. (DRYE *pushes a heart-shaped button. A horn sounds. The machine gurgles, whizzes and whines. A chime plays "Country Gardens" and from behind the computer left, umbrella raised above her head, comes* MARY POPPINS.)

ROBIN HOOD: Yoicks! What is this creature with the black mushroom over her head?

MIXIE: It's Mary Poppins, Robin.

ROBIN HOOD: I like her not.

MARY POPPINS: Indeed, Mr. Hood. Fancy that. Well, I am not fond of you either. Running about in a dirty forest in those ridiculous green rompers, without a proper governess. And I dare say you haven't washed your hands in a week. Now, off with you. Spit-spot. (*She grabs* ROBIN *by the ear and marches him down left*)

ROBIN HOOD (*As they exit*): Gadzooks! Help! Help me,

merry men. Help, Sheriff of Nottingham! King John!
Anybody—help!

MINGLER: Poor Robin.

MENTOR: Beautiful. A neat balance of personalities.

CUTT and DRYE: Neat. Very neat.

MENTOR: Now, shall I choose the next card?

PIXIES: No!

MENTOR: I'm glad you said that. (*Takes card from* CUTT)
Ah, Cleopatra!

HOBNOB: Oh, please—not the glamorous, exotic Cleopatra.

MENTOR (*To* CUTT, *briskly*): Compute Cleopatra. (CUTT
*puts the card in the slot. The machine gulps, the beeper
sounds, and a chime plays an oriental tune as* CLEO-
PATRA, *hands outstretched and feet facing left in an
Egyptian pose, appears right of machine.*)

CLEOPATRA: Is it my own true love who hath summoned
the Queen Cleopatra? Ah, true love, I have built a
great barge with silken sails that you and I may float
upon the Nile. I have filled it with gold and jewels just
for you.

MENTOR: Compute Cleopatra's mate. (DRYE *pushes the
heart-shaped button. The horn sounds. The machine
gurgles, whizzes and whines and a fog horn sounds dis-
mally, as* SCROOGE *enters left of the machine, hunched
over and frowning.*) Your Majesty, may I present Mr.
Ebenezer Scrooge, your ideal mate.

CLEOPATRA (*Flinging her arms out dramatically*): My love,
all that I own is yours.

SCROOGE: Bah, humbug. Young woman, you and I are going to put the kingdom of Egypt on a sound financial
basis. No more barging up and down the Nile, flinging
gold around. No more jewels. And while we're at it—
sell those useless pyramids.

CLEOPATRA: But what about my feelings? You have hurt
my feelings, O Scrooge. (*She starts to cry*)

SCROOGE (*Pulling her off right*): Feelings—bah, humbug! If I had my way, everyone who babbles about feelings would be boiled in tear drops! (*They exit.*)

MENTOR (*Smugly*): It's a pleasure to see two such scientifically matched personalities.

CUTT *and* DRYE: Oh, very scientific. Very.

MENTOR: Now then, shall we compute another couple, just for the record?

PIXIES: No!

MENTOR: I'm glad you said that. Cutt, choose a card. (CUTT *shuts his eyes and riffles the cards, choosing one. He hands it to* MENTOR.) Interesting—very interesting. Sleeping Beauty.

MINGLER: Oh, I beg you. Leave Sleeping Beauty alone. You mustn't interfere with Prince Charming.

MENTOR: Silence. Compute Sleeping Beauty. (CUTT *inserts the card. The machine gulps. The beeper sounds and the chime plays Brahms' "Lullaby."* PAGES *carry* SLEEPING BEAUTY *in on a litter down right of the machine. They stand with arms folded, waiting.*) And now, let Cupivac find a mate for Sleeping Beauty. (DRYE *pushes the button. The horn sounds. The machine wheezes, whines and the chimes play Brahms' "Lullaby" as* TROLLS *carry in stretcher with* RIP VAN WINKLE, *snoring loudly, down left.*)

MINGLER: Rip Van Winkle! But, but what kind of a love story is that? They'll never wake up.

MENTOR: Perhaps not. But what a masterpiece of logic. Sleeping Beauty and Rip Van Winkle. Absolutely pluperfect.

CUTT *and* DRYE (*Shaking hands with each other and then with* MENTOR): Pluperfect! A masterpiece! (PAGES *take* SLEEPING BEAUTY *off right, followed by the* TROLLS, *who exit with* RIP VAN WINKLE, *still snoring.*)

HOBNOB: You're a meddler, Mentor. Daniel Cupid will never forgive you.

MENTOR: Fiddle-dee-dee. System is all that matters. Each little pigeon in its hole. Why, there's no end to the tidy new arrangements CUPIVAC will create. Romeo and Mrs. Wiggs of the Cabbage Patch. (*The pixies groan.*) Snow White and the Jolly Green Giant. (*The pixies moan*) Lady Macbeth and Little Lord Fauntleroy. (*The pixies begin to cry.* CUPID, *dressed in safari outfit, runs in from right and stands downstage, lifting his hand commandingly.*)

CUPID: Stop! I demand to know what is going on here.

MENTOR: Daniel Cupid!

PIXIES (*Ad lib*): Daniel Cupid. Hurrah! Just in time. (*Etc.*)

MENTOR: See here, Cupid. Your day is over. The day of the computer is at hand. CUPIVAC is the greatest boon to mankind since the invention of spinach.

CUPID: Aha. A computer. I suppose this machine can put one and one together and make two as well as I can?

MENTOR: Better. You stick people together with gooey sentiment.

CUTT: CUPIVAC gets to the root of the matter.

DRYE: The square root of the matter.

CUPID: Very impressive. (*The pixies shake their heads.* CUPID *takes the program cards*) May I see the program cards? Do you mind if I compute a few?

MENTOR: Not at all. Be my guest. (CUPID *puts three cards in the slot. The machine gulps three times. The beeper sounds and a rasping voice sounds over a megaphone*)

CUPIVAC: Card number 1234: Technician Cutt. Card number 5678: Technician Drye. Card number 9101112: Dr. Mentor.

CUTT *and* DRYE: That's us!

MENTOR: What is the meaning of this? What are you doing, Daniel Cupid?

CUPID: Each little pigeon in its hole. Why, there's no end to the new arrangements CUPIVAC will make.

MENTOR: Oh, no.

CUPID: Button, button, now where is that little button?

CUTT: Don't—

DRYE: Don't push the button—

CUPID: I'm glad you said that. Here goes. (*He pushes the button. The horn sounds. The machine wheezes and whines and out from left of the machine bound Cinderella's* TWO STEPSISTERS *and* STEPMOTHER.)

MENTOR: Good heavens. What ghastly looking creatures. Who are they?

STEPSISTERS: Don't you recognize us?

1ST STEPSISTER (*Embracing* CUTT): I'm Cinderella's adorable first stepsister. I've been waiting centuries for someone like you.

2ND STEPSISTER (*Hugging* DRYE): And I am Cinderella's enchanting second stepsister. Your lovely computer brought us together.

STEPMOTHER (*Linking arms with* MENTOR): You must remember me—Cinderella's gentle, kind, understanding stepmother. Of course you do. And I'll take just as good care of you as I did of little Cinderella. Come!

STEPSISTERS: Come! (*They drag* CUTT, DRYE *and* MENTOR *down left.*)

CUTT, DRYE *and* MENTOR (*On their knees before* CUPID): Help! Save us!

CUPID: Fiddle-dee-dee. Systems are all that matter. My, my. I hope you three live logically ever after. (*They exit, protesting*)

HOBNOB: Phew, Mr. Cupid. Are we glad to see you again!

MIXIE: But what will happen to that beastly CUPIVAC?

CUPID: Listen. I think we're going to have a visit from some moving men. (CUTT *and* DRYE *enter from left. They pick up the computer.* MENTOR *enters and panto-*

mimes directions, waving them off left again.) Going somewhere, Dr. Mentor?

MENTOR: We're going to improve the computer. It needs a few adjustments. Just a few adjustments. (*He exits left. There is a loud crash, tinkle of glass, a broken beeping sound and a scattering of nuts and bolts*)

PIXIES: What was that?

CUPID: I think that's what you call an adjustment. (*The three telephones ring. The pixies scamper to the table. CUPID sits on the table near HOBNOB.*)

HOBNOB (*Answering phone*): Hello, Cloud Nine. Oh, yes, he's here. (*He holds the phone out to CUPID*)

MIXIE (*Answering phone*): Good morning, Cloud Nine. Mr. Cupid? Just a moment, please. (*He holds the phone out to CUPID.*)

MINGLER (*Answering phone*): This is Cloud Nine. Call for Mr. Cupid? I'll put him on. (*He holds the phone out to CUPID. CUPID speaks into all phones at once.*)

CUPID: Daniel Cupid, at your service. (*The curtains start to close.*) Love Makes the World Go 'Round—

PIXIES: And around and around and around! (*Curtain*)

THE END

A Tale of Two Drummers

Characters

DAME HELENA CHANNING
MERRYBELLE ⎱ *her children*
OLIVER ⎰
MONSIEUR BEAUCHAMPS, *a dancing master*
TABITHA, *the maid*
GENERAL GEORGE WASHINGTON
GENERAL PHILANDER KNOX
LT. ALEXANDER HAMILTON
COLONEL STERNE ⎰
AIDE ⎟
SERGEANT-MAJOR ⎬ *British soldiers*
PVT. HOPKINS ⎭

TIME: *September 15, 1776.*
SETTING: *The parlor of the Channing town house on Bloomington Road, New York.*
AT RISE: DAME HELENA *stands up center, her back to the audience, looking anxiously out a bay window.* MONSIEUR BEAUCHAMPS *is sitting up left, with hand raised, as* MERRYBELLE *and* OLIVER *stand down right, ready to dance a minuet.*

BEAUCHAMPS: Clasp hands. (MERRYBELLE *and* OLIVER *clasp hands.*) Raise hands. (*They raise clasped hands.*

BEAUCHAMPS *begins to hum a minuet, waving his hand in time, as they start to dance.*)

DAME HELENA: Oh! (*Children stop and all look at her.*)

BEAUCHAMPS: What is it, Madame Channing?

DAME HELENA (*Turning*): I fancied I heard gunfire.

OLIVER: 'Twas only the blacksmith down the street, Mother. (DAME HELENA *turns back to window.*)

BEAUCHAMPS: Once again, children. The minuet. And you, Monsieur Oliver, lightly, lightly on the toes. You are not marching clump, clump, in heavy boots.

OLIVER: I wish I were marching. (*The clock strikes two.*)

DAME HELENA (*Jumping*): Oh! 'Twas only the clock. How it startled me.

BEAUCHAMPS: Ah, madame is not well. Perhaps I should conclude the lesson.

DAME HELENA: Perhaps it would be best, Monsieur Beauchamps. Oliver has his mind on that dreadful drum of his and I am not myself. 'Tis the strain of this war. Please, feel free to leave early.

BEAUCHAMPS (*Rising and bowing*): Thank you, madame. (*He takes his cloak from a rack up center and dons it.*) Please, do not worry. There is a brave militia to defend New York, is there not? And the British General Howe is far away in Boston, is that not so?

DAME HELENA: I devoutly hope that the British are in Boston. If they should march on New York with our feeble militia, I tremble to think of the consequences.

BEAUCHAMPS: Take courage, Madame Channing. Many things we fear never come to pass. (*He bows.*) Au revoir, children.

MERRY *and* OLIVER (*Bowing and curtsying as he exits up right*): Au revoir, Monsieur Beauchamps. (OLIVER *runs to his mother, who seats herself in chair up left and fans herself with a lace handkerchief.*)

OLIVER (*Stoutly*): Don't you worry, Mother. If the worst comes, I'll join the militia. I'm already a good drummer.

DAME HELENA: Don't worry! Oh, Oliver! You would march with a great noisy drum? What a target you'd make for a British musket! Promise me you will never play that—that demon drum, again!

OLIVER: But, Mother— (TABITHA *enters down right, and bobs a curtsy.*)

TABITHA: If it please you, Dame Helena, there are some workmen at the kitchen door. They wish to see you.

DAME HELENA: Workmen? I didn't send for any workmen.

TABITHA: I thought not, ma'am, but they were most insistent. They said to tell you this: They've come to mend the house.

MERRY: To mend the house?

TABITHA: There was more. They've come to mend *the house of liberty.*

DAME HELENA (*Aside*): *Liberty.* The password of independence. (*To* TABITHA) I shall come immediately. (*Casually, to the children*) I had forgotten. Some repairs to be made on the attic. Amuse yourselves, children. (*She exits down right swiftly, followed by* TABITHA)

MERRY: How odd. Mama just had the attic repaired not a month ago.

OLIVER: Perhaps the squirrels have been at the shingles again. (*He lifts window seat beneath bay window*) Hist, Merry—look. (*He brings out a drum and sticks from the window seat.*)

MERRY: Oh, Oliver, your drum. Where did you find it? I thought Mama had hidden it from you.

OLIVER: She did. In a pickle barrel. I hope it won't sound sour! Listen, I'll play you a roll the way the British do.

Very long and pompous-sounding. Listen. (*He plays a long roll.*) Now, here's a Yankee beat. Very smart and to the point. (*He plays a quick, lively beat.*)

MERRY: Oh, do let me try. This is much more fun than that tedious minuet. Is this the British way? (*She bangs on drum a few times*)

OLIVER: Longer, harder, like the boring voice of King George saying, "Taxes-taxes-taxes." (*She tries again.*) Good, Merry. That's the way. Now try the Yankee beat. (MERRY *hesitantly raps out the Yankee beat.* DAME HELENA, *followed by* GENERAL WASHINGTON, GENERAL KNOX, *and* LT. HAMILTON, *their uniforms hidden by shabby cloaks, enters down right and crosses to long table at left.* OLIVER *quickly hides the drum behind him.*)

DAME HELENA: Pray, gentlemen, be seated. (*Men sit at table,* WASHINGTON *at the head.*)

MERRY: Gentlemen! Who can they be?

WASHINGTON: Who are these children, good dame? Can they be trusted?

DAME HELENA (*Crossing to children and bringing them to table*): They are my own children, sir. I would trust them with my life. Children, pay your respects. These are no ordinary workmen. They are American officers— Lt. Hamilton, General Knox, and our commander, General George Washington. (*They throw back cloaks, revealing uniforms.*)

MERRY *and* OLIVER: General Washington! (*Children bow and curtsy.*)

WASHINGTON: Thank you for your hospitality, Dame Helena. It is not every household we can trust these days.

OLIVER (*Eagerly*): What's the news, sir?

WASHINGTON: Bad, I fear.

KNOX: Lord Howe has moved a fleet of ships into New

York Harbor. (*He takes out a map*) Many of his troops are at Staten Island—here.

HAMILTON (*Pointing*): But a contingent of British riflemen has crossed the East River here—and driven our militia back.

DAME HELENA: I was certain I heard gunfire! Have you been followed?

WASHINGTON: No, I think not. We have a plan to delay the occupation of New York by the British until we can regroup our forces.

HAMILTON: A certain Mrs. Murray, who is sympathetic to our cause, has opened her mansion to the officers of the British army, and to the commander, Lord Howe. While they are delayed, sipping tea and nibbling crumpets, we shall slip north to Harlem Heights.

KNOX: It is most vital, madam, that we be undiscovered.

WASHINGTON: New York must not fall into the hands of the British. If New York falls, the revolution fails. Above all, we three must not be captured.

DAME HELENA (*Going to window and glancing out nervously*): Pray, gentlemen, let me make you safe upstairs in the study. This street is full of Loyalists, prying and snooping. I dare not close these curtains at midday, and I fear someone will discover you. Moreover, there is a back staircase to a side street, should you need to leave quickly.

WASHINGTON: As you wish. Now I must beg two favors of you. First, if any one should visit, keep everything as usual and try not to betray nervousness. Second, lend us your son to guide us through New York.

OLIVER: General Washington wishes *me* to be his guide? Let me do it, Mother. Let me!

DAME HELENA: Oh, he's such a little boy. (OLIVER *stands on tiptoe.*) Very well, but do be careful.

OLIVER: Thank you, Mother. *(Bringing out the drum)* And I shall take the drum too. May I, General?

WASHINGTON: Take the drum if it pleases you, lad. Perhaps it will be useful.

DAME HELENA: Oliver—your drum! You promised! *(Shakes her head)* Ah, well. Come this way, gentlemen. *(She leads men off left. As she exits, TABITHA enters fearfully from right, crossing to MERRY.)*

TABITHA: Oh, miss, is it true? Cook says the city is swarming with red-coated rascals. Cook says the British are dreadful men. Cannibals, they are.

MERRY: Oh, pooh, Tabitha. The British are dreadful, 'tis true, but not cannibals, I think. Besides, they'll not be eating Yankee pot roast—'twill give them indigestion. *(TABITHA smiles. DAME HELENA re-enters, crossing to the girls.)*

DAME HELENA: Now, we must heed the General, Merry and Tabitha. Everything must appear cheerful and calm. *(A knock is heard at the door up right.)* A guest. I would guests would pay their respects elsewhere today. Tabitha, answer the door. *(TABITHA goes to answer it)* 'Tis the Mayhews, no doubt.

TABITHA *(Opening the door and falling back in alarm as COLONEL STERNE, followed by his AIDE, SERGEANT-MAJOR and PVT. HOPKINS, strides in)*: Oh, alack! The British have come!

MERRY: Mama!

DAME HELENA: British soldiers!

COLONEL: British indeed, ma'am. Colonel Sterne, of His Majesty's infantry. What, are there no tea and crumpets here?

DAME HELENA: Why should there be tea? I did not expect you!

COLONEL: Tsk, tsk. Then you are not as hospitable as a certain Mrs. Murray, who even now entertains General

Howe and his brother officers. But I have no time for chitchat. I have reason to believe that General Washington is hiding hereabout.

DAME HELENA (*Pretending to be faint*): Oh! General Washington. Oh! I must get my smelling salts upstairs. (*She starts to cross left*)

COLONEL: Halt! Stay where you are. (*She stops.*) Soldier, guard this hall. (HOPKINS, *musket raised, stands down left.* TABITHA *sidles down right.*) Sergeant-Major, guard that exit! (SERGEANT-MAJOR, *pike raised, goes down right.* MERRY *backs to the door upstage*) Aide, see to the front door. (AIDE, *tipping his hat to* MERRY *apologetically, stands at the front door, hand on sword.*)

AIDE: Begging your pardon, miss, but we can't be too careful.

COLONEL: Aide, stop begging her pardon. A British officer never begs. He commands. Now then, we shall use your house as a headquarters from which to conduct a thorough search.

DAME HELENA: Of course. Certainly. What a splendid idea. We shall give you all the help we can, shan't we? (*The girls nod*) Now, I suggest that you search the stable next door. 'Tis full of stalls and lofts. An excellent place for those—er—rebels to hide.

MERRY: Oh, yes. The very place. My brother and I often hide there when we play "I spy."

TABITHA: 'Tis true. And Cook says that runaway servants often hide there.

COLONEL: Indeed? 'Tis heartening to see such a display of loyalty to the Crown. I shall dispatch someone to search this stable you speak of, directly after I have searched this house.

DAME HELENA: Search my house? My private house? Sir, you have no warrant!

COLONEL: I need no warrant. You seem disturbed, madam.

Is there something you wish to conceal? (DAME HELENA *is taken aback.*)

TABITHA: Oh . . . (*She begins to cry.*) You must not search. You will see the beds are not made. 'Tis my fault.

MERRY (*Beginning to cry*): My room is in frightful disorder.

COLONEL: Nonsense. I am not searching for dust curls. I am searching for generals.

AIDE (*Helplessly*): There, there, don't take on, ladies.

COLONEL: Soldier, come with me. (*He starts left.* DAME HELENA *begins to weep loudly.*)

DAME HELENA: Oh! Oh! The world is upside down! (*She waves her arms and shrieks.*)

COLONEL (*Rushing to her, and seating her at the table, down left*): Aide, come here. (*To* MERRY) What is this, girl—a fit? (AIDE *pours water from pitcher on table.* DAME HELENA *sips it. The* COLONEL *fans her with his hat.*)

MERRY: 'Tis an attack of the vapors. (*Indignantly*) You should have let her have the smelling salts. I shall go and fetch them now. (*She marches left*)

COLONEL: Stop! Go no further. Come over here, girl. I'll send the soldier. Where are the salts?

DAME HELENA: Never mind. 'Tis not necessary. I have recovered. Merry, come soothe my head. (MERRY *strokes her mother's head. They whisper together, facing front so that the* COLONEL *does not hear*) What shall we do? They must not search upstairs. We must warn General Washington to leave this house immediately.

MERRY: I have an idea. 'Tis farfetched, but it is our only chance. Play along with me, Mama. (*She crosses to center, smiles at the* COLONEL) Pray, sir, 'tis not often we entertain the officers of His Majesty here. May I offer you some music?

COLONEL (*Annoyed*): *Music?* We are here on business, girl. Now sit down and knit—or whatever you do.

DAME HELENA (*Beginning to shriek again*): Music! I must have music!

COLONEL (*Hastily*): Very well. No more hysteria. Music, it is.

AIDE: Shall I open the spinet, child, or tune your harp?

MERRY: Nay, sir. I play the drum. (*She beats with her fists on the table in a long, loud drum roll. She does this again and again.* COLONEL *puts his hands to his ears*)

COLONEL: Stop! Halt! I command you to cease! Aide, stop that drumming!

AIDE (*Shouting*): Sergeant-Major, stop the drumming!

SERGEANT-MAJOR: Soldier, stop the drumming!

HOPKINS (*At the top of his lungs*): *Stop the drumming!* (MERRY *smiles demurely, stops, curtsies.* DAME HELENA *and* TABITHA *applaud.*)

COLONEL: What a household. Weeping mother and a lunatic child! Oh, my sainted ears. Soldier, you search upstairs. I shall stay down here and pacify these Yankee-Doodle dunderheads. (HOPKINS *salutes and exits left*)

MERRY: Now that I have played for you, may I sing for you?

ALL (*Hastily*): No! (*Offstage, the Yankee drum beat is heard faintly, with a voice calling out orders gruffly*)

AIDE (*Cocking his ear*): Sir—I hear a drum.

COLONEL (*Angrily*): I do not find that funny, Aide. Do not speak of drums again. My head aches. (*The drum sounds louder.*)

AIDE: But, sir— (HOPKINS *enters and salutes.*)

HOPKINS: Private Hopkins reporting, sir. I found nobody upstairs. (DAME HELENA, MERRY *and* TABITHA *sigh with relief*)

COLONEL: Drat! They are in this vicinity, I know it. (*The drum sounds again.*)

SERGEANT-MAJOR: Your pardon, Colonel, but I hear a drum, too.

COLONEL: Sergeant-Major, that's enough. You hear nothing. Nothing! (*The drum sounds again.*)

HOPKINS: But I hear it, too. A Yankee beat. (*The drum sounds outside the door up right.*)

OLIVER (*Offstage; gruffly*): Fix bayonets. Surround the house!

COLONEL: Alack! The militia! Why did nobody tell me? (*To* TABITHA) You, wench—lead us out of here. Is there another exit?

TABITHA: Yes, sir. Through the kitchen to the alley.

COLONEL: Take us there.

TABITHA: Yes, sir. (*She leads them off down right. Before exiting,* HOPKINS *bows to* MERRY.)

HOPKINS: You need not have feared, miss. Your room is in perfect order. Not a curl of dust anywhere! (*He salutes and runs off.*)

DAME HELENA: We are saved! The militia is here! (*They embrace each other, cheering.*) Let them in, Merry. Let in all the hundreds of brave soldiers. We shall have a reception and a ball for them.

MERRY: Yes, Mama. (*She opens the door. Both* MERRY *and* DAME HELENA *curtsy very low, as* OLIVER, *grinning broadly, enters playing a drum roll*)

OLIVER (*Bowing as they rise*): Your obedient servant, ladies.

BOTH (*Astonished*): Oliver!

OLIVER: 'Tis not King George!

MERRY: But where is the militia?

OLIVER: I am the militia. Captain and private. Listen. (*He calls out orders*) Left flank, march! Fix bayonets! Surround the house!

DAME HELENA: But General Washington? His staff?

OLIVER: Safely on their way to Harlem Heights on a

wagonload of hay. They bid me return home. When I heard Merry thumping that British drum roll, I knew the redcoats were here. 'Twas well done, Merry.

DAME HELENA: But you could have been shot!

OLIVER: I would not leave you here alone. So, I summoned up my courage and made myself sound like three hundred men. Now, tell me what a clever fellow I am.

MERRY: What a clever fellow you are!

DAME HELENA (*Sighing and shaking her head*): Oh, Oliver!

OLIVER: What is it, Mother? (*Curtains begin to close.*)

DAME HELENA: Do play us something on the drum. I have always said that a drum is the most tuneful, most melodious, most beguiling of instruments!

OLIVER: Now I ask you—isn't that just like a mother! (*Curtain*)

THE END

The Exterior Decorator

Characters

MADAME JACQUES FROST
MONSIEUR JACQUES FROST
DR. EQUINOX
MONSIEUR PRINTEMPS
FOUR GREENSMOCKS

FOUR BLUESMOCKS
TWO SUNLIGHTERS
TWO WEST WINDS
FOUR ROBINS

TIME: *The month of March.*
SETTING: *The Chateau Glacé.*
AT RISE: MONSIEUR *and* MADAME JACQUES FROST *are downstage.* MADAME FROST *is sitting in a sheet-draped lawn chair, moaning. Downstage right is a sign reading, "Chateau Glacé." Upstage, right and left, are bare gray trees and bushes. At back is a cloudy, gray sky.*

MADAME FROST: Oh, how dismal it all is! Oh, how gloomy the world is! (*She coughs loudly.*)
JACQUES FROST: Please, my dear. Try to calm yourself. I have called Dr. Equinox. He will be here in a few moments. Meanwhile, is there something that might please you? Perhaps a fresh, cold icicle?
MME. FROST (*Shuddering*): No, I couldn't eat another one.
JACQUES: But you must keep your strength up. I have it!

I'll bring you a delicious Eskimo pie stuffed with diced snowflakes.

MME. FROST: No, not a bite!

JACQUES: A cup of glacier tea?

MME. FROST: No, not a drop!

JACQUES: Then, shall we listen to the concert of the wild winds on the hi-fi? North Wind himself is conducting his Symphony Number One in Absolute Zero.

MME. FROST: Oh, that old North Wind. He bores me.

JACQUES: Then can I do *anything* for you?

MME. FROST (*Sniffling and groaning*): No, not a thing!

JACQUES (*Pacing up and down*): Oh, I shall surely wear myself to a shadow with this worry. Where can that Dr. Equinox be keeping himself? (DR. EQUINOX *enters right, with doctor's bag.*) Ah, Dr. Equinox! Just in time. I have been so worried about Madame Frost.

DR. EQUINOX: What seems to be the difficulty, my dear Jacques Frost?

JACQUES: Look at her—for weeks now she has been moaning and sighing. Nothing amuses her. She will not even take the tiniest mouthful of food.

DR. EQUINOX: I see. Tsk, tsk. Suppose I examine her. (*To* MADAME FROST) Good afternoon, dear Madame. I am most concerned to hear of your illness. Can you tell me what is troubling you?

MME. FROST: I can hardly lift my head from the pillow.

DR. EQUINOX: Aha! Let me feel your pulse. (*He takes her wrist.*) Throb . . . throb . . . throb. . . . Hmm, very slow. Like a sluggish brook.

MME. FROST: And then there is the cold. The chilly weather seemed so bracing in January. But now it goes through my bones and I sh-shiver and I sh-shake.

DR. EQUINOX: Let me take your temperature. (*He puts a large outdoor thermometer in her mouth.*)

JACQUES: Is it serious, Doctor?

DR. EQUINOX: We shall see what we shall see. (*Takes thermometer from* MADAME FROST *and reads it*) Um-hum! Twenty degrees above zero. Just as I thought.

JACQUES: What do you think?

DR. EQUINOX: Madame has a most uncomfortable case of the doldrums.

MME. FROST (*Hysterically*): Oh! Oh! The doldrums! Oh, I shall never recover! Oh, what a dreadful disease! Oh! (*In a puzzled tone*) What are the doldrums?

DR. EQUINOX: Calm yourself, Madame. The doldrums are a very common complaint. They occur about the middle of March. The patient complains of depression and weakness. Everything seems too gloomy to bear. (DR. EQUINOX *takes out a large prescription pad and begins to write with crayon.*)

MME. FROST: My symptoms exactly! Shall I have to take pills? I adore pills.

DR. EQUINOX: No pills.

MME. FROST: A tonic then? Oh, do prescribe a rich, red tonic.

DR. EQUINOX: No tonic.

MME. FROST: No tonic? No pills? What will you prescribe for me? (DR. EQUINOX *shows pad to audience and* MADAME FROST. *It says,* "Rx: MONSIEUR PRINTEMPS")

DR. EQUINOX:
Madame Frost, attend and heed,
Monsieur Printemps is what you need!

JACQUES: Monsieur Printemps? Why, that means Mr. Springtime.

MME. FROST: You are prescribing this Mr. Springtime for me instead of a lovely tonic? I never heard of such medicine! (*She coughs again.*)

DR. EQUINOX: Monsieur Printemps will do wonders for you. He's better than pills for the doldrums. Aha! I hear him coming now. (MONSIEUR PRINTEMPS, *in smock and beret, bounds in left. He clicks his heels and bows.*)

MONSIEUR PRINTEMPS: Bon jour, Monsieur Frost. And Madame Frost. My friend, Dr. Equinox, has asked me to come to assist you out of the doldrums. I trust you will soon be in the green, as the saying goes. Allow me to present my card. (*He hands them a large card.*) Monsieur Printemps: Exterior Decorator Supreme.

MME. FROST (*Reading the card*): What a very odd profession. An *exterior* decorator. No, don't tell me. Let me guess. If an interior decorator decorates insides . . . then an exterior decorator decorates outsides.

PRINTEMPS: Exactly, Madame. You are exceedingly clever.

MME. FROST: Did you hear that, Jacques? Monsieur Printemps considers me clever. Why, I believe I could sit up a bit.

JACQUES: Excellent, my dear.

DR. EQUINOX: I must be on my way now. If I know the good work of Monsieur Printemps, Madame will no longer need my services. Adieu! (*He doffs hat and exits right.* MONSIEUR PRINTEMPS *stands at center, hands on hips, and shakes his head, as he views Chateau Glacé.*)

JACQUES: What is the matter, Monsieur?

PRINTEMPS: I do not like to criticize your taste, Monsieur Frost, but this chateau is distinctly dreary. The whole color scheme is gray on gray on more gray. Even Madame is gray. And the carpet!

JACQUES: What is wrong with our carpet? When it came to us in December it was a lovely white.

PRINTEMPS: Look at it, I beg you. Bits of brown earth showing through. Soiled snow lying in heaps upon it. Oh, this carpet must go! Ho! Greensmocks! (*He claps his hands.* 1ST *and* 2ND GREENSMOCKS *run in, bringing a sample of green paper grass.*) Here is a sample of our latest well-to-well carpet.

MME. FROST: What a fresh green color it has.

PRINTEMPS: Feel the cool, smooth texture. Imagine running barefoot over acres and acres of this.

MME. FROST: But does it come in a pattern? I really prefer carpets with patterns.

PRINTEMPS (*Rolling his eyes ecstatically*): Does it have a pattern? Ooh-la-la! Tell her, Greensmocks!

1ST GREENSMOCK: In April, Madame will be pleased to note that this carpet has a fine pattern of pastel-colored crocuses and snowdrops, bordered with tiny purple violets.

2ND GREENSMOCK: In May, the pattern will change, and Madame will be delighted to observe that brilliant yellow daffodils will form an old-fashioned motif with vibrant purple pansies.

1ST GREENSMOCK: In June, another pattern will emerge and Madame will observe with rapture the most elegant interweaving of red, yellow, and pink roses.

MME. FROST: Oh, say no more. An ever-changing carpet! Oh, I simply must have it. (3RD *and* 4TH GREENSMOCKS *enter. The four unroll the flowered grass border across the stage. The music of "Spring Song" is heard until they are finished. They bow and take places right and left.*)

PRINTEMPS: Très bien. Already I observe a flush of health in Madame's cheeks. (*He looks at the trees, cocking his head to one side thoughtfully.*) Now . . . upholstery. Ugh! These trees are as bare as skeletons in a Halloween graveyard.

JACQUES (*Stiffly*): Our other decorator, Monsieur L'Hiver, assured us that bare trees were very modern-looking.

PRINTEMPS: Ah, Monsieur L'Hiver. I might have known it was Mr. Winter. He has no taste at all. Ho! Greensmocks! Show Madame our most artful slipcovers for trees. (GREENSMOCKS *run offstage and bring back crepe*

paper bunches of leaves which they present to MADAME
FROST. *She looks at them closely and rubs leaves be-*
tween fingers, then nods approval. The GREENSMOCKS
attach leaves to trees and bushes. Music, "Rustle of
Spring," is heard. When they have finished, they pull the
sheets off the lawn furniture and stand left and right of
stage.)

MME. FROST: Oh, how very charming. The trees now
match the lawn.

PRINTEMPS: Harmony, dear Madame. Harmony is the key
to successful decorating. And now I shall redo your impossible ceiling.

JACQUES (*Sputtering*): Impossible ceiling? How can you
say that? We've had some glorious snowfalls from that
ceiling.

PRINTEMPS: I dare say. But snowfalls are quite out of
fashion after the 21st of March. Let me think. (*He looks*
upward, squinting.) I seem to see your ceiling in a light
pastel tint.

MME. FROST: I've always been fond of heavenly blue.

PRINTEMPS: Madame, you have an eye for color. Heavenly
blue it shall be. Ho! Bluesmocks! (*He claps his hands.*
FOUR BLUESMOCKS *enter and bow.*) Bring from my ware-
house one heavenly blue ceiling for Madame. (*They*
exit, and return with "clouds," blue backdrop with
white sun. 1ST *and* 2ND BLUESMOCKS *set up the backdrop*
as "Blue Skies" is heard.) May I make one small altera-
tion?

MME. FROST: Anything, clever Monsieur Printemps.

PRINTEMPS (*Pointing to backdrop at various places*): Let
us put a few puffy white clouds here . . . here . . .
and here . . . (3RD *and* 4TH BLUESMOCKS *pin the clouds*
where MONSIEUR PRINTEMPS *indicates.*)

MME. FROST: Marvelous. Don't you think it looks marvelous, Jacques?

JACQUES: Changes . . . changes. So many changes. I am quite confused about the whole thing. I liked everything the way it was.

PRINTEMPS: Naturally. But you must admit that Madame has a gay sparkle in her eye and a new zest for life. Speaking of sparkles, I don't care one bit for the light here. Very dim, indeed. Now, Madame, I have a most interesting lamp. A single direction, golden-ray lamp that gives a pleasant rosy glow in the morning, and a multicolor sunset every night.

MME. FROST: It sounds remarkable. May I see it?

PRINTEMPS: Ho! Sunlighters! (SUNLIGHTERS *enter left and change the white disc on the backdrop to a gold one, after which they pretend to polish the sun with gold dustcloths.* 1ST BLUESMOCK *changes the sign from "Chateau Glacé" to "Chateau Soleil." The music, "You Are My Sunshine," is heard.* MONSIEUR PRINTEMPS *nods at signs.*) Good! We are changing the name of the palace from "Ice Palace" to "Sun Palace." (*Sniffing*) The air seems damp and stale. Ho! West Winds! (WEST WINDS *enter, with large fans, and dance about stage to the music of "Sweet and Low."*)

MME. FROST (*Sniffing*): What a lovely aroma. It smells like green buds uncurling, and fresh-mown grass and lilies of the valley all in one bouquet. It's getting warmer. (*Rises, takes off her cloak.* 1ST *and* 2ND GREENSMOCKS *bring her a flowered robe.*)

JACQUES: Whew! (*Mops his brow. The* GREENSMOCKS *offer him flowered robe.*) Oh, no. I shan't need that. I prefer my old coat. (*He hugs his coat proudly.* SUNLIGHTERS *shake gold dustcloths at him.* WEST WINDS *fan him. He opens his coat.*) Oh, well, perhaps I could unbutton the coat. (SUNLIGHTERS *and* WEST WINDS *come closer.*) Perhaps I could take it off for a moment—just a moment mind you. (GREENSMOCKS *bring the flowered robe. He examines it.*) Well . . . it is a very pretty cloak. I'll try it on . . . just for a moment, mind you. (*He puts it on.*)

ALL: Hurrah! (1ST *and* 2ND BLUESMOCKS *crown* MONSIEUR *and* MADAME FROST *with garlands.*)

PRINTEMPS: Ah, I have the final touch. Music! We need a Spring Quartet. (*Claps his hands*) Ho! Robins! (FOUR ROBINS *enter, carrying flutes or whistles and music stands. They play a few short trills.*)

MME. FROST: Oh, splendid, splendid! I feel wonderful. My feet hardly touch the ground. I could dance.

JACQUES: Be careful, my dear. You were quite ill.

MME. FROST: Was I? I don't remember. The whole world looks so green and pleasant to me now. A party, we'll give a party for these delightful people. Good people, Monsieur Frost and I invite you to a ball in honor of the redecoration of our chateau. Our guest of honor shall be Monsieur Printemps!

PRINTEMPS (*Clicking his heels and kissing her hand*): I am flattered, dear lady.

MME. FROST: Take your partners, please, for the Grand March. Quartet, strike up a melody! (ROBINS *begin piping, as music begins. Company marches off.* MONSIEUR PRINTEMPS *remains on stage. He puts hands on hips and looks over stage, head cocked to one side.*)

PRINTEMPS: A masterpiece, if I do say so myself. (*He clicks heels and bows to audience as the curtain closes.*)

THE END

Lion to Lamb

Characters

LION WIND, *a boy*
LAMB WIND, *a girl*
CHORUS, *10 boys and 10 girls*

SETTING: *Ten chairs are at each side of stage, and a weather vane is at center. Upstage is a ladder beside backdrop of sky, which may have lighted "stars."*

AT RISE: CHORUS *is sitting in chairs, one group at left, the other at right.* (SOLOS 1 *through* 10 *are in* LEFT CHORUS; SOLOS 11 *through* 20, *in* RIGHT CHORUS.)

CHORUS (*Both sections; roaring*): Wheeee! Whooooo! Wheee! Whooooo! (LION WIND *enters upstage, swaggers to center and spins the weather vane very fast.*)

GIRLS (*In* LEFT CHORUS):
Oh, the wind has come to our town

BOYS (*In* LEFT CHORUS):
With a whistle, with a roar . . .

LEFT CHORUS (*Looking up and holding hands on heads*):
There never was such blowing
In the skies before!
All the clouds are leaving heaven
Like a flock of frightened sheep,

1ST SOLO:

For the wind has blown the stars out—

(LION WIND *climbs ladder and "blows out" stars.*)

2ND SOLO:

And the darkness is so deep

3RD SOLO:

That the moon is hiding, hiding

Where the rainbow is asleep.

CHORUS (*Both sections*): Wheeee! Whooo! (4TH SOLO, a
*boy, steps forward, putting up umbrella, and holding it
before him as if bracing it against the wind*)

4TH SOLO:

Oh, it's gales and gusts and tempests,

Topsy-turvy all about!

(LION WIND *takes umbrella by the sides, shakes it play-
fully, and turns it inside out.*)

Help! Help! Police!

Wind's turning my umbrella

Inside out!

(LION WIND *takes hat from 5TH SOLO, a girl, and ex-
changes it with hat of 6TH SOLO, a boy.*)

5TH SOLO:

That wild wind is a trickster . . .

6TH SOLO:

He's a prankster, look and see—

5TH SOLO:

That silly boy has *my* hat,

6TH SOLO:

An old bonnet's stuck on me!

(*They exchange hats quickly.*)

7TH SOLO (*Rising as* WIND *grabs newspaper from his
hands*):

Stop thief! (*Sitting*) He snatched my paper!

8TH SOLO (*Shaking finger, as* WIND *blows newspaper*):

A most disgraceful caper!

9TH SOLO (*Holding up pieces of shingle*):
    I found my roof in ruins,
    There were shingles everywhere—
10TH SOLO (*As* WIND *messes her hair*):
    Oh, Mommy, Mommy, Mommy,
    Wind is bothering my hair!
    (LEFT CHORUS *rises. All stand with hands on hips and
    frown at* WIND, *who dances away.*)
GIRLS (*In* LEFT CHORUS):
    He's been howling, growling, blasting
    With a noise that's everlasting.
BOYS (*In* LEFT CHORUS):
    He's been bawling, squalling, whiffling,
    He's been snarling, snoring, sniffling.
LEFT CHORUS:
    He's a bold wind, he's a cold wind,
    He's a dusty, blusty old wind,
    And we wish he'd curl his windy self
    Into a windy ball,
    And bl-ow away, and bl-ow away
10TH SOLO:
    And never come back at all, at all,
LEFT CHORUS:
    And never come back at all!
LION WIND (*At center*):
    Woooo-well! Woooo-well!
    Whirlwind, whirliblast,
    Whirli-whirli-cane,
    I swoop to the North Pole,
    I swoop back again. . . .

    I'm the *khamsin* of Egypt,
    The *mistral* of France,

Typhoon, monsoon—
I make the oceans dance.

I'm a fast wind, a blast wind,
A beam wind, a scud,
When I buzz through the blizzard—
Hide, little bud!
(*He zooms to chorus member farthest left. Chorus member quakes and hides head.*)
I strip the trees in autumn,
I roil the winter sea. . . .
Now, has someone, anyone
A good word for me?
RIGHT CHORUS (*Rising*): We have.
Fresh breeze, helpful breeze,
Merry, airy friend,
We have the *best* words
For you, Mr. Wind.
(11TH SOLO *steps forward, holding kite to the side.* WIND *takes it, dances with it higher and higher, climbs ladder upstage, and hangs kite on backdrop.*)
11TH SOLO:
Wind took my kite
With a tug . . .
RIGHT CHORUS:
With a tug,
11TH SOLO:
Wind took my kite to the sky.
He pulled it aloft where the clouds hang soft
And the sun with her eye, with her bright yellow eye,
Watched my kite as it went a-bobbing by.
RIGHT CHORUS:
And the sun with her eye, with her bright yellow eye,
Watched the kite as it went a-bobbing by.

(12TH SOLO, *dressed as sailor, steps forward, holding sail-boat.* WIND *takes boat, blows on it and carries it about stage.*)

12TH SOLO:

Whenever I go a-sailing, a-sailing, a-sailing,
Whenever I skim across the brine,
Tip-tossed and running free,
Beside me is a partner . . .

RIGHT CHORUS:

A partner, a partner,

12TH SOLO:

Beside me is a partner,
A friend I cannot see.

He huffs and puffs a galeful,
A spinnaking, spanking sailful,
Then like a playful whale, full
Speed ahead we go. . . .

RIGHT CHORUS:

Ahoy! Full speed ahead we go. . . .
(WIND *sets down boat at left.* 13TH *and* 14TH SOLOS *exit right briefly and return carrying laundry basket containing laundry strung on clothesline. They hold laundry basket between them.*)

13TH SOLO:

Oh, Mrs. Smith, oh, Mrs. Smith,
The sun has gone away.
If we hang them high, will the overalls dry,
Shall we hang the clothes today, today?

RIGHT CHORUS:

Shall we hang the clothes today?
(13TH *and* 14TH SOLOS *set down basket, and hold up clothesline.* WIND *blows on clothes and shakes them.*)

14TH SOLO:

Oh, Mrs. Jones, oh, Mrs. Jones,

The overalls will dry, dry, dry.
There's a good stiff breeze in the tops of the trees.
Heave ho! And let them fly, fly, fly.
RIGHT CHORUS:
Heave ho! Let the overalls fly!
BOYS (*In* RIGHT CHORUS):
Hot . . . hot . . . hot . . . hot.
15TH SOLO (*Mopping brow with red bandanna*):
When it's half past twelve on a steaming day,
16TH SOLO (*Mopping brow*):
And the heat is like a hammer on your head,
17TH SOLO (*Mopping brow*):
When you're hot and thirsty and the sun beats down
18TH SOLO (*Mopping brow*):
And you're cross and tired and red . . .
(WIND *comes up, takes out fan, and fans these four* SOLOS.)
QUARTET (SOLOS 15 *through* 18):
Then along comes a breeze
From a shady, green pool,
Refreshing as a waterfall,
18TH SOLO:
Invigorating . . .
19TH SOLO:
Cool. . . .
RIGHT CHORUS:
Ah-h-h-h! There is nothing in the world
That's a brisker, better boon
Than a zestful ocean zephyr
On an August afternoon.
(WIND *makes O.K. sign.* 20TH SOLO, *dressed as a miller, steps forward holding small windmill.* WIND *turns the arms of mill.*)
20TH SOLO:
Up . . . down . . . and over she goes . . .

RIGHT CHORUS:
Over she goes . . . over she goes . . .
20TH SOLO:
Up . . . down . . . and over she goes, my gristy-grindy mill.
Huff, puff and push her around,
RIGHT CHORUS:
Push her around, push her around,
20TH SOLO:
Huff, puff, push her around
With a windy, windy will.
This is the way he grinds my corn
On a blowy morn,
RIGHT CHORUS:
On a blowy morn,
20TH SOLO:
This is the way he grinds my corn
With never a worry to stay him,
He turns the fan like a working man
And never a penny I pay him. . . .
RIGHT CHORUS:
And never a penny,
Oh, no, never any,
Oh, never a penny
We pay him.
CHORUS (*Both sections*):
Oh, the wind has come to our town.
(WIND *quiets down, turns the arms of mill slowly, then exits up center.*)
GIRLS:
With a whisper, with a sigh,
BOYS:
He hardly makes a stirring
In the big, still sky.

1st Solo:

He entered like a lion,

20th Solo:

Full of mischief, full of noise,

2nd Solo:

He set himself to working

19th Solo:

With the mills and boats and boys,

3rd Solo:

Now he is a tame wind . . .

18th Solo:

But, can he be the same wind?

(Lamb Wind *enters with a basket of flowers and petals.
She dances lightly down center.*)

Lamb Wind:

I'm the southerly wind,
I'm the springtime wind,
I whiffle and eddy and stir.
I flutter and flow
Down the warm, green hills,
I murmur and sing and whir.

I'm an easy wind, and a bee-zy wind,
A fragrant flowers and tree-sy wind,
(*She tosses petals on the stage.*)
A perfectly placid and please-y wind,
I hum and whisper and purr . . .

I'm a favorable wind
And a trade-y wind,
A woodsy glen and glade-y wind,
I'm a balmy wind, and a calm-y wind
And sailors call me a lady wind.
In short, I am a lamb,

I am.

In short I am a lamb!

CHORUS (*Both sections*):

Aha! Now we have wind of it,

So this must be the end of it.

BOYS:

The lion who "Marched" in bold as brass

Is gamboling through the April grass.

GIRLS:

A perfect little lamb—

LAMB WIND (*Curtsying*):

I am!

A perfect little lamb!

(*She scatters flowers to the audience as she exits. Curtain.*)

THE END

Cinder-Riley

Characters

LEPRECHAUN	FAIRY GODMOTHER
CINDER-RILEY	JACK O'CLOCK
THE STEPMOTHER	DANCERS
AGGIE ⎫ stepsisters	PROP BOYS
MAGGIE ⎭	

BEFORE RISE: *The piano sets the scene with a lively Irish jig. While the music is playing, the* LEPRECHAUN *pokes his head through the curtain opening. He turns his head first to one side, then to the other. Then he leaps out and seats himself on the apron of the stage, cross-legged. The music stops.*

LEPRECHAUN: Whist now, it's a fine audience ye are! We have a grand play for you to watch this day. 'Tis the old Hibernian legend, "Princess Cinder-Riley, or The Lost Brogan." Our actors are guaranteed to make you split your sides with laughter one minute, and cry your way through three handkerchiefs the next! But first, we'll need your cooperation. In order to make the play begin, we'll need some loud clapping. This clears the air for the actors. Now, would you mind applauding, please? (*He taps his stick, and all applaud. The curtains open.*)

*   *   *

SETTING: *The stage is bare. The backdrop is hung with drawing of large knives, forks, spoons and skillets.*

AT RISE: *Two* PROP BOYS *carry in a large screen which they set at center.* BOYS *walk behind the screen, so that they are not seen, and remain there. A table covered with a cloth reaching to the floor is "walked" onstage by* FAIRY GODMOTHER *and* PROP BOY, *who are hidden beneath it, giving the magical effect of a walking table. On the table are a pile of papers, a quill pen and an inkstand.*

LEPRECHAUN (*Stopping the applause*): Sure, that was fine! Now, just applaud a bit more and our actors will come out and begin the play. Ready? Let's clap for the Princess Cinder-Riley, her wicked stepmother, and her two disgustin' stepsisters. (*He taps his stick again. All applaud.* STEPMOTHER, AGGIE, *and* MAGGIE *enter, noses in the air. They are followed by* CINDER-RILEY, *who wears a long gown, a crown, and silver slippers.* CINDER-RILEY *is crying and wringing her hands.*)

STEPMOTHER: Now, Princess Cinder-Riley, it's no good cryin' at all, at all! You must keep to the schedule. Riding lesson at two o'clock. Music lesson at three. Etiquette lesson at four. Dancing lesson at five. And at six, the royal state banquet with the Duke of Downderrydown, the Earl of Earlyrise and your betrothed, the King of West Muffinland!

CINDER-RILEY: Must I, stepmother? Oh, please don't make me marry the King of West Muffinland! He has turned-up toes and a wart on his nose, and he's as fat as a tub of butter!

AGGIE *and* MAGGIE (*Linking arms and dancing around mockingly*): Ha! Ha! Cinder-Riley's going to marry the King of West Muffinland!

AGGIE: With turned-up toes!

MAGGIE: And a wart on his nose!

AGGIE *and* MAGGIE (*Together*): Fat as a tub of butter! (*They pantomime big stomachs and puffed-out cheeks.*)

STEPMOTHER: Now, don't carry on so, Cinder-Riley. After all, you are a princess, and I am your regent. Princesses must marry kings. I shall see to it that you do! While we're at it, you must send out a proclamation that your stepsister Aggie shall marry the Duke of Downderrydown.

AGGIE: The Duke of Downderrydown—ah! He's so handsome!

STEPMOTHER: And your stepsister Maggie shall marry the Earl of Earlyrise.

MAGGIE: The Earl of Earlyrise—ah! He's so rich!

STEPMOTHER: And speaking of proclamations, here are thirty-three dozen more matters of proclamation to be signed before sundown. (*She points to a large stack of papers on the table.*) Come, girls, we must go rest ourselves for the royal banquet this evening. Princess Cinder-Riley, I'd advise you to hustle your bustle if you wish to be finished before the sun goes down! (STEPMOTHER *exits.* AGGIE *and* MAGGIE *follow, noses in the air.* LEPRECHAUN *bounces to the side and shouts "Boo," encouraging audience to do likewise. As* CINDER-RILEY *comes downstage, he puts finger to lips, shushing audience.*)

CINDER-RILEY: Alas! Alack! Well-a-day! Sure, and woe is me! (*She sobs.* LEPRECHAUN *takes out large red hanky and pantomimes wiping away tears.*) I do not love the King of West Muffinland. Nay! Nay! A thousand times nay! I love handsome Jack O'Clock. But oh, bitter fortune, Jack O'Clock is only a kitchen boy. Would that I were a simple scullery maid. I would give all my satins, all my jewels, yes, my very crown itself, just to be a kitchen maid. For this is the night of the Pantry Frolic. All the lads and colleens who work in the kitchen will be dancing and singing. And Jack O'Clock, my own true love, will be crowned Prince of the Potatoes! I cannot be there. Oh, my heart is breaking!

FAIRY GODMOTHER (*Poking head out from under the tablecloth*): Pssst! Cinder-Riley! (CINDER-RILEY *looks around, startled, and sees* FAIRY GODMOTHER.)

CINDER-RILEY: My goodness! Who might you be? (GODMOTHER *steps out, dressed in kitchen outfit and carrying a broom and reticule.*)

GODMOTHER: Sure, I'm your fairy godmother, I am, I am. I've come to help you out of your miserable plight. Dry your tears, me pretty. We must be quick. Now, let me see.

CINDER-RILEY: But, fairy godmother, I have thirty-three dozen matters of proclamation to sign before the sun goes down!

GODMOTHER: Pish posh, macushla! That's a simple thing for a fairy to fix. Here now—just write your name in the air, whilst I wave me wand. (CINDER-RILEY *writes her name in the air.* FAIRY GODMOTHER *waves broom as she chants.*)
Dimple-dee, dample-dee, dumple-dee dined
Proclamations—Be ye signed!
(CINDER-RILEY *claps hands in amazement as she looks at papers.*)

CINDER-RILEY: Oh, how *marvelous!* They're all signed! 'Tis a miracle to be sure!

GODMOTHER: Tonight you shall be a simple kitchen maid. First, you need a raggedy dress . . . aha! Me magic shears. (*Takes huge pair of shears from reticule, snips at* CINDER-RILEY's *dress, turning it into a short gown with a ragged hem.*) Now, a mob cap. (*She takes off her cap. Underneath it, she wears another cap, so that she always stays perfectly dressed.*) And a sweet little apron. (*Takes off her own apron. There is another apron beneath it.*) Now you are all ready to go to the Frolic! (CINDER-RILEY *takes off crown, puts it on table. She puts on cap and apron, looks down at feet.*)

CINDER-RILEY: Ah—but my shoes!

GODMOTHER: Sure, I almost forgot. You need some nice comfortable brogans. You could never dance the night in those slippers. (*She takes off her own shoes. Underneath she has another pair.* CINDER-RILEY *takes off her slippers, puts them on table, and puts on the brogans.*) There is only one more thing, Cinder-Riley. You must be home at twelve o'clock to the minute. Are you ready now?

CINDER-RILEY: Indeed I am, fairy godmother.

GODMOTHER (*Waving broom*):
Rimple-dee, rample-dee, rumple-dee row
Bring us the Pantry Frolic now!
(PROP BOYS *behind the large screen move it off so that it looks as though it is moving by itself.* PROP BOY *under table moves it off. The music of an Irish jig is heard, and the* DANCERS *enter, clapping hands to music. They may dance a reel. When music stops,* JACK O'CLOCK *enters, dressed in tatters, with a crown of potatoes.* CINDER-RILEY *and* GODMOTHER *stand to one side, watching.*)

DANCERS:
Here's Jack O'Clock, let's give him a cheer,
He's the Potato Prince without a peer!
Hip, hip, Potato! Hip, hip, Potato! Hip, hip, Potato Prince!

(LEPRECHAUN *cheers and leads audience in cheers and applause for* JACK O'CLOCK.)

DANCER: Lead us in a jig, Jack!

JACK: That I will! (*Piano begins jig.* DANCERS *freeze in pose.* JACK *spots* CINDER-RILEY, *holds up hand. Piano changes to "When Irish Eyes Are Smiling" which is played sentimentally throughout remainder of scene between* JACK *and* CINDER-RILEY.) Wait! Here's a colleen the like of whom I've never seen. She's as lovely as a May morning. 'Tis herself I shall dance with and none other. Come, me little flower. (GODMOTHER *exits, as* JACK O'CLOCK *and* CINDER-RILEY *dance together. At end of dance,* JACK *goes downstage and speaks in an aside to the audience.*) Me heart! Me heart is not in its rightful place! Sure, it's been stolen! Stolen by the maid with the raggedy dress. Dare I speak me deepest thoughts to her? (LEPRECHAUN *nods eagerly.* CINDER-RILEY *goes downstage other side, speaks in an aside to the audience as she holds her hand on her heart.*)

CINDER-RILEY: My heart! My heart is beating like the drums in a marching band! Ah! He's so manly! Ah! Dare I speak my mind to him? (LEPRECHAUN *nods and takes* CINDER-RILEY *by the hand, goes to center, beckons to* JACK, *who joins them. He joins their hands, then holds his finger to his lips to warn audience not to make noise.*)

JACK: Oh, lovely kitchen maid!

CINDER-RILEY: Oh, Jack! (*They strike a pose.* LEPRECHAUN *beams and claps hands, motioning audience to applaud, also. Chime sounds twelve times.*) Oh, dear! 'Tis midnight. I must go! (*On the stroke of twelve the screen and table are walked back on again.* GODMOTHER *is beneath table again.* DANCERS *go behind screen.* CINDER-RILEY *leaves one shoe on stage as she runs back near screen.* JACK *picks up shoe, scratches head, goes behind screen with shoe.* STEPMOTHER, AGGIE *and* MAGGIE *enter, noses in air.*)

STEPMOTHER (*Horrified*): Princess Cinder-Riley, where in the great rollin' world were you this evening?

AGGIE: We looked hither and yon for you!

MAGGIE: And the King of West Muffinland was so angry, he popped three gold buttons off his coat!

STEPMOTHER: Cinder-Riley! What are you doing in that dreadful rag? Take off that apron! (*She snatches the apron off* CINDER-RILEY.)

AGGIE: Put on your crown! (*Takes cap off* CINDER-RILEY's *head and thrusts crown on*)

MAGGIE: Put on your slippers! (*Tosses the slippers to* CIN-DER-RILEY, *who puts them on, hiding other brogan behind table.*)

STEPMOTHER: And throw my cloak over that tattered dress! (*Puts cloak around* CINDER-RILEY's *shoulders*) Foolish girl! You must prepare to marry the King of West Muffinland immediately!

CINDER-RILEY: Oh, no! Please! Wait! The marriage cannot be official unless there is a proclamation.

STEPMOTHER: I took care of the proclamation. It was in this great pile. You signed it yourself.

AGGIE *and* MAGGIE (*Together*): So there!

CINDER-RILEY: Oh, woe! Alas! 'Tis true. Oh, I shall fade away and die. I'll be in my grave with the sorrow of it all!

STEPMOTHER: Come, Cinder-Riley. (*Starts to lead her off.* JACK *comes around the screen, puts his hand up and shouts.*)

JACK: Wait! (*They turn and stare.* STEPMOTHER *eyes him icily.* CINDER-RILEY *sighs longingly.* LEPRECHAUN *signals for cheers, and piano plays a fanfare.* JACK *bows.*) I beg your pardon, me ladies and Your Royal Highness, but I have a boon to ask ye.

CINDER-RILEY (*Aside*): Handsome Jack O'Clock. My own true love! (*To* JACK) Speak, young man, I command you.

JACK: I have in me hand a darlin' little brogan which a fair lass, the pride of me life, wore to the Pantry Frolic. And I swore to meself that I would not rest until I tried it on the foot of every maid in the kingdom.

AGGIE (*Giggling*): Oh, isn't he a fine broth of a lad! Let him try it on my foot!

JACK: I must try every maid until I find her. (*He puts the brogan on* AGGIE's *foot. The toe of the shoe is slit so that her stocking, stuffed with cotton, protrudes visibly.*)

MAGGIE: You silly colleen! Your foot is the size of an elephant's! Here, young man—try my dainty foot! (JACK *puts shoe on her. The same thing happens.*)

JACK (*Sadly*): Well, I suppose that is that! Your ladyship is the last girl in the kingdom—except of course you, Your Highness. I suppose I shall never find my lost kitchen maid. (*He turns to go.*)

CINDER-RILEY: Wait! Try the shoe on my foot.

JACK: But, Your Highness!

CINDER-RILEY: Please.

JACK: Very well, but I hardly think the shoe could belong to Your Royal Highness. (*He slips the shoe on* CINDER-RILEY. DANCERS *come from behind screen and cheer.*)

DANCERS (*Cheering*): Hip, hip, Potato Prince! (LEPRE-CHAUN *leaps up and down and leads cheers. All show astonishment as* GODMOTHER *comes out from under table, slips cloak off* CINDER-RILEY, *and replaces the cap and apron.*)

JACK: Princess Cinder-Riley! You are me lost love!

STEPMOTHER: Lost love? The likes of you, Jack O'Clock, speakin' about the Princess Cinder-Riley as your lost love! What impudent nonsense! The Princess is promised to the King of West Muffinland. It is officially proclaimed! (GODMOTHER *waves broom over the papers.*)

GODMOTHER (*Stepping up and curtsying*): Begging your pardon, madam, but if you will examine this proclamation (*Picks up paper and waves it*), you will find that she is promised to someone quite different.

STEPMOTHER (*Snatching paper angrily*): Indeed! Let me read it! Why, I wrote the proclamation myself. I certainly should know what I have written! (*Righteously*) Ahem! (*Reads*) "Hear ye! Hear ye! The Princess Cinder-Riley is hereby promised in marriage to the Prince of Potatoes, Jack O'Clock." (*She stares at paper, astonished.*) All is lost!

GODMOTHER: And 'tis signed by the Princess' own hand. That makes it official. (LEPRECHAUN *cheers in pantomime.*)

STEPMOTHER: But what shall I tell the King of West Muffinland?

GODMOTHER: Dear me, the good King still needs a wife, does he not? (*Snaps fingers*) Ah! The very thing. Another proclamation. (*Hands one to* STEPMOTHER *with a flourish*)

STEPMOTHER: Ahem! (*Reading*) "To Whom It May Concern." (AGGIE *and* MAGGIE *poke their noses over the paper to see better as she reads*) "The King of West Muffinland shall be married this morn to her ladyship, the former regent of the realm, stepmother of Princess Cinder-Riley." (*She screams.*) Oh, no!

AGGIE: And 'tis signed by Cinder-Riley's own hand!

MAGGIE: That makes it official!

STEPMOTHER (*Throwing up hands*): Oh, no! Oh, woe! He has turned-up toes and a wart on his nose.

AGGIE *and* MAGGIE (*Together*): And he's fat as a tub of butter!

STEPMOTHER: Help me, daughters, I am about to faint! (*She faints in their arms. They drag her offstage.* LEPRECHAUN *boos and invites all to boo.*)

JACK: Come, Cinder-Riley, let us prepare for our joyous weddin'. Oh, happy day! (*Piano may play "Wedding March" as they strike a pose.*)

CINDER-RILEY: Yes, dear Jack. And you shall be my prince regent and the king of my heart, forever!

GODMOTHER: Faith now, I've done a full day's work. I've banished the wicked stepmother and the disgustin' stepsisters; I've joined the lovers, and I've even found a wife for the King of West Muffinland. (*She strikes a pose as* LEPRECHAUN *steps up and shakes her hand. All form tableau as* LEPRECHAUN *motions for applause, then runs to help close curtain. Piano concludes with fast jig. Curtains close.* LEPRECHAUN *turns his head from right to left, then waves goodbye and disappears.*)

THE END

The Snowman Who Overstayed

Characters

SNOWMAN

CRAB APPLE TREE

MR. BLUEBIRD

MRS. BLUEBIRD

SUPERWIND, *the March wind*

SPRINKLE, *the April shower*

HELIOS, *the sun*

PRINCESS SPRING

MARCH PAGE, *a boy*

APRIL PAGE, *a girl*

MAY PAGE, *a girl*

DANDELION CHORUS

TIME: *The middle of March.*

SETTING: *A bare garden.*

AT RISE: *The* CRAB APPLE TREE, *leafless and scowling, stands up left, shivering.* DANDELION CHORUS *sits dejectedly down center, wearing green hoods. At center stands the* SNOWMAN *wearing his top hat at a rakish angle and a big grin on his face.*

CRAB APPLE TREE *and* DANDELIONS:
Brrr! Brrr! Brrr!
It's cold, cold, cold! (*All shiver.*)
Brrrrrrr!

TREE (*Gruffly*) : Here it is, the middle of March—

DANDELIONS: The middle of March!

TREE: Here it is, the beginning of spring—

DANDELIONS: Spring is beginning to begin to begin.

TREE:
> And that tardy old slow man
> That poky old snowman,
> Won't go and won't go and won't go away.

DANDELIONS:
> Do you hear what we say?
> He won't go away.

SNOWMAN: I'll stay.

ALL: Go away!

SNOWMAN: I'll *stay*.

ALL: Brrr! Brrr! Brrrr! (*They shiver again.*)

TREE (*Scowling*):
> I'm a sad apple, mad apple,
> Bad apple tree. (*Holds out arm*)
> See that branch? Not a blossom on it.
> I'm a rough apple, gruff apple, crab apple tree
> Getting crabbier every minute!
> Snowman, snowman, listen to me, snowman—
> Why won't you go, man? Go, go, *go*, man!

DANDELIONS:
> We are poor little dandelions
> Cold little dandelions,
> Snowman, go, and let us be
> *Gold* little dandelions.

ALL:
> Snowman, snowman, listen to us, snowman.
> Please get up and go, man. Go, go, *go*, man!

SNOWMAN:
> I'll not. I can't.
> I won't. I shan't.

ALL: Go home to the North Pole, you old chill-joy.

TREE: Look—here come the bluebirds. Who ever heard of a snowman sticking around when the birds fly back? (MR. *and* MRS. BLUEBIRD *flutter on left.*)

MR. BLUEBIRD: Hello, hello, hello. We're back, friends.

Back to the old nest.

MRS. BLUEBIRD: Aha. There's our favorite tree. (*She flut-ters around the* TREE.) Oh, dear. What happened to you, tree? Where are your leaves? Where are your blossoms?

TREE: They won't come out. It's too cold. Ask him. (*Nods toward* SNOWMAN)

DANDELIONS: Ask him why he's staying in *our* garden.

MR. BLUEBIRD (*Hopping around* SNOWMAN, *cocking his head*): Brrr. He looks like snow. (*Touching* SNOWMAN) He feels like snow.

MRS. BLUEBIRD: How upsetting. He *is* snow. A snowman! We can't nest in this garden. The eggs would never hatch.

MR. BLUEBIRD: How curious. Snowman, please tell me. Why are you in this particular garden at this particular time, doing nothing in particular?

SNOWMAN: I am waiting.

ALL: For what? What are you waiting for?

SNOWMAN: For spring.

ALL: For spring!

TREE: You silly old slush pile. Spring won't come while you're here. Meanwhile, get off my roots. They're freezing.

MR. BLUEBIRD: Just a minute. You say that spring won't come while the snowman is here? (*They nod.*) Well, I say Princess Spring is just the person to deal with the snowman. I say, let's give her an SOS.

SNOWMAN: An SOS? What's an SOS?

TREE: Save Our Sap!

DANDELIONS: Save Our Seeds!

BLUEBIRDS: Save Our Springtime!

MR. BLUEBIRD: This is how the code goes. Three long beeps. Three short beeps. Three long beeps. Ready? All together now.

ALL: Beeeep. Beeeep. Beeeep. Beep. Beep. Beep. Beeeep. Beeeep. Beeeep. (*They listen*).

MR. BLUEBIRD: Once more. Loud and strong. (*They all signal again. The* MARCH PAGE *enters right and makes a low bow.*)

MARCH PAGE: Greetings, subjects of Princess Spring. Her Highness has heard your SOS.

TREE: Is she here, I hope?

MARCH PAGE: Princess Spring sends her regrets. She cannot be here in person. She's opening cherry blossoms in Japan. But she has heard about the abominable snowman. She has sent the March wind to take care of that winter left-over. (SUPERWIND *runs in from up left.* MARCH PAGE *exits.*)

ALL: It's not a bird! It's not a plane! It's Superwind!

SUPERWIND: That's me. The March wind with muscles. Where's Frosty? I'll blow him to smithereens. (*He blows hard at the* TREE, *who bows low.*)

TREE: Help! Stop! I'm not a snowman. I'm a tree.

SUPERWIND: Oh. Sorry about that, tree. Ah—there you are. (*He circles the* SNOWMAN.) Don't try to hide from me.

SNOWMAN: I wasn't.

SUPERWIND: Stand away, birds. I might blow you to the moon. (*The* BLUEBIRDS *move away up left*) All right, snowman. This is the end of you. On a count of three, I'll make snowflakes out of you. Here we go. One. Two. Three. (*He blows mightily. Nothing happens. The* SNOWMAN *grins impudently.*) Let's try a count of four. One. Two. Three. Four. (*He blows hard again.*) Whoo. Whew. Wooo. Wheee. (*He huffs and he puffs so hard that he finally blows himself out, and lies, toes curled up, on the floor.*)

MR. BLUEBIRD: Look at that. He blew himself out.

MRS. BLUEBIRD: How dreadful for him. Do let us take him

out of the garden. Perhaps he will recover if we get him away from that snowman. (*The* BLUEBIRDS *drag* SUPER-WIND *off left, returning immediately.*)

MR. BLUEBIRD: Call SOS, quickly.

ALL: Beeeep. Beeeep. Beeeep. Beep. Beep. Beep. Beeeep. Beeeep. Beeeep. (*The* APRIL PAGE *enters right.*)

APRIL PAGE (*Bowing*): Greetings, subjects of Princess Spring. Her Majesty has heard your SOS.

DANDELIONS: Is Princess Spring here, we hope, we hope?

APRIL PAGE: Alas, no. Princess Spring sends her regrets. She is in England, coaxing the daffodils out of the ground. But the news about the March wind has reached her. So she sends Sprinkle, the April shower, to help you with your snow disposal problem. (APRIL PAGE *exits down right, as* SPRINKLE *enters up right, carrying watering cans. Appropriate tinkling music is played, as* SPRINKLE *dances, and with watering cans, pantomimes first a gentle drizzle, then a heavier rain, finally a frantic downpour. At the end, she sinks in a heap to the floor.*)

MR. BLUEBIRD: Another one down. How extraordinary. She rained herself out.

MRS. BLUEBIRD: Poor thing. We must get her out of this garden.

MR. BLUEBIRD: Once more. Send one more SOS to Princess Spring. (*As the* BLUEBIRDS *drag* SPRINKLE *off up left, the* TREE *and* DANDELIONS *chant*)

ALL: Beeeep. Beeeep. Beeeep. Beep. Beep. Beep. Beeeep. Beeeep. Beeeep. (*The* MAY PAGE *enters down right.*)

MAY PAGE (*Bowing*): Greetings, subjects of Princess Spring. I bring news of Princess Spring.

ALL: Is she here? Is spring finally here, we hope, we hope, we *hope*?

MAY PAGE: Princess Spring is on her way. She was most distressed to hear of the failure of the March wind and

April shower. This time she sends you a red-hot, sure-fire snow remover. (HELIOS *enters slowly up left.*) Presenting Helios, the sun! (MAY PAGE *exits.*)

HELIOS (*Slowly passing by* SNOWMAN): Hello, snowman. Remember me?

SNOWMAN: Of course. You're the thin, pale little sun that used to hide behind the clouds in February.

HELIOS: Times change, snowman. I have changed, snowman.

SNOWMAN: Come closer. Let me see how you have changed.

HELIOS: Are you sure you want me to do that?

SNOWMAN: The March wind could not blow me away. The April shower could not drown me. What can a yellow ball high up in the sky do to me?

HELIOS: You'd be surprised, snowman. (HELIOS *moves closer to* SNOWMAN, *who takes off his top hat and fans himself. He wipes his brow, and puts hat back on.*)

SNOWMAN: Whew. I'm feeling a strange sort of feeling. A sticky, drippy sort of feeling. (*He moves up left a little*) Help! I'm shrinking. I'm fading. What has happened to me?

HELIOS: You are melting, poor old snowman. That is what happens to snow in the springtime. It turns to water. Now, surely you don't want to see spring.

SNOWMAN (*Stubbornly*) : But I do. I do want to see spring. I will stay to see spring even if I melt down to a mud puddle! (*The three* PAGES *enter down right as* PRINCESS SPRING *enters up right.*)

PAGES: Attention! Attention, if you please. Announcing the arrival of Primavera, Keeper of the Blossoms, Her Royal Highness, Princess Spring. (*All bow. The* SNOWMAN *takes off his hat.*)

PRINCESS SPRING (*Going to the* SNOWMAN): So you are the famous spring snowman.

TREE: Melt him, Your Highness!

DANDELIONS: Banish him, Your Majesty.

PRINCESS SPRING: Wait. I am curious to know why a snowman should wish to stay when he is in danger of melting. There are two sides to every question, and I wish to hear the snowman's point of view. Speak, snowman.

SNOWMAN (*Going down center*): Thank you, Gracious Majesty. I have not done the tree any real harm. I have not stopped the dandelions from blooming forever. I wouldn't hurt any living thing. I only—well—delayed them a little. Please understand, Princess Spring. When I was only knee-high to a snowflake, I heard about how green the spring was. I've never seen any color but white, and that's not even a color. I heard that trees have rustling things called leaves. I've only seen bare trees. And they told me that the birds make music in the springtime. I've never heard a bird sing because I've never seen a bird in winter. Oh, there are a few, but they won't come near a cold, old snowman. So I decided I must see these things, and hear these things. Was it a bad thing to do? Was it wrong to wait for you?

PRINCESS SPRING: Oh, I do understand. Now I understand at last. No, my out-of-season valentine, it was not wrong of you to wait. It was just a little out of the ordinary. You have touched my heart. You cannot stay for long. But I will grant you one moment, and one moment only, to see the spring come to this garden. You will be the first snowman in the history of the North Pole to welcome spring.

SNOWMAN: Thank you, Your Highness. Wait until I tell the polar bears!

PRINCESS SPRING (*Touching* TREE *with her wand*): Crab apple tree, awake! I command you to put forth your leaves and blossoms. Bloom! Bloom!

TREE (*Bringing out branches with leaves and blossoms from his long sleeves*): Look at me! I'm blooming, I'm blooming!

PRINCESS SPRING (*Touching* DANDELIONS): Dandelions, rise and show your golden heads. (*The* DANDELIONS *stand, stretch, and throw off the green hoods, disclosing yellow pompon hats.*)

DANDELIONS: Look at us! Look at us! We're blooming! We're blooming!

PRINCESS SPRING: Bluebirds, come and build your nest. The sun will shine every day and make a warm place for the new birds. (BLUEBIRDS *enter and stand by* TREE.)

BLUEBIRDS: We're coming! We're coming! Here we are. (*The curtain begins to close.*)

PRINCESS SPRING: Now, what do you say, snowman?

SNOWMAN: Welcome, spring!

ALL (*Forming a tableau*): Welcome, spring. (*Curtain*)

THE END

All Hands on Deck

Characters

ASIA BRISTOW ⎫
EUROPA BRISTOW ⎬ *a sea captain's*
INDIA BRISTOW ⎭ *daughters*
AUNT PATIENCE BRISTOW, *their great-aunt*
BETTY APPLE, *the maid*
RAMU SINGH, *a young Indian prince*
CAPTAIN DREAD, *a pirate*
MATEY ⎫
SQUID ⎬ *his men*
NAVAL OFFICER
SAILOR

TIME: *An afternoon in the summer of 1830.*
SETTING: *The parlor of Captain Bristow's home in Salem, Massachusetts. Heavy curtains are drawn across a large window at right, which looks out on the harbor. Up left is a long cradle with a baby blanket in it.*
AT RISE: *AUNT PATIENCE is seated in a rocking chair at center, embroidering a pillowslip. Her cane is on the floor beside her, and a newspaper is folded on her lap. ASIA sits on a stool nearby, and EUROPA and INDIA are sitting on the floor at her feet, with a sewing basket beside them. The three girls are each embroidering a*

section of a small coverlet. Behind them, up center,
BETTY APPLE *is dusting the mantel and bookcases with
a feather duster.*

AUNT PATIENCE (*Reciting as she sews*): Up . . . down
. . . knot the little knot.

GIRLS (*Reciting in unison*): Up . . . down . . . knot the
little knot.

INDIA (*Stopping her sewing, and turning to* AUNT PA-
TIENCE): Aunt Patience, this is all such a jumble. What
are we embroidering?

AUNT PATIENCE: Can't you see, India? 'Tis your father's
own flag, the very flag his ship carries so bravely at sea.
It will be a most appropriate coverlet for your new
baby cousin's cradle. (INDIA *stands, takes coverlet from*
EUROPA *and* ASIA, *and holds it up, upside down. The
coverlet is a ship's flag, drawn in ink and partially embroidered.*)

ASIA: Oh, India! You're holding the flag upside down!

AUNT PATIENCE: That is certainly *not* appropriate for a
baby!

INDIA: And why not?

AUNT PATIENCE (*Looking at her, horrified*): India Bristow! The daughter of a great sea captain should know
that a ship's flag hung upside down is a distress signal.
(INDIA *quickly turns the flag right side up.*)

EUROPA (*Laughing*): That's better, India.

AUNT PATIENCE (*Sharply; sewing again*): That is quite
enough, girls. (INDIA *sits, and each girl takes her corner
of the coverlet and starts to embroider. After a moment,*
AUNT PATIENCE *pauses, and looks at cradle.*) Think of
it, girls. Your new cousin will rest his head in the cradle
you slept in. (*Turning to* BETTY APPLE) Betty Apple,
did my nephew say when his servants would come to
fetch the cradle to his home?

BETTY APPLE (*Coming down center and curtsying*): Yes, ma'am. He did, ma'am. (*Curtsies again*) They will come this afternoon, ma'am. (*Curtsies again*)

AUNT PATIENCE: Gracious, Betty Apple, you need not curtsy so much. You'll make us all seasick.

BETTY APPLE (*Curtsying again*): Yes, ma'am. (*Girls laugh as she returns to her dusting.*)

AUNT PATIENCE (*Rapping her thimble sharply on the arm of her rocker*): Girls! Young ladies do not guffaw in the parlor. You must try to make a pretty picture. I remember a time in 1776—or was it '77? 'Twas during the Revolution at any rate, and General Washington said —(INDIA *yawns.*) India! Are you a great gaping fish?

INDIA (*Closing her mouth*): No, Auntie. (EUROPA *and* ASIA *giggle.*)

AUNT PATIENCE: Ladies do not yawn in the parlor. Now, while you work, I shall read you tidbits from the *Chronicle.* (*Unfolds newspaper which she holds in her lap*) Ladies should strive to be well informed. (*Girls sigh, as* AUNT PATIENCE *peers over her glasses at paper.*) Oh! Upon my soul! How dreadful! (*Girls drop their work and surround rocker, looking over* AUNT PATIENCE's *shoulder.* BETTY APPLE *stops dusting and listens.*)

ASIA: What is it, Auntie? Not bad news about Father's ship, is it?

EUROPA: His ship is not due in Salem until next week.

INDIA: Has there been a storm at sea?

AUNT PATIENCE: No, 'tis not about your father, thank heaven. But none of us is safe. There are pirates abroad! Listen! (*Reads*) "A wicked deed by foul pirates has been reported to this paper. Some months ago the young prince, Ramu Singh, was taken from his father's palace in Delhi, India, and placed aboard a three-masted schooner. A note demanding ransom was sent to the

Raja, his father. It is believed the pirate ship set sail for New England."

GIRLS: New England!

AUNT PATIENCE (*Reading*): "Merchant men and coastal frigates are warned to beware of any unmarked ship resting in hidden coves, and to report any such to the Admiralty at Salem."

BETTY APPLE: Pirates! Oh, I shall stay away from hidden coves.

ASIA: Poor little prince. I hope they find him soon.

AUNT PATIENCE: Indeed. Ah, me. I feel quite exhausted. I think I shall go to my room and take a short nap. My cane, India. (INDIA *hands her the cane.*) Good afternoon, girls. I trust you will finish the coverlet this afternoon and engage yourselves in profitable conversation. During the Revolution we had the most stimulating conversation. I remember General Washington said —or have you heard that tale?

ASIA: Many times, Auntie. 'Twould tire you to tell it again.

AUNT PATIENCE: True. (*She wags her finger at them as she starts to exit down left*) No idle gossip. And— (*Over her glasses to* INDIA) no loud guffaws!

GIRLS (*Meekly*): Yes, Auntie. (*They bend their heads obediently over their needlework as* AUNT PATIENCE *exits left. When she is out of sight,* INDIA *flings down the embroidery and does a hornpipe.* EUROPA *takes a large spyglass out of the sewing basket, and* ASIA *stretches.*)

INDIA: Avast, you lubbers. She's shoved off. Europa, my dear, say something profitable.

EUROPA (*Opening the spyglass*): Sixpence plus sixpence makes a shilling. There—that's profitable. (*She goes to window, draws back the curtains, and peers out through spyglass.*)

ASIA (*Sitting in rocker*): Poor Aunt Patience. She means well, truly she does. But she doesn't realize that this is 1830—not 1776. Girls aren't china dolls any more.

INDIA (*Giving the rocker a push*): Indeed not. They are China clippers. (*She rocks the rocker very fast.*) Hoist your mainsail!

ASIA: Stop it, Indy. (INDIA *stops. She takes a handful of ribbons from the sewing basket and waves them in front of* ASIA.)

INDIA: I'm an octopus. I'm an octopus.

EUROPA: Hush, India. I can't think. (*Peering through glass intently.*) Why, there's a new ship in the harbor. *The Pearl of the Sea*, she's called, under Dutch colors with a new flag. Three-masted, too.

ASIA (*Going to the window*): How very strange. I know every ship that plies these waters and I never saw that one before. (*They gaze out window.*)

INDIA (*Sneaking up behind* BETTY APPLE): Turn to, good ship Betty Apple. (BETTY APPLE *whirls around, giggling.*) I'm a pirate and I want your cargo. Your feather duster, or your life!

BETTY APPLE (*Playing the game*) : Oh, have mercy upon me, sir. You wouldn't take away me precious duster, would you? I've seen it grow from a pinfeather to this fine clump of turkey ticklers. Take me jewels, or me money, but not me dear duster.

EUROPA (*Excitedly, still looking through glass*): Oh, some men have come ashore from the schooner with a great hamper. (INDIA *and* BETTY APPLE *run to window, and look out.*) Look, Asia! (ASIA *takes spyglass and looks out.*)

ASIA: Why, they're heading up our street!

BETTY APPLE: Perhaps they're coming to the inn next door. (*Fearfully*) There's strange goings-on there these days. Why, the serving girl told me how a great, fierce

stranger with a black beard took rooms there this week
and he keeps his door locked all the time.

ASIA: Hush, Betty Apple. Don't go worrying us with tales
of fierce strangers.

INDIA: Let me look, Asia. (*She takes glass and looks out*)
Oh, help! They're coming to our very door with that
hamper. (*Closes glass and looks about fearfully*)

EUROPA: I know! It must be a present from Father. He
sent it by a fast ship, to reach us before he came home.

ASIA: Of course. Father has often sent us gifts before he
came himself. (*A heavy knock on the door at right is
heard, startling the girls, who draw close together.*)

EUROPA (*Fearfully*): It *must* be from Father. (*Another
loud knock is heard.*)

MATEY (*Shouting from off right*): Ahoy, inside there—
open up! (*Girls gasp.* ASIA *and* EUROPA *hide behind
curtains while* INDIA *hides behind rocker.* BETTY APPLE
looks uncertainly at door.)

ASIA (*In a loud whisper*): Answer the door, Betty Apple.
(BETTY APPLE *walks hesitantly to door and opens it.*
MATEY *and* SQUID *push in a large hamper.*)

MATEY (*Roughly*): Be you the serving girl?

BETTY APPLE: I am.

SQUID: Here's the hamper, then. (*She starts to open hamper, and* SQUID *slaps his hand down over hers.*) Hands
off, if you know what's good for you.

BETTY APPLE: Oh! You're rude, you are. (*She shakes her
hand.*)

MATEY: Now, now, Squid. Don't upset the maid. 'Tis only
odds and ends, girl. Come on, Squid. We've done our
bit. Now let's shove off. (*They exit right. The girls
come from behind chair and curtains and gather around
the hamper.*)

ASIA: Are you all right, Betty Apple? I never saw such

rude sailors. I shall report them to Father. Odds and ends, indeed!

EUROPA: Open it, Asia. It's Paris hats, I know it!

INDIA: No, it's miles and miles of Chinese silk. Oh, hurry, Asia.

ASIA: On a count of three I'll open it. Then we'll all see at the same time. Ready? (*They nod.*) One . . . (*She opens latch.*) Two . . . (*She slowly raises lid.*) Three . . . (*She throws back the lid, and* RAMU SINGH, *wearing a turban and a brocaded tunic, jumps up, his hands over his face.*) Oh, mercy! (*All gasp in amazement.*)

INDIA: Upon my soul, it's a boy. A real live boy!

EUROPA: What a jolly idea of Father's to send us a playmate. Do come out, boy. (*She helps* RAMU SINGH *over the side of hamper.*) Let us look at you.

RAMU SINGH: Please . . . please to help me.

ASIA (*In dismay*): This is no ordinary boy!

INDIA: Of course not. Father wouldn't send us an ordinary boy.

ASIA: He's wearing a turban . . . jeweled rings . . . silks. Boy, what is your name?

RAMU SINGH (*Bowing*): Ramu Singh is my name, memsahib.

ASIA: Ramu Singh! The Indian prince Auntie just read about.

EUROPA: 'Tis unbelievable!

INDIA: 'Tis marvelous!

RAMU SINGH (*On his knees*): I beg you, memsahib, hide me! I am in great danger. Those men who brought me here are pirates. They have kept me prisoner for many months. Let me stay with you. Please!

INDIA: Of course you may stay with us. (RAMU SINGH *gets to his feet.*) But, Asia, why do you suppose those men left him here, at our house?

BETTY APPLE: I think I know, miss. 'Twas a mistake. He was meant to be left next door, at the inn. With that strange, fierce man.

ASIA: That must be it. And if it's true, we have to work quickly. Those seamen will come back here for the prince when they discover their mistake. Europa, go to the window and keep a sharp lookout. (EUROPA *runs to window, and peeks out from behind curtains.*) Now, Betty Apple, you put some books in the hamper and close it fast. Perhaps those seamen will take it without looking too closely. (BETTY APPLE *hurries to bookcase, takes an armload of books, dumps them into the hamper and closes it.*) Now, where to hide you, little prince.

INDIA (*Pointing to grandfather's clock up left*): In the clock?

ASIA: Too small.

INDIA: In Auntie's room, under the bed?

ASIA: No, if Auntie wakens, there will be a most dreadful fuss.

EUROPA (*Drawing the curtains back and gasping*): They're coming back, and they're bringing a great fierce man with them. He has a beard black as ink!

RAMU SINGH: It is Captain Dread! Oh, he is a wicked man, memsahib. He is a shark who makes men walk the plank or sets them adrift without oars. (*He cringes behind rocker.*) Hide me! Hide me! (*There is a loud knock on door right.*)

BETTY APPLE: Oh, Miss Asia, they are at the door!

INDIA (*Grabbing* RAMU SINGH *by the hand and running with him to the cradle*): I have an idea. Come, Ramu, lie down in the cradle. (*He climbs in and she covers him with blanket.*) Don't move. I'll stay by you.

ASIA: Well done, India. Listen, all of you. Sit as you do when Auntie is here. Be as natural as possible. Keep your wits about you. And let me do the talking. (ASIA *composes herself in the rocker;* EUROPA *sits at her feet, takes up coverlet and starts to sew.* INDIA *rocks the cradle.* BETTY APPLE *stands fearfully by the hamper, her feather duster clasped to her. Knocking is heard again.*)

BETTY APPLE: Oh, they'll break the door down!

ASIA: Answer it, Betty Apple, quickly.

BETTY APPLE: Oh, Miss Asia! My knees don't want to hold me up. (*In a quavering voice*) Come in, if it please you. (INDIA *puts a warning finger to her lips and bends over the cradle.* CAPTAIN DREAD *swaggers in, making a low bow. He is followed by* MATEY *and* SQUID, *who stand with arms folded.*)

CAPTAIN DREAD: Pardon this unseemly intrusion, ladies. I be the captain of the schooner you may see from your window—*Pearl of the Sea.* These are Dutch seamen come to help me fetch a hamper they left here by mistake. Just odds and ends, it is. (MATEY *and* SQUID *wink at each other.*)

ASIA (*Coolly, rising and curtsying*) : Your hamper is here, Captain. Pray take it as soon as you can. We are ladies and we do not care for odds and ends in our parlor. (*She sits firmly.*)

CAPTAIN DREAD (*To* MATEY *and* SQUID): Up with it, you scurvy dogs. When we are outside, the cat-o'-nine-tails will give you a lesson in reading addresses. (SQUID *and* MATEY *push the hamper right toward door.* MATEY *stumbles, and overturns the hamper, spilling out the books.*)

MATEY: Shiver me timbers! It's full of books!

GIRLS: Oh! (*They look at each other with terror.*)

CAPTAIN DREAD (*Picking up one of the books and looking slowly around at each girl with an unpleasant grin*) : So it is. An educated family of genteel ladies, I see. And to think I was planning to say farewell to these learned lassies. Now, Matey and Squid, what do you say we settle down here for a while? Perhaps they can teach us something. Tell me, my pretty little dears, what do you know about princes, eh? What have you done with our property, eh?

GIRLS (*Shocked*): Oh!

ASIA (*Rising and going to face him*): Captain, I must ask you to leave. I do not like the tone of your voice.

CAPTAIN DREAD (*Snarling*): Oh, you don't, don't you? (*He grasps* ASIA's *wrist.*) I'm Captain Dread, the pirate, and these are my men. Don't any of you cross me, or you'll find your bones feeding the fishes. My ship is the terror of the sea and she flies the Jolly Roger. (*Letting go of* ASIA) Now, where is the boy? (*The girls remain silent.*) Matey, search the room, and you, Squid, guard the door. (MATEY *looks behind chair and curtains as* SQUID *stands in front of door, arms folded.*) I'll give you ladies just five minutes. If you don't produce my property by then, I'll *scuttle* ye!

BETTY APPLE: Oh, I don't want to be scuttled! (MATEY *goes to cradle and bends over it.*)

MATEY: A baby! Now isn't that sweet.

INDIA (*Leaning over the cradle protectively*): Stay away from our baby!

MATEY: Aw, now I mean him no harm. I just want to chuck him under his little chin. (*He starts to put his hand in cradle.*)

INDIA: Stop! Do you know what happened to the last man who chucked him under the chin? The baby bit him! (MATEY *takes his hand from the cradle in a hurry.*)

MATEY (*Indignantly*): All right, then. It's a sad world when little babies are unfriendly. (*He looks off left.*) Here's another room, off here. (*As he moves left,* ASIA *intercepts him and bars the way.*)

ASIA: 'Tis our great-aunt's room. I pray you, do not disturb her. She is over eighty and she'll do you no harm.

CAPTAIN DREAD: Leave her. If she gives us trouble, Squid can take care of her.

SQUID: Hist, Cap'n. I can hear voices outside.

CAPTAIN DREAD (*Pointing to* EUROPA): You, girl. Go to the window and see who it is. If they are coming here, tell them to go away. (EUROPA, *still carrying the coverlet, goes to the window, and looks out.*)

EUROPA: 'Tis servants from my uncle's house. They've come for—for— (*She looks at cradle and* INDIA *puts her finger to her lips*) a piece of furniture that was promised to him.

CAPTAIN DREAD: Wave them away. Go on. Do as I say. (EUROPA *looks at the coverlet in her hands, then leans out the window and waves it.*)

EUROPA (*Calling out*): You, down there. Go away. 'Tis not ready. Come back tomorrow. (*She turns around. The coverlet is no longer in her hands.* BETTY APPLE *goes to her.*)

BETTY APPLE (*In a loud whisper*): Miss Europa, what have you done with the coverlet?

EUROPA: Shh! I can't tell you now.

CAPTAIN DREAD: You two. Stop that whispering.

BETTY APPLE (*Curtsying*): Oh, yes, sir. Yes, sir. (*She goes to the mantel and begins to dust frantically.*)

RAMU SINGH (*From cradle*): Ah-h-h chooo!

MATEY (*Turning around*): What was that?

INDIA (*Quickly*): 'Twas just the baby. Betty Apple's dusting made him sneeze. (RAMU SINGH *sneezes again.*)

CAPTAIN DREAD: The baby, eh? (*He goes to cradle.*) What a very large sneeze—(*Pulls blanket from* RAMU SINGH) for such a very small baby. (*He seizes* RAMU SINGH *and pulls him from cradle.* INDIA *jumps up and huddles at one side with her sisters and* BETTY APPLE.)

RAMU SINGH (*Struggling with* CAPTAIN DREAD): Help, help, memsahib!

CAPTAIN DREAD (*Holding him tightly*): Some baby, eh, mates? Worth a prince's ransom. It's back to the ship with you, boy, and this time I'll put you in the hold with the bilge water. (*To* MATEY) Put him in the hamper.

SQUID: What'll we do with the girls, Cap'n?

CAPTAIN DREAD: Bring them with us. They know too much, so we can't leave them here to set the Navy after us. We'll set sail with the tide in an hour, and once we're on the high seas (*Laughs evilly*), we'll take care of them.

MATEY: The plank, Cap'n?

CAPTAIN DREAD: Aye. The dear little ladies will walk the plank. (*Motioning toward the door*) Now, ladies, move quickly, all of you. Act as if we were your kindly old uncles, taking you for a stroll. (*To* MATEY) Put the prince in the hamper, Matey. (MATEY *takes* RAMU SINGH's *arm and pulls him to hamper, which he turns upright. The girls do not move.*)

SQUID (*Gruffly*): You heard the Cap'n. Move! (AUNT PATIENCE, *cane in hand, enters briskly left, and looks around, bewildered. While others look at her,* RAMU SINGH *ducks down behind hamper.*)

AUNT PATIENCE: Girls, what is going on out here? I heard loud guffaws. Oh! Who are these gentlemen?

INDIA: Oh, Auntie, Auntie, they aren't *gentlemen!*

GIRLS: They're pirates! (MATEY *and* SQUID *take a step toward* AUNT PATIENCE.)

AUNT PATIENCE (*Hand upon her heart*): Pirates! In my parlor? Oh, mercy!

ASIA: Auntie, please don't faint. Not now.

AUNT PATIENCE (*Recovering herself*): Faint? Of course I shan't faint. I didn't faint during the Revolution when General Burgoyne put a cannon right on my front lawn.

Here, you pirates, you're trespassing. (*She waves her cane at* CAPTAIN DREAD.) Begone!

CAPTAIN DREAD: Put that cane down, old lady, or I'll scuttle ye.

AUNT PATIENCE: Girls, remember that you are daughters of a fighting sea captain. Battle stations, girls. All hands on deck and don't give up the ship! *En garde, pirate!* (*She assumes a fencing position, using her cane as a sword, and thrusts it at* CAPTAIN DREAD, *who backs away, trying to defend himself.* BETTY APPLE *thrusts feather duster in* MATEY'S *face, and dusts him. He sneezes and coughs and tries to escape her.* INDIA, EUROPA, *and* ASIA *surround* SQUID, *push him into rocker, and* ASIA *binds him with ribbons from the sewing box as the others hold him firmly.*)

MATEY: Stop that, I say! Ha, ha, it tickles. I can't see for the dust!

BETTY APPLE: Put up your hands, or I'll give you another dusting.

MATEY (*Sneezing and coughing*): Stop. I surrender. (*Puts his hands in the air. Girls finish tying* SQUID, *and* INDIA *puts a large blue hair ribbon on his head.*)

SQUID: Here now! Take off that ribbon. What'll my mates say? (AUNT PATIENCE, *one hand behind her back, forces* CAPTAIN DREAD *to the wall, and pins him against it with her cane.*)

CAPTAIN DREAD (*Putting his hands in the air*): This old lady fences like a French champion!

AUNT PATIENCE: Of course. 'Twas Lafayette himself who taught me, back in 1776—or was it '77? Now stay there or I'll scuttle *you!* (*A loud knock is heard on door right, then* NAVAL OFFICER *and* SAILOR *run in.*)

OFFICER: Ahoy, Miss Bristow, the Navy is here.

AUNT PATIENCE (*Pointing her cane at* CAPTAIN DREAD): And just in time. We have three pirates ripe and ready for the brig. Oh, I haven't had such a jolly time since the Boston Tea Party.

OFFICER (*Looking the pirates over*): Upon my soul—Captain Dread. And Matey and Squid. Congratulations, ladies. You've captured the three most notorious pirates since Captain Kidd. Ho, seaman, put them in irons. (*The* SAILOR *puts handcuffs on each pirate.*)

CAPTAIN DREAD: One favor, one favor I beg ye.

OFFICER: What's that?

CAPTAIN DREAD: If it's all the same to you, don't tell anyone how we were captured.

MATEY: That's right. We'll never live it down. The "terrors of the sea" we used to be called—and now look at us.

SQUID: Done in by little girls and an old lady. Oh, the shame of it!

OFFICER: Ha, ha! But of course I'll tell the tale of these gallant ladies. You invited yourselves here, now take the consequences. Seaman, stow them in the brig.

SAILOR: Aye, aye, sir. (*He lines pirates up and they march out right.*)

OFFICER: 'Twas a lucky thing we sighted your distress signal, ladies.

AUNT PATIENCE: Distress signal? What distress signal? (EUROPA *runs to window, and brings in coverlet, which she holds up, upside down.*)

EUROPA: This, Auntie.

OFFICER: That's right, ma'am. The ship's flag, hung upside down from your flagpole—the seamen's distress signal.

BETTY APPLE: Oh, Miss Europa, what a clever notion!

INDIA: If you please, sir, we have an even bigger surprise than those old pirates. (*She looks around room and sees* RAMU SINGH *peering over edge of hamper. She takes his hand and leads him to the* OFFICER.) May I introduce

Prince Ramu Singh, formerly of Delhi, India, now the
guest of the Bristows of Salem?

AUNT PATIENCE: A prince! Oh, nicely introduced, dear
India.

OFFICER (*Looking carefully at* RAMU SINGH): Ramu Singh.
It is! Upon my word, the entire Admiralty has been
scouring the coast for this child. Are you all right?

RAMU SINGH (*Bowing*): I am most happy now. (*To the
girls*) Thank you, memsahibs. I will not forget you when
I return to Delhi. My father, the Raja of Singh, will
reward you with the greatest gift a Raja can give.

INDIA: Oh, lovely. We adore gifts. What might it be, pray?

RAMU SINGH: The largest—

GIRLS (*Eagerly*) : Yes?

RAMU SINGH: And the noblest—

GIRLS: What? What?

RAMU SINGH (*Triumphantly*): Sacred elephant! (*Girls
squeal with joy.*)

AUNT PATIENCE: An *elephant*? Mercy, mercy! A great
galumphing elephant? Girls! (*She thumps her cane on
floor.*) You are not to let that elephant *in my parlor!*
(*All laugh, as the curtain falls.*)

THE END

The Crocus Who Couldn't Bloom

Characters

MOTHER NATURE
FATHER NATURE
TWO PROP BOYS
MAMA ROBIN
PAPA ROBIN
ROBERT ROBIN
KATY CATERPILLAR
SWEET PEA
PANSY

MORNING GLORY
IRIS
CROCUS
WEED
TWO MARCH WINDS
MR. SUN
MISS SHOWER
GERTIE GREENTHUMBS

TIME: *A fine September day.*

SETTING: *A garden. A wall runs along the back. On the wall, attached to a tree, is a large nest. In front of the wall is a flower bed, with a wheelbarrow near it. Down left is a celestial clock-calendar, a clock marked with the months.*

AT RISE: MOTHER *and* FATHER NATURE *are snoozing in lawn chairs at center. Behind the clock-calendar stand* TWO PROP BOYS. 1ST PROP BOY *moves clock hand to nine, and* 2ND PROP BOY *chimes triangle nine times. On the ninth stroke,* 1ST PROP BOY *unfurls a large signal flag, which reads "Autumn."* MOTHER *and* FATHER NATURE *waken and rub their eyes.*

FATHER NATURE: Happy September, Mother Nature. (*Yawning*) We nearly overslept. Look at the celestial clock-calendar. It's time to do our autumn chores and get ready for spring.

MOTHER NATURE: Dear me! The fall is already upon us, and not a seedling tucked away in the flower bed. We'll never be ready in time for spring.

FATHER NATURE: We'd better hop to it. (*Shivers*) Hm-m-m. The earthly furnace has cooled down. There's a chill in the air. Time to turn the leaves. (*He goes to the tree and turns the leaves, which are green on one side and autumn-colored on the other, as* MOTHER NATURE *trundles the wheelbarrow offstage.* MAMA, PAPA, *and* ROBERT ROBIN *enter left, carrying small valises.*)

MAMA ROBIN: Hurry, hurry, hurry, Robert Robin! We must meet the other Robins the second week in September. Last year you poked along and poked along, and we ended up flying south with those noisy sparrows.

PAPA ROBIN: Do hurry, hurry, hurry, Robert. Do you want to freeze your feathers?

ROBERT ROBIN: Cheer up! Cheer up! We may be the last robins in the garden in the fall, but when spring comes we're always the first to fly north. (KATY CATERPILLAR *enters. She humps along, singing a melancholy refrain.*) Oh, look, Papa! A caterpillar!

KATY CATERPILLAR (*Humping up*): Hump-a-diddle. (*Flattening out*) Dump-a-doodle. (*Up*) Hump-a-diddle. (*Down*) Dump-a-doodle. (*She sees the* ROBINS *watching her, and strikes a dramatic pose.*) Oh, woe is me! Oh, the sadness of a caterpillar's life! Children scream when they see me. Ladies faint. Even strong men run at the sight of me!

ROBERT ROBIN (*Looking closely at* KATY): I don't think you're so awful—for a bug.

KATY CATERPILLAR: Oh, I am ugly. I am clumsy. I am one hundred per cent hopeless.

MAMA *and* PAPA ROBIN: Hurry, hurry, hurry! It's half past September.

MAMA ROBIN: Do you have your flight plans, Robert? (ROBERT ROBIN *bends down and pats* KATY's *head in sympathy.*)

ROBERT ROBIN: Yes, Mama. Goodbye, little caterpillar. (ROBERT *picks up his valise and flies off left with the other* ROBINS. MOTHER NATURE *wheels in wheelbarrow, with burlap cloth, sheets, and cocoon in it.* SWEET PEA, PANSY *and* MORNING GLORY *follow her.*)

KATY CATERPILLAR: Nobody wants me. (*Breaks down*) Oh, humpity, bumpity, boo, hoo, hoo!

MOTHER NATURE: Why, Katy Caterpillar, are you crying again? Shame on you—a big insect like you.

KATY CATERPILLAR (*Sniffling*): I have my reasons.

FATHER NATURE (*Offering* KATY *his handkerchief*): Wipe your eyes, you silly caterpillar. I have a surprise for you. Katy, you are going to have a metamorphosis!

KATY CATERPILLAR (*Raising herself up in surprise*): A whoo-si-which-i-what?

FATHER NATURE: A great change is going to come over you. Soon you will spin a warm cocoon. Then you will go to sleep for the whole winter. When you waken, presto-chango! You will be something heavenly—something wonderful.

MOTHER NATURE: It will be such a marvelous change, Katy, that you won't believe it.

KATY CATERPILLAR: I don't believe it now. A change! Things are bad enough now. A metagoofusus is coming. Oh, it's the end.

FATHER NATURE: Trot up to the tree and rest now, Katy. Mother Nature and I will help you spin a cocoon as soon as we set the seedlings in place. (KATY *goes to tree*.)

MOTHER NATURE: Here are Sweet Pea, Pansy, and Morning Glory, Father Nature. The others are near the shed. I'll put these away, while you get the others. (*MOTHER NATURE helps the flowers into the second row of flower bed, where they all huddle down. FATHER NATURE brings in* IRIS, WEED, *and* CROCUS. *He puts them in the first row, with* IRIS *first*, WEED *middle, and* CROCUS *on the right*.)

FATHER NATURE: We'll leave Crocus until the last. She needs special care. Spring can't officially begin until Crocus blooms. (*When they have put the other flowers in place, they both make a chair with their hands for* CROCUS, *and lower her into the space next to* WEED.)

MOTHER NATURE: Now, we'll cover the little dears with some good soil. (*They put burlap around the flowers. The clock strikes October and the triangle chimes ten times*.)

FATHER NATURE: October. Time for the leaves to fall. (*He takes the leaves, which are loosely attached, and lets them sail to earth*.)

MOTHER NATURE: Now, Katy Caterpillar, we must help you spin your cocoon.

KATY CATERPILLAR (*Sleepily*): Oh, what is it now? Why can't people leave me alone? (*MOTHER and FATHER NATURE unfurl the cocoon and attach it to tree, close enough to the exit so that* KATY CATERPILLAR *can go offstage, and return, unseen, later on*.)

FATHER NATURE: That is your cocoon, Katy. Soon you'll be so sleepy that you'll sleep through the whole winter.

KATY CATERPILLAR: I don't believe it. (*She yawns*.) Nobody sleeps through the whole winter, especially caterpillars. (*She snores loudly as the cocoon is lowered and screens her from view of audience*.)

FATHER NATURE: You know, Mother Nature, the almanac said this would be an unusually cold winter. Perhaps we'd better tuck those seeds in with a blanket of snow.

MOTHER NATURE: Good idea. We mustn't take a chance of freezing our Crocus. Why, spring could be delayed for years if she didn't bloom. (*As they tuck sheets around flowers, the clock hands move to November and the triangle chimes eleven times. MOTHER NATURE hangs up a sign, "Do Not Disturb Flowers until Spring." Then MOTHER and FATHER NATURE resume their seats in the lawn chairs.*) I think we can settle ourselves, Father Nature. Everything seems to be in order. We're all ready for spring.

FATHER NATURE: We'll just have our winter nap now. Did you set the calendar for spring?

MOTHER NATURE: Yes, I did. The March Winds said they'd wake us. (*They pull white sheets up over themselves. The clock moves to December. A few bars of Christmas music are heard. Triangle chimes twelve times and a white flag with red and green letters, "Winter," is unfurled. MOTHER and FATHER NATURE doze. Clock moves to January. "Auld Lang Syne" is heard. New Year's noisemaker sounds and chime strikes one. Clock moves to February. "Let Me Call You Sweetheart" is heard and the triangle sounds twice. Clock moves to March. At half past March, triangle sounds three times and a bicycle siren sounds up. A green flag with white letters announcing "Spring" is waved, and TWO MARCH WINDS, dressed as lions, roar on stage. They growl and roar, striding about stage, flinging covers off the flowers and WEED and sheets from MOTHER and FATHER NATURE. Then they run off stage waving the covers as they go. MOTHER and FATHER NATURE rub their eyes and sit up. Along the garden wall comes MISS SHOWER. She has a large sprinkling can from which she flings out hand-*

fuls of foil raindrops. The flowers and WEED *begin to grow, putting out their feet from the seed covers, and shaking themselves.* MOTHER *and* FATHER NATURE *go to the flower bed to watch them.*) Isn't it exciting? The babies are beginning to put down their roots.

FATHER NATURE: All they need is a good, long spell of sunshine. Then, when Crocus blooms, spring will finally be here. (MISS SHOWER *exits.* MR. SUN *comes along the wall. He stands on the wall at center and holds out his hands while the flowers grow. The flowers all cast off their seed pods, to show green costumes. At first their hands stay stiffly by their sides, but, as the* SUN *raises his arms, they raise their arms, like leaves unfolding.* WEED *slips out of the weed pod. He goes behind* CROCUS, *ready to choke her.*)

MOTHER NATURE (*Gently, to* CROCUS): All right, Crocus. You may bloom now. You may begin spring. (CROCUS *does not move.* SUN *leaves the stage.*)

FATHER NATURE: Perhaps she didn't hear you. (*Speaking louder*) Come, Crocus, it's time for spring! (CROCUS *still does not bloom. The* ROBINS *re-enter, led by* ROBERT.)

ROBERT: Hurry, hurry, hurry! I can't wait to see the old nest. See? We're the first robins to come back to the garden.

FATHER NATURE (*Barring the way*): Stop! You can't come any further!

PAPA ROBIN: Why not? Isn't it spring?

MOTHER NATURE: Oh, dear, this is so embarrassing. The fact is, Crocus hasn't bloomed yet!

MAMA ROBIN: Hasn't bloomed yet? The slowpoke. Do tell her to hurry, hurry, hurry. I have spring nest cleaning to do. (*They go down right and wait.*)

KATY CATERPILLAR (*From behind cocoon*): Help! Let me out of this contraption. How did a self-respecting butterfly ever get into such a thing? Let me out, I say!

FATHER NATURE: Now, now, Katy. Just be patient. Spring hasn't started yet.

KATY CATERPILLAR (*From cocoon*): Hasn't started? I demand an explanation!

MOTHER NATURE (*Sadly*): Crocus hasn't bloomed yet.

KATY CATERPILLAR (*From cocoon*): Crocus hasn't bloomed?

FATHER NATURE: Hold your antennae, Katy. As soon as we find the trouble, you can come out of your cocoon.

MOTHER NATURE: I'm sure I don't know what is worrying little Crocus. (GERTIE GREENTHUMBS *appears on the wall behind the flowers. She sits cross-legged on the wall, listening.*) We gave her plenty of good soil—

FATHER NATURE: Plenty of showers, plenty of sun—

KATY CATERPILLAR (*Crossly, from cocoon*): Plenty of *time!*

MOTHER NATURE: What did we do that was wrong? What's missing?

GERTIE (*Hopping off wall*): Maybe it's me!

MOTHER NATURE: Who are you?

GERTIE: I'm a human being. Every garden needs one. Let me introduce myself. I'm Gertie Greenthumbs, the girl gardener extraordinary. I'm extraordinary because I have not one green thumb—but two. See? (*Holds up her green thumbs*) My special talent is with crocuses. May I look at your problem child?

MOTHER NATURE: Indeed you may.

FATHER NATURE: Anything you can do to help Crocus would be so much appreciated. (GERTIE *goes to* CROCUS, *who hangs her head.* WEED *puts his hands around her neck.* CROCUS *bends her knees as if wilting.* GERTIE *looks very wise as she shakes* CROCUS *gently.* ROBINS *come up, heads cocked to the side, and watch curiously.* KATY *pokes her head out of the cocoon.*)

GERTIE (*Wisely*): Aha!

ALL: She says, "Aha!"

GERTIE (*Going down on hands and knees to examine roots*): Oho!

ALL: She says, "Oho!"

GERTIE (*Peeking behind* CROCUS): I have it!

ALL: She has it! (GERTIE *takes* WEED *by the collar.* WEED *hangs his head, ashamed.*)

GERTIE: Look! The culprit!

ALL: What is it?

GERTIE (*Shaking* WEED): A weed!

ALL: A weed!

GERTIE: He was choking the Crocus. No wonder she couldn't bloom.

ALL (*Shaking fists*): Shame! Shame on the weed! (*The* WEED *wilts, slithers to the floor and lies still.*)

GERTIE: Into the barrow with you! (FATHER *and* MOTHER NATURE *pick* WEED *up by hands and feet and put him in the barrow.*) Now, let's see about the Crocus. (*She examines her.* CROCUS *stands straighter.*) The sun is shining. (MR. SUN *appears on wall.*) The robins are singing. (ROBINS *open mouths.*) The beautiful, bountiful spring is springing. So, hocus pocus—open, Crocus! (*She pulls open the flower on* CROCUS' *hat.*)

MOTHER NATURE: Thank you, thank you, my child. Now spring can begin.

FATHER NATURE (*Pulling out whistle and blowing it*): Ladies and gentlemen, birds and flowers! May I have your attention, please? (GERTIE *goes to each flower and opens it.* ROBINS *go to the nest in the tree.*) Thanks for your patience, all and one. Spring officially has begun!

PAPA ROBIN: Come along, we'll help Father Nature open the blossoms on the apple tree.

MAMA ROBIN: And then we'll all pitch in with the nest building. Hurry, hurry, hurry!

ROBERT ROBIN: Cheer up! Cheer up! Spring is here, here, here!

KATY CATERPILLAR (*Miffed*): Everyone has forgotten about me.

FATHER NATURE: Oh, hello, Katy. Do you need some help? (*He takes down the cocoon.* KATY, *now dressed as a butterfly, stands on the wall. She touches her wings with a baffled air.*)

KATY CATERPILLAR: I'm different! (*She scratches her head.*) How do I look?

FLOWERS: You're beautiful, beautiful, beautiful!

KATY CATERPILLAR: I am?

MOTHER NATURE: Here, Katy, look at yourself. (*She hands her a mirror from her pocket.*)

KATY CATERPILLAR (*Entranced*): Oh! I'm heavenly. Oh, I'm ravishing! Oh, gorgeous me! I'm something! I'm somebody! I'm—I'm the queen of the air!

FATHER NATURE (*Chuckling*): Now, now, Katy Caterpillar, don't let your metamorphosis go to your head.

KATY CATERPILLAR: Katy Caterpillar? Who is that? I was never a caterpillar. Never! I'm Belinda Butterfly. Beautiful, bonnie, bewitching, bedazzling Belinda Butterfly! (*She flies around stage.*)

MOTHER NATURE (*Sighing*): Butterflies never remember they were once caterpillars. So temperamental. Every year it's the same thing.

FATHER NATURE: I wouldn't worry about her. When Belinda meets the birds and the bees and the other creatures of the air, she'll settle down. Right now, she thinks she's the only thing with wings. (*He takes* MOTHER NATURE's *arm and they go back to their lawn chairs. The* ROBINS *and* KATY *open the pink blossoms on the tree.* GERTIE *goes to the lawn chairs.* FATHER NATURE *yawns.*) Did you set the calendar for summer, my dear? (*He and* MOTHER NATURE *seat themselves.*)

MOTHER NATURE: I certainly did. The Fourth of July promised to wake us.

FATHER NATURE: This has been the strangest spring, hasn't it?

MOTHER NATURE: We never worked harder, but it was worth all the trouble. All we needed was good soil . . . a few showers . . .

FATHER NATURE: A good spell of sunshine . . . Father Nature . . .

MOTHER NATURE: And Mother Nature.

GERTIE (*Sitting cross-legged at their feet*): And a girl human being with two green thumbs. (*She puts up both thumbs and smiles. Curtain*)

THE END

Sun Up!

Characters

Chorus of Puddle Jumpers
Commander
Coaxer
Witch
Father Time
Sun

Time: *The end of April.*
Setting: *An outdoor scene.*
At Rise: Commander, Coaxer *and* Chorus of Puddle
  Jumpers *are standing in a semicircle. They are dressed
  in rainwear and hold open umbrellas.*

Half Chorus: Drip—
Half Chorus (*Answering*): Drop!
Half Chorus: Drip—
Half Chorus: Drop!
1st Solo: Drip—
2nd Solo: Drip—
Chorus: Drop!
Half Chorus: Drip—
Half Chorus: Drop!
Half Chorus: Drip—
Half Chorus: Drop!

3RD SOLO: Drip—
4TH SOLO: Drip—
CHORUS: Drop!
1ST QUARTET (*Twirling umbrellas in time to rhythm*):
    The rain keeps a-coming,
    A-dripping and a-drumming,
    And a patter-patter-pattering down . . .
2ND QUARTET (*Twirling umbrellas*):
    The wind keeps a-roaring,
    And the water keeps a-pouring,
    And it's wetter, wetter, wetter in town.
1ST SOLO (*Quickly twirling umbrella*):
    Each raindrop's the same
2ND SOLO (*Twirling umbrella*):
    As the same one that came
3RD SOLO (*Twirling umbrella*):
    With two thousand and four
4TH SOLO (*Twirling umbrella*):
    Just a moment before.
1ST SOLO (*Yawning*):
    What a bore!
CHORUS:
    What a bore!
    What a b-o-r-e
    Bore!
1ST QUARTET:
    Here we sit in our wet galoshes
2ND QUARTET:
    And our mackintoshes,
3RD QUARTET:
    With moist umbrellas—
4TH QUARTET:
    Damp little fellas—
2ND SOLO:
    With mud on our toes

3RD SOLO:
And a cold in our nose.
Ah choo!
CHORUS: Ah choo!
We are waiting, waiting, waiting
For the slowpoke sun.
1ST QUARTET:
Oh, the slowpoke sun
2ND QUARTET:
In the last-of-April sky;
4TH SOLO:
Wish it were May Day
1ST SOLO:
Or the Fourth of July!
2ND SOLO (*Shivering*):
Wish it were warm;
3RD SOLO:
Wish the birds would sing;
4TH SOLO:
Wish the grass were green;
1ST SOLO:
Oh, where is spring?
CHORUS:
Oh, where—oh, where—
Oh, where is spring?
COMMANDER (*Stepping out of circle to address* PUDDLE
JUMPERS): Friends, have you had enough of this fizzle-
drizzle?
CHORUS: We have!
COMMANDER: Do you want some action from that hide-
and-seek sun?
CHORUS: We do!
COMMANDER: Then follow me, friends.
We'll demand—
We'll command that sun to come out!

CHORUS:
  We'll demand—
  We'll command that sun to come out!
COMMANDER: We'll lay it on the line.
  We'll get down to brass tacks.
  We'll talk turkey to that sun!
CHORUS: Gobble, gobble, gobble! We'll talk turkey to that sun.
COMMANDER: Attention! Furl umbrellas. (CHORUS *furls umbrellas in unison.*) Shoulder bumbershoots! (CHORUS *shoulders umbrellas like rifles.*) Puddle Jumpers, about face! (CHORUS *turns and faces backdrop.*) Now hear this!
CHORUS: Now hear this!
COMMANDER: Listen, sun. Come out and shine!
CHORUS: Come out and shine.
COMMANDER: Attention, sun! I'll give you a countdown of three—
CHORUS: Count of three.
COMMANDER:
  One—
  Up and at 'em, sun,
  Two—
  Start a-moving, sun,
  Three—
  Rise and shine!
CHORUS:
  Rise and shine.
  Rise and shine.
  Rise and shine, shine, shine,
  Shine, shine!
COAXER (*Turning around and stepping out of group*): No, no, no! (COMMANDER *rejoins* CHORUS)
CHORUS (*Turning around*): No?
COAXER: Never, never, never!

CHORUS: Never?

COAXER: Everybody knows you can't *command* that great big sun.

CHORUS: You can't?

COAXER:
Gently, gently you must coax him—
He is sensitive, shy and mild.

CHORUS: Oh-h-h-h!

COAXER:
Sweetly, sweetly you must beg him—
He is like a sulky child.

CHORUS: Ah-h-h-h!

COAXER: Allow me to demonstrate. (*Calling*) Yoo-hoo, Mr. Sun.

CHORUS (*Imitating* COAXER): Yoo-hoo, Mr. Sun.

COAXER:
If it isn't too much trouble,
If you're so inclined,
If it somewhat pleases you,
If you do not mind . . .

CHORUS:
Will you, would you,
Might you, could you
Send a little sunshine down?

2ND SOLO:
Just a little stray ray—

3RD SOLO:
Just a little one-beam sunbeam—

4TH SOLO:
Won't you dry the sky a little
So the town won't drown?

COAXER: Please—

CHORUS: Please—

COAXER: Pretty please—

CHORUS: Pretty please—

Come out, come out, wherever you are. (WITCH enters, *carrying umbrella.*)

WITCH (*Cackling*): "Pretty please," indeed. Everybody knows you can't coax or command that sun. You have to bewitch it! (COAXER *rejoins* CHORUS.) Hissst! (*She beckons, and* CHORUS *crouches around her.*)
Get an old black cat with a bony bobtail.
Get a big black hat. Get a silver pail.
Find a log in a dell. Find a frog in a well.
Stir them all together with a sorcerer's spell.

CHORUS (*In whispered chant*):
Old black cat . . . bony bobtail,
Big black hat . . . silver pail,
Log in a dell . . . frog in a well—
Stir together with a sorcerer's spell!

WITCH (*Using umbrella as a wand*):
By the dizzy demons with the mean green eyes,
By the darning needles and the dragonflies,
By the hoot owl's whistle, and the hound dog's whine,
I conjure thee and spell thee—
Shine, sun, shine!

CHORUS (*Waving umbrellas like wands*):
We conjure thee and spell thee—
Shine, sun, shine!
(*All wait expectantly.* CHORUS *groans disappointedly.*)
Aw-w-w-w!
(WITCH *shrugs shoulders and exits.* FATHER TIME *enters, carrying calendar.*)

FATHER TIME (*To audience*): This is a job for Father Time! (*To the* CHORUS) Hi, there, Puddle Jumpers. What's the trouble?

CHORUS:
The sun won't shine,
Won't shine, won't shine,
The sun won't shine at all . . .

1ST SOLO:
    We don't know where he is biding—
2ND SOLO:
    We believe that he is hiding—
CHORUS:
    For we haven't seen his face since the fall!
3RD SOLO:
    Every play day is a gray day—
4TH SOLO:
    A dismal stay-away day.
FATHER TIME: Well . . .
CHORUS: Well?
FATHER TIME:
    How about a May Day?
CHORUS:
    That's a hip-hooray day!
FATHER TIME:
    Perk up, Puddle Jumpers—
    The world has rolled on:
    Muddy March has muddled past,
    Dripping April's gone. . . . *(He tears off leaves from his calendar to illustrate.)*
    Now turn around,
    And twist around;
    Look sky-high, each one.
    Give a shout, and call him out—
    (FATHER TIME *shouts up to the backdrop.*)
    Howdy, Mr. Sun! (CHORUS *turns.*)
CHORUS (*Putting umbrellas on floor, taking off raincoats and hats, revealing bright, summer clothes*):
    Turn around, (*They turn front.*)
    And twist around; (*They turn again to face backdrop.*)
    Look sky-high, each one.
1ST SOLO:
    Give a shout—

2ND SOLO:
Call him out—

CHORUS (*With hands to mouths, like megaphones, loudly*):
Howdy, Mr. Sun! (*Slowly, the clouds on backdrop roll
away, revealing rainbow and large gold disc with cutout
for* SUN's *face.* SUN *appears in disc, wearing straw
boater.*)

SUN: Howdy, Puddle Jumpers!

CHORUS: Hooray! (*They turn front, put arms on each
other's shoulders, and sway to rhythm of the verse.*)
Oh, the sun keeps a-beaming,
A-shining and a-gleaming,
And a-sparkle, sparkle, sparkling down.
Each cloud is like a feather,
And it's calmy, balmy weather,
And it's brighter, brighter, brighter in town!

3RD SOLO:
Each day is a gay day—

4TH SOLO:
A summery heyday—

1ST QUARTET:
A hip-hip-hooray day—

CHORUS:
A May Day!
A May Day!
It's spring! spring! spring! (*They drop arms and extend
hands in greeting to* SUN, *and they hold positions.*)

SUN (*Tipping hat and winking*): Howdy! (*Curtain*)

THE END

The Punctuation Proclamation

Characters

HARK } *heralds* HO	ROYAL TREASURER
	ROYAL COOK
KING PISH-POSH	TWO BOY COURTIERS
ROYAL TUTOR	TWO GIRL COURTIERS
ROYAL STORYTELLER	OTHER COURTIERS
ROYAL SCRIBE	

SETTING: *The throne room of King Pish-Posh, in the kingdom of Bosh.*

AT RISE: KING PISH-POSH *is snoring noisily on his throne.* HARK *is patrolling the stage from right;* HO *is patrolling from left, and they meet at center.*

HARK: Come on, now. It's your turn to waken him, Ho.

HO: Oh, no. I distinctly remember that I woke him the last time, Hark.

HARK: Go on. It's half past the hourglass. He'll miss his reading lesson.

HO: That reading lesson! He's always in such a fearful temper when he has to read. Here, let's toss a coin. (*He takes coin from pocket, tosses and catches it and puts it on the back of his hand.*)

HARK: Heads.

Ho: Tails. (*Looks at his hand*) Whew! It's tails. Go ahead, Hark. I'll stay right behind you to catch you when he flattens you. (ROYAL TUTOR *enters timidly from left, with easel, large lesson pad, and book.*)

HARK: Wait. Here's the Royal Tutor. Let him have the honor of telling the King it's time to read. (*Heralds tiptoe down right, sit on stools, and watch.* TUTOR *places easel, with lesson pad on it, up left, near throne. He opens book, crosses to throne, and pulls gently at* KING's *sleeve.*)

TUTOR: Your Majesty.

KING (*Snoring*): Bluhuhuh.

TUTOR (*A little louder*): It is time for your daily reading lesson, King Pish-Posh. (KING *sits bolt upright.*)

KING: Humph! Reading, is it? I knew there was some reason why this was a bad day.

TUTOR: If Your Majesty would only relax. Reading is fun.

KING: Fun! I'd rather be boiled in green, gurgling oil. All those letters huddling together, staring at me like black cats—

TUTOR: The letters are trying hard to mean something to you, Sire. Here—(*He uncovers sentence written on the lesson pad. It reads "I am the King."*) Here is the sentence we have been trying to read for the last three months. Do let us see now how well you can read it.

KING (*Scowling*): Tutor, that sentence is too hard. There are (*Counts on fingers*) ten letters in that sentence. Why can't I have a sentence with *one* letter? I could read that.

TUTOR (*Sighing*): Impossible, Sire. Come now, please. I know you can read this. I beg you to try.

KING: Botheration! (*He thrusts out his lip as he glares at sentence.*) Um-um-um.

TUTOR: The first word is—(*Points to himself*)

KING: The first word is "you." There. I read a word.

TUTOR: No, no, Majesty. The word is "me"—I mean, "I."

KING: I knew that. I was jesting with you. Let me read it, now. "I"—

TUTOR: Sound it out, Gracious Highness.

KING: A-M. A-M. Aha! I have it. LALLAPALOOZA!

TUTOR (*Throwing up his hands*): No, Sire—"am." Now, try the next word. And I suggest that you really *look* at the word.

KING: You never let a poor king rest, do you? Very well, I'll look. I'll stare a hole through the paper. (*He stares at easel. He rises, takes a step closer, and stares again. Then he goes up and tries to brush the period off the paper.*)

TUTOR: What is the matter, Majesty?

KING: There is some sort of beetle on the paper. (*Slaps easel*) There! I got it! No, I didn't. He's still there.

TUTOR (*Coming to easel*): Let me see. Oh, I beg to differ with you, Sire. That is not a beetle. That is a "period."

KING (*Walking back to throne*): I don't care what kind of insect it is. It doesn't belong in my nice, neat palace. (*KING sits on throne*)

TUTOR: But a period is a punctuation mark. It is part of the sentence.

KING: What? Do you mean to tell me that, in addition to twenty-six letters of the alphabet, I shall have to remember an inky blob?

TUTOR: There are many punctuation marks, Sire. There are commas, exclamation marks, question marks, colons, and apostrophes.

KING (*Holding his ears*): Enough! Stop! I won't have it. No. Twenty-six letters are troublesome enough.

TUTOR: But there is nothing I can do, Sire. Punctuation was part of the language before we were even born.

KING: Well, *I* can do something about it. I shall abolish it.

TUTOR (*Wringing his hands*): That is not possible!

KING: Am I, or am I not the King? I am the King! (*Pom-*

pously) There. That's a good sentence. You ought to have that sentence on the easel: "I am the King." I can abolish anything I wish. (*To the heralds*) Heralds! Heralds! (*They rise and run to* KING.)

HARK: Front and center, Sire!

HO: At your service, Majesty!

KING: Draw up a proclamation of abolishment. (*Heralds cross to table with scrolls and quill pens, and prepare to write proclamation.*) Ahem. (KING *dictates.*) "His Royal Highness, King Pish-Posh, of the kingdom of Bosh—" Do you have that?

HARK: Yes, Sire.

KING: "Hereby proclaims that all punctuation marks shall be abolished throughout the land, forever and ever and a day." Seal it with the Royal Seal, and proclaim it immediately.

HO: Immediately, Your Majesty. (*Heralds bow and exit with scrolls,* HARK *at left,* HO *at right.*)

KING: There. That is that. Now, let us be done with reading. It is time for the court to assemble. Tutor, bid my courtiers and the Storyteller enter. (*The* TUTOR *goes off right and returns with* COURTIERS.) Now, we must have a jolly story. Where *is* my Storyteller? (COURTIERS *sit on chairs to left and right of throne.* ROYAL STORYTELLER *runs in from right with large book under his arm.*)

STORYTELLER: The Royal Storyteller begs to announce his presence in the court of King Pish-Posh.

KING: Humph. Very good. Let us have a story.

TUTOR (*Aside*): I do hope it isn't "Goldilocks and the Three Bears" again.

KING: Let us have "Goldilocks and the Three Bears," again.

COURTIERS (*Groaning*): Oh, no!

1ST BOY COURTIER: Please, Sire, not that story today.

1st GIRL COURTIER: Please, Sire, we have heard that story three hundred sixty-five times.

KING: Humph. I suppose it is the fashion to be democratic. Very well. What other story would you like to hear?

2ND BOY COURTIER: Might we hear about Robin Hood?

COURTIERS: Yes, yes!

KING: Robin Hood? That's a frightful story. Think what that outlaw did to good King John. Some other tale, think of some other tale.

2ND GIRL COURTIER: Then, Your Majesty, may we hear the story of Sleeping Beauty? We ladies would enjoy it so much.

KING: Would you?

GIRL COURTIERS: Yes, yes!

KING: Does it have a bad fairy in it?

2ND GIRL COURTIER: Oh, yes. She is most dreadfully wicked.

KING: Then we shan't have it. Bad fairies make me nervous.

GIRL COURTIERS (*Sadly*): Oooh.

KING: It is my turn. Royal Storyteller, open your book to the story of Goldilocks and the Three Bears. (*As* STORYTELLER *opens book,* Ho *enters from right, and* HARK *enters from left, to announce proclamation. They read from scrolls.*)

Ho: Hear ye! Hear ye! His Royal Highness, King Pish-Posh, of the kingdom of Bosh, hereby proclaims—

HARK: That all punctuation marks shall be abolished throughout the land, forever and ever and a day. (*Heralds exit,* HARK *left and* Ho *right.*)

STORYTELLER: What? No more punctuation?

KING: Never mind. It doesn't concern you. Continue.

STORYTELLER: Very well, Your Highness. (*He begins to read in a singsong fashion with no pauses. As he reads, the* COURTIERS *yawn, and fall asleep, and the* KING *grows more puzzled.*) "Once upon a time there lived a little girl named Goldilocks she was an adventurous child she lived in a great wood her parents said do not go into the forest alone but she said pooh pooh I am old enough to take care of myself—"

KING: Stop!

STORYTELLER: This is impossible, Your Majesty. There are no commas or periods. It is like being in a wilderness with no signposts.

KING (*To* TUTOR): Is this true?

TUTOR: It is true, Sire. I tried to warn you. (HARK *enters from left with* ROYAL SCRIBE *and* ROYAL COOK, *who carries large menu and wooden spoon. Ho enters from right with* ROYAL TREASURER, *who carries small abacus.*)

HARK: Your Highness! There is terrible chaos in the land. The people clamor for you to restore punctuation. Thousands of requests are pouring in. The Royal Scribe is desperate.

SCRIBE (*Bowing*): Honored King, the records of the kingdom are snarled and confused. We need our apostrophes urgently. Without apostrophes we do not know what belongs to whom, or whose things are which.

HO: The Royal Treasurer is in a tizzy. He cannot figure out the taxes.

TREASURER (*Bowing*): Moneyed Majesty, I must have periods in abundance. We use them by the carton for decimal points. (*Holding up abacus*) I cannot tell now whether you have one million gold ducats or only one millionth of a ducat.

KING: My treasury is in danger? This *is* serious.

HARK: What's more, Your Majesty, the Royal Cook is frantic.

COOK (*Tartly*): Highness, I demand that you put commas back.

KING: Humph. I see no need for commas. I don't eat commas.

COOK (*Advancing to* KING *and thrusting menu under his nose*): Look at this menu. Does this sound appetizing? Beef soup salad creamed chicken ice cream coffee cigars.

KING: Coffee cigars? Blah. Very well. I declare a state of emergency. I seem to have made a mistake. Kings do make mistakes.

TUTOR: Sire—

KING: You shouldn't interrupt in the middle of my mistake.

TUTOR: But, I merely wanted to tell you that you *can* put things right again. (*In stage whisper, as he points to heralds*) The heralds.

KING: I can? Yes, yes, of course I can. Heralds. (*They bow.*) Punctuation is in again. Go spread the word.

ALL: Hooray! (*Heralds exit.*)

KING: And now we can get on with our story.

ALL: Ugh.

KING: On second thought, ever since I heard that story without the punctuation, I am not nearly so fond of it. (*To* 2ND GIRL COURTIER) What was the title of that tale you declared was so interesting?

2ND GIRL COURTIER: "Sleeping Beauty," Your Majesty.

KING: "Sleeping Beauty" it shall be, then. After all—(*He stares at the easel.*) I-AM-THE-KING. Period! I read it. I read the sentence. There was nothing to it. It was fun!

ALL: Hooray for King Pish-Posh!

KING: I'm a Royal Reader! Why didn't someone tell me it was fun?

TUTOR: We tried, Sire. We certainly did try! (*Curtain*)

THE END

Terrible Terry's Surprise

Characters

TERRY
GRANDMA
APRIL FOOL
SEVEN LITTLE FOLLIES
MR. HOGAN

MISS BLYTHE
MISS GARVEY
MR. ARDEN
MR. RULE

TIME: *April Fools' Day.*

SETTING: *Terry's living room.*

AT RISE: GRANDMA *is sitting in her rocker and knitting,
as* TERRY *enters, carrying a notebook. The edge of his
report card is sticking from his sleeve. He tries to sneak
behind her as she speaks.*

GRANDMA (*To herself*): This sock is almost finished. My,
it's getting late. Terry should be home soon. April first!
Land o' Goshen, it's report card time again. I hope the
dear boy has improved his behavior! Every year he tries
to sneak right by his old grandma. He goes up to that
window and tries to hide behind the curtain. (TERRY
does this.) Come out from behind that curtain, grandson. (TERRY *shrugs and starts to tiptoe off left.*) Then
he tries to go right to his room, hoping I'll forget that

report card. Come here, Terry! (TERRY *sighs, shakes his head and goes to* GRANDMA.)

TERRY: Oh, hi, Grandma. I guess I didn't see you.

GRANDMA: Didn't see me! Why, I was sitting here as plain as a plum in a vanilla pudding. All righty. Where is it?

TERRY: Where is what, Granny?

GRANDMA (*Exasperated*): We have to have a guessing game every time. Turn out your front pocket. (TERRY *turns it out.*) Turn out your back pocket. (TERRY *turns it out.*) Open your notebook. (TERRY *opens his notebook.* GRANDMA *riffles through it.*) What's that up your sleeve?

TERRY: It must be my shirt cuff, Granny. (*He pushes card up sleeve.*)

GRANDMA: Since when does your cuff have the signature of the principal on it? Hand it over, grandson. (TERRY *pulls the card out and hangs his head as* GRANDMA *puts her spectacles on and studies the card.*) You just stay put there. Don't go wiggling off somewhere. Let's see. Mr. Arden, your teacher, says: "Reading: D. Writing: D. Arithmetic: D. Behavior: Minus zero." Minus zero? How can that be? I thought zero was the lowest mark.

TERRY: It was—until I came into the class.

GRANDMA: Terrible! Simply terrible. What does Mr. Hogan, your gym teacher, have to report? (*Reading*) "Gym: Terry does not pay attention. He constantly disrupts the class."

TERRY: I can explain, Granny. We were playing basketball, and I made a basket through the principal's window.

GRANDMA (*Rocking agitatedly*): Through the principal's window! Mercy!

TERRY: I didn't mean to. I was trying my double-swisher-special-bounce-dribble. It didn't hit the basket. The principal was awfully angry, too, about all that water on the floor.

GRANDMA: What water on the floor?

TERRY: The ball bounced into the principal's fishbowl while he was feeding his tropical fish. He was awfully wet.

GRANDMA: Shameful! Simply shameful. Well, I suppose I'd better have a look at the bad news from Miss Blythe, your music teacher. (*Reading*) "Terry does not pay attention. He disrupts the class."

TERRY: I try to behave, Granny, but somehow things always go wrong. I guess Miss Blythe is still angry about the trumpets.

GRANDMA: What about the trumpets?

TERRY: I was trying to be helpful. She asked me to clean out the trumpets. So I thought of an original way to do it. I dunked them in lots of soap and water. I guess I didn't get it all out, though. When the band started to play, they blew soap bubbles to the tune of *Yankee Doodle*.

GRANDMA: Soap bubbles! (*Looks at card*) Why, here's a note from the cafeteria supervisor, Miss Garvey. "Please inform Terence—"

TERRY: Uh-oh. Nobody calls me Terence unless he's really angry!

GRANDMA (*Reading*): "Please inform Terence that he can no longer eat in the cafeteria. We do not think it was very polite of him to put salt in the sugar bowl."

TERRY: Oh, that. I was only trying to help. I was helping set the table that day, and saw a big empty bowl with an S on it, so I filled it up with salt. Boy, did Miss Garvey scream when she tasted her coffee later on.

GRANDMA (*Shaking her head*): Terry, do you remember what I said would happen if you didn't improve your report card?

TERRY (*Crestfallen*): Yes, Granny. No television for a week—

GRANDMA: No television for a month!

TERRY: Yes, Granny. No television for a month. Come straight in after school and stay in my room for half an hour.

GRANDMA: Stay in your room for an hour and a half!

TERRY: Yes, ma'am. An hour and a half. And mow the lawn once a month.

GRANDMA: Mow the lawn twice a month.

TERRY (*In a small voice*): Yes, Granny.

GRANDMA: And in addition, young man, you are going to write an apology note to each one of those teachers. You begin this minute. There is paper on the table, and a fountain pen and ink. So don't you fiddle and twiddle around. I'll go fix dinner. But I'm going to look in on you from time to time. So don't try your famous vanishing act! (*She gathers up her knitting and bustles off left.*)

TERRY: Boy! Boy, oh boy! Apology notes. I don't know why I have to apologize for being a normal, mischievous boy. Everybody makes a little noise sometimes. I'm not so bad. (*He sits at table left and starts to write.*) I guess I'll begin with Miss Garvey. She's the angriest. Dear Miss Garvey, I am sorry I put salt in the sugar bowl. Next time I will put sugar in the salt shakers. . . . (TERRY *laughs. As he does so, the lights flash on and off, music is heard, and* APRIL FOOL *and his* SEVEN LITTLE FOLLIES *come down center aisle, unseen by* TERRY. 3RD LITTLE FOLLY *carries a pair of men's shoes. They climb up over the apron of the stage.* APRIL FOOL *steals in back of* TERRY *and claps his hands over* TERRY'S *eyes.*) Hey, Granny! What are you doing? (SEVEN LITTLE FOLLIES *pantomime laughter.*)

APRIL FOOL (*Taking his hands away and hopping to the front where* TERRY *can see him.*): April Fool!

TERRY: Who are you? Who let you in?

APRIL FOOL: We came through the walls to hex and perplex you. I am the April Fool, and these small pixilated people are my Seven Little Follies. (*Each of the* FOLLIES *bows in turn.*)

1ST LITTLE FOLLY: I'm Mischief.

2ND LITTLE FOLLY: I'm Madcap.

3RD LITTLE FOLLY: I'm Sillybilly.

4TH LITTLE FOLLY: I'm Fiddlefaddle.

5TH LITTLE FOLLY: I'm High Jinx.

6TH LITTLE FOLLY: I'm Hobbledehoy.

7TH LITTLE FOLLY: I'm Tomfoolery.

TERRY: I didn't invite you!

APRIL FOOL: We invited ourselves. Whenever there is an April Foolish boy who is up to tricks, we come around to teach him a lesson.

TERRY: I don't need a lesson.

LITTLE FOLLIES: Oh, yes, you do! (LITTLE FOLLIES *push* TERRY *to the front of the stage, some holding his arms and some his legs.*)

TERRY: Granny! Granny! Come quick!

APRIL FOOL: She can't hear you. We sent her on a wild goose chase for her spectacles. (*To* LITTLE FOLLIES) That's enough. Let him go. He can't get away. (*They release* TERRY.) As you have observed, we are in control here. Now (*Clapping hands*), Sillybilly, bring out the shoes. (3RD LITTLE FOLLY *shows shoes.*) Do you see these?

TERRY: Sure. They're a pair of men's shoes.

APRIL FOOL: Teacher's shoes. We are going to put *you* in your teacher's shoes. Off with his sneakers! (1ST *and* 2ND LITTLE FOLLIES *remove his sneakers and put the large shoes on him.*) Now, Terry me lad, give me your honest opinion. How would you like to teach school?

TERRY: I wouldn't! I couldn't! I'm only a little boy.

APRIL FOOL: You are big enough to make mischief. Little Follies! Bring in the schoolroom. (*The music is heard*

again, as the LITTLE FOLLIES *exit and return with blackboard, chalk, five desks and chairs.*) Terry me boy,
we'll need a simple magic spell to turn you into a full-
fledged teacher. This spell can be broken only when
one child in your class learns one fact. Until you teach
something to someone, you must remain in the teacher's
shoes!

TERRY: Why, that doesn't sound so hard. I'll teach them
one and one makes two, and I'll be out of these old
shoes in a jiffy.

APRIL FOOL: Prepare to cast the spell, Little Follies. (LIT-
TLE FOLLIES *form a circle around* TERRY, *pointing at
him.* APRIL FOOL *makes a diagram in the air with his
finger.*)
By the seven wonders on lands and seas,
Plus and minus—

LITTLE FOLLIES (*Chanting in unison*):
Twos and threes.

APRIL FOOL:
Longitudes, latitudes.

LITTLE FOLLIES:
Spelling bees.

APRIL FOOL:
Lunchrooms, coatrooms.

LITTLE FOLLIES:
Blackboards, chalk.

APRIL FOOL:
Geography, history.

LITTLE FOLLIES:
Silence, talk.

APRIL FOOL:
Till someone learns, till eternity,
Forever a teacher you shall be.

LITTLE FOLLIES: Forever a teacher you shall be. (APRIL
FOOL *and* LITTLE FOLLIES *exit walking backward, point-*

ing their fingers at TERRY *as they go off. Then* MR. AR-
DEN, MR. HOGAN, MISS BLYTHE, MISS GARVEY, MR.
RULE *enter. A bell rings as they take their seats.*)

TERRY: What do I do now? Umm. Good morning, boys
and girls.

ALL: Good morning, Mr. Terence.

TERRY: Whew! So far so good. This will be a cinch. Class,
this morning we will learn some arithmetic.

MISS GARVEY (*Waving her hand*): Teacher! Teacher! I
have something for you!

TERRY: You shouldn't interrupt me.

MISS GARVEY: But it's very important.

TERRY: Oh, all right. (*She flounces up to the desk with a
large red apple.*) Say, you look like Miss Garvey, my
cafeteria supervisor. No! You couldn't be.

MISS GARVEY: I have a big red apple for you.

TERRY: Well, thank you, but I think you could have waited
until after class. (*He starts to take a bite, then yelps as
he pretends to see a worm on the apple.*) Ugh! There's
a dirty old worm on this apple! You should be more
careful!

MISS GARVEY (*Snatching the apple away*): Of course there's
a worm on my apple. That's Winifred. She's *my* worm.
You almost bit my cute little worm. She's not dirty, are
you, Winifred, dear? I'll bet she's cleaner than you are.
There! She's going back into her little hole. You hurt
her feelings. (*She flounces back to her seat.*) Shame on
you!

TERRY: Oh, please. Let's get back to our lesson. Wait a
second. I know something even quicker than arithmetic.
I'll teach you boys some summer sports.

MR. HOGAN (*Waving his hand*): Would you repeat that,
Mr. Terence?

TERRY: You have to listen! Say, you look familiar, too.
You look like Mr. Hogan, my gym teacher. Isn't that

strange. (*He scratches his head.*) All right, I'll repeat it just once more. I'm going to teach you boys some summer sports.

MR. HOGAN: Yippee! Somersaults! Come on, fellows, the teacher says we should all do somersaults! (MR. HOGAN, MR. ARDEN, *and* MR. RULE *turn somersaults on stage, with* MISS GARVEY *and* MISS BLYTHE *clapping and cheering.* TERRY *runs back and forth trying to stop them. At length he grabs* MR. HOGAN's *whistle and blows it; they resume seats reluctantly.*)

TERRY (*Mopping his forehead*): Whew! This is tougher than I thought it would be. Never mind the sports. (*Looks at* MISS BLYTHE) Say, you look like Miss Blythe, my music teacher. That's it! I'll try music. (*Brightening*) How about learning *Jingle Bells?*

MISS BLYTHE (*Groaning*): I just hate *Jingle Bells.*

TERRY: Now look here, you have to obey the teacher. I said *Jingle Bells,* and *Jingle Bells* it's going to be! Ready, everybody? The first line goes: "Dashing through the snow—" Now you sing after me— "Dashing through the snow—"

MISS BLYTHE (*Blowing pitch pipe*): Dashing through the rain—

TERRY: No! "Dashing through the snow." It doesn't make sense to sing "Dashing through the rain."

MISS BLYTHE: But I thought we should try to be original.

TERRY: You can't be original with somebody else's song.

MISS BLYTHE: Why not?

TERRY: Because . . . because I said so. Now, let's begin again.

"Dashing through the snow,
In a one-horse open sleigh,
O'er the fields we go,
Laughing all the way—"

MISS BLYTHE (*Blowing pitch pipe*):
Dashing through the rain,
In a one-jet open plane
Through the clouds we fly,
Crying in the sky— (*Students applaud loudly.*)

TERRY: Oh, what did I ever do to deserve a class like you! Why, when I was a student, I always paid strict attention. I always—I always— (*He stops, shamefaced.*) Well, let's go back to arithmetic. (*The students groan.*) That will be enough of that, class! Now look at this simple problem and pay attention. (*He writes "1 plus 1 equals 2" on blackboard.*) One plus one equals two. Does everyone understand that?

MISS GARVEY: One what, teacher?

TERRY: What do you mean, one what? One anything.

MISS GARVEY: But, teacher, one dozen eggs and one dozen eggs doesn't make two eggs. It makes twenty-four eggs.

TERRY: One plus one equals twenty-four? I never heard anything so silly. (*He thinks a moment.*) But . . . but that's right.

MR. RULE: No, it isn't. The way I figure it out, one package of gum and one package of gum equals ten sticks of gum.

TERRY: One plus one equals ten. But it can't!

MR. ARDEN: Of course it can't. Everybody knows that if you take one twelve-hour period and add one twelve-hour period, you get one day.

TERRY: One plus one equals one! That's impossible.

MISS BLYTHE: It certainly is impossible. The way I heard the problem, you take one quarter note and add another quarter note; together these make one half note.

TERRY: No, it can't be! One plus one equals one half? That's five different arithmetics. I'm getting so confused I can't even think straight.

MR. RULE: Hooray! The teacher can't think straight. Let's have an airplane race. (*He takes five large paper planes from inside his desk and gives them to the others.* TERRY *dashes to* MR. RULE's *desk.*)
TERRY: Give me those airplanes. (MR. RULE *hides his behind his back.*) Why—you're the living image of my school principal, Mr. Rule. But Mr. Rule wouldn't sail paper airplanes. (*Looks at* MR. ARDEN) And you look like my teacher, Mr. Arden! What's going on here?
MR. RULE (*In a singsong voice*): Teacher can't teach!
ALL: Teacher can't teach. (*They all aim their planes at* TERRY, *who looks from side to side frantically.*)
TERRY: April Fool! April Fool! Please come back, April Fool. I need your help. These students won't pay attention. They won't learn. I'll be in these shoes for the rest of my life! (*He breaks down, and sits on floor, sobbing, then rises with a sudden inspiration.*) Wait a minute! You said that if I taught one child one single fact, the spell would be broken. Well, I'm a child, and as a teacher, I taught myself something. I taught myself a real fact: a child can't learn anything unless he pays attention to his teacher. (*The lights flash on and off. The music begins. The students leave the stage.* APRIL FOOL *and* LITTLE FOLLIES *re-enter and remove the blackboard, chalk, desks and chairs.* TERRY *changes back to his own shoes during one of the blackouts. When lights stop flashing,* TERRY *is all alone, sitting at table asleep.* GRANDMA *enters, wearing her spectacles.*)
GRANDMA: The queerest thing just happened, Terry. I looked high and low and in between for my spectacles, but I couldn't find them anywhere. Do you know where I finally located them? Right on top of my forgetful old noggin. Now, isn't that a good April Fool joke on me, Terry? Why, bless me. The boy's fast asleep.
TERRY (*Waking, rubbing his eyes*): I'm home! I'm really

home! Oh, Granny, Granny, I'm so glad to see you.

GRANDMA: You must have had a bad dream.

TERRY: I sure did. I dreamed I had to teach a whole class of students who were just like me.

GRANDMA: My, my. That must have been a real nightmare.

TERRY: Say—those apologies. I'll start to work on them. Now let's see. (*Starts to write*) Dear Miss Garvey, I am very sorry that I misbehaved in the cafeteria. Somehow, I think I know just how you felt when you tasted that salt in your coffee. . . . You can bet your boots I won't do it again. (GRANDMA *smiles and pats* TERRY *on the shoulder.* APRIL FOOL *and the* LITTLE FOLLIES, *putting fingers to lips, enter on tiptoe in time to the music, slip silently over the apron and dance up the center aisle as the curtains close.*)

THE END

Trouble in Tree-Land

Characters

FOREST RANGER
THREE BIRCH TREES
THREE PINE TREES
THREE MAPLE TREES
PROFESSOR OAK

ARTIE
WILLY, *his younger brother*
LUCY
SEEDLING CHILD

BEFORE RISE: FOREST RANGER *enters, holding a seedling wrapped in burlap.*

RANGER (*To audience*): Hi, there. I'm a forest ranger, and I take care of a mighty forest preserve here. You know, an ancient people called the Druids once thought that spirits lived inside of trees. Now, I've tended trees and studied them for many years, and sometimes I have a feeling that those ancient folks were right. (*Gesturing*) Come along. I'll show you. (*He sets down seedling at right as the curtain rises.*)

*　　*　　*

TIME: *Arbor Day.*
SETTING: *A forest grove.*
AT RISE: *The "trees" are grouped upstage, with* PINES *at right,* BIRCHES *at center, and* MAPLES *at left;* PROFESSOR OAK *stands down left. The* RANGER *crosses to center.*

RANGER: Here we are in my favorite grove. (*Pointing out each group as he names it*) Pines . . . birches . . . maples . . . and my wise old oak over here. These trees have real personalities for me. For instance, these sturdy pines: Strong against wind and snow, always green, they are the sentries of the forest. The maples, on the other hand, remind me of pioneer homesteaders, putting down deep roots and settling over the land, giving comfort and shade to all kinds of creatures. But the birches, now, are different. Delicate and slender, they look like young ladies in graduation dresses. (*He crosses to* OAK.) Down here is my favorite tree—the oak. He towers above the others. I like to think of him as a thoughtful old philosopher of the forest. (*Confiding*) I call him "Professor Oak." (*He crosses to right and picks up seedling.*) Well now, I'd better find a spade and plant this young fellow before the sun goes down. (*He exits right.*)

OAK (*Clearing his throat*): Ahem! Fellow dwellers in Tree-Land. . . .

1ST BIRCH: Listen, trees, Professor Oak is about to make his Arbor Day speech.

TREES (*Clapping*): Speech! Speech!

OAK: On this great woodland occasion, I should like to take the opportunity of giving you a lecture on nature.

PINES: Hear! Hear!

1ST MAPLE: Professor Oak, tell us about those funny-looking animals. You know—people.

OAK: Wait! I shall do better than merely talk about people. I shall introduce you to some. I feel a tingling about my roots which means that some real people are coming this way.

TREES (*Ad lib*): Real people! How exciting! (*Etc.*)

OAK: Sh-h! Stop whispering now, so the people won't be frightened by your rustling. They are very nervous creatures. As they walk through the grove, I will explain some of their more interesting features. (ARTIE, WILLY *and* LUCY *enter up left, carrying toy axe, camping equipment and picnic baskets. The trees hold their positions.*)

ARTIE (*Walking to center*): Hey, Willy . . . Lucy, bring the picnic things here. I've found a nice clear spot in this grove. Lucy, you put the picnic out, and, Willy, you help me gather some sticks for firewood.

WILLY: Aw, Artie, some big brother you are. I don't want any of that old broken stuff on the ground. I want to use my new axe. I'm going to get myself a whole tree.

ARTIE: Oh, all right. Go chop a tree. But chop softly. We don't want a ranger snooping around. After all, we aren't even supposed to build a fire in this part of the woods. (ARTIE *goes left and gathers sticks.*)

LUCY (*Putting picnic things out carelessly*): Those old rangers are such spoilsports. Always telling you to pick up this and pick up that. Who sees the litter in the middle of the woods anyhow? The dumb old trees don't have any eyes.

2ND BIRCH: Yoo-hoo, Professor Oak. What are the people doing?

OAK: I'm not sure, Miss Birch, but I don't like the looks of it. (*He leans in and cups his ear to hear better.*)

WILLY: O.K., you trees. Ready or not, here I come. I'm a big logger, and I'm going to cut you down in one stroke. (*He lifts his axe to one of the* PINES.) Timber-r-r-r!

PINES (*Drawing back in fright*): Professor Oak!

OAK: Quickly, Pines—he's about to attack you. Let him feel your sharp needles, or he will cut you to kindling! (PINES *bend branches, brushing their needles against* WILLY.)

WILLY (*Backing away*): Ouch! Those needles are sharp! Who wants an ugly pine anyhow? I'll get a maple or a birch. (*He lifts axe and threatens* MAPLES.)

OAK: Maples! Keep him away with your roots. (MAPLES

extend their roots. WILLY *stumbles, looks bewildered, then heads for* BIRCHES, *who scream and huddle together.*) Birches, sweep him away with your long branches! (BIRCHES *shriek and push* WILLY *away with their branches.* WILLY *goes to* ARTIE.)

WILLY: Artie! Artie! This place is haunted. I can't get near those trees.

ARTIE: Sh-h! Pipe down. Do you want a ranger breathing down our necks? Come on, we can use these sticks (*Picks some up*), and let's get the fire started. I'm starving.

WILLY (*Picking up rest of sticks*): Where shall we put them?

ARTIE (*Leading the way*): Pile them over here on the pine needles. You watch your big brother, Willy. I'm even smarter than a Boy Scout. I can make the biggest bonfire you ever saw. Now, where are the matches? (*Searches his pockets*) Oh, here they are. (*Takes out box of matches*)

OAK: Matches? Fire? Oh, no! We must stop him. Calling all trees! Emergency! Fire!

TREES (*Together*): Fire! Fire! (*They sway back and forth in agitation.*)

OAK: Come, come. We must be calm. Perhaps we can save ourselves from that pumpkin head. When he lights that little stick, each of you rustle your leaves. The flame may go out. (ARTIE *pretends to strike match, and the trees wave their arms as if to blow it out.*)

ARTIE: Hey, the match won't light. I'll try another one. (WILLY *and* LUCY *join him as he pretends to strike another. The trees rustle, and match does not light. Trees scowl and take a step forward.*)

LUCY (*Glancing around, shivering*): Artie, I'm scared.

TREES (*Folding arms forbiddingly and chanting as they step forward again*): People, go home. . . . People, go home. . . . People, go home. . . .

WILLY: Artie, l-l-look. The trees seem to be getting closer. Let's go home!

ARTIE (*Nervously*): You're right. It *is* getting kind of gloomy here. Let's pack up and go. (*They pick up equipment speedily, as trees continue to chant.* LUCY *leaves paper cups, napkins, etc., on the ground.* ARTIE *notices them.*) Hey, Lucy, you left some stuff on the ground.

LUCY: So what? Somebody else will pick it up. I want to get out of here. (*They start to leave.*)

3RD BIRCH (*Horrified*): Professor Oak! Is she going to leave that rubbish in our grove?

1ST PINE: It looks disgusting.

2ND MAPLE: How would she like it if a maple tree dropped leaves on her parlor rug?

OAK (*Angrily*): It takes a lot to make a mighty oak angry. But this does it! Trees may seem helpless to most people, but we have ways of protecting ourselves. I'll make them leave in a hurry. I'll throw an acorn at that girl. (*He pantomimes throwing an acorn at* LUCY.)

LUCY: Artie, that tree threw an acorn at me.

ARTIE: Don't be silly, Lucy. Trees don't throw acorns. (OAK *pantomimes throwing acorn at* ARTIE, *then at* WILLY.) Ow! What *is* this?

WILLY (*Trying to hide behind* ARTIE): Don't let him hit me, Artie! Ow!

ARTIE: It's a barrage! Come on. Let's get out of this place. (LUCY *and* WILLY *exit hurriedly, trying to avoid acorns and yelling "Ouch!" as* OAK *turns and continues to pelt them.* ARTIE *pauses downstage, turns to trees and makes a fist.*) If I had my way, I'd make you all into pencils! Just wait until the Park Department hears about you! (*Exits*)

OAK: Whew! Well, so much for them.

2ND BIRCH (*Holding up her hands, shaking*): Look at me.

Every last leaf is shaking. I'm nervous clear down to my taproot.

3RD MAPLE: Make pencils of us, indeed. And after all the maple syrup I've given to those ungrateful people.

2ND PINE: Do they all behave like that? If I had my way, no human being would ever set foot in this forest again.

TREES (*Ad lib*): Hear, hear! Fine idea! Yes, indeed! (*Etc.*)

OAK: Now, now, everybody settle down. I'll admit those were most unattractive specimens of humanity, but people are not all like that. There are humans who really care about trees.

3RD PINE (*Sniffing*): I find that hard to believe. (RANGER *enters, carrying spade and seedling.*)

OAK (*To trees*): How about our ranger?

RANGER (*Kneeling to examine pile of wood left by picnickers*): What's this? Hmm . . . I think somebody was about to start a fire. Why, he could have burned down my favorite grove . . . maybe a whole forest. I'd like to get my hands on him. I'd teach him a thing or two!

OAK: See, our ranger is angry at those other people. Wait till he notices the trash.

RANGER: And look at this—old paper cups, napkins, garbage thrown around any old place. (*He picks up trash.*) It's a good thing those careless people left before I arrived on the scene.

1ST BIRCH: Oh, thank goodness. He's picking it all up.

OAK: He does many splendid things for us. He keeps away fire, and sprays us for insects, and keeps out people with axes and saws. And best of all, look what he brings us: company!

3RD PINE: What is it? (RANGER *pantomimes digging hole down left, by the* OAK. *He sets the seedling in place.*)

3RD MAPLE: It is certainly very tiny.

3RD BIRCH: He made a hole for it, so it must have roots like us.

RANGER (*Standing back to look at seedling and addressing trees*): There you are, ladies and gentlemen. An Arbor Day present for you. Now the oak won't be alone any more. (*Pauses*) I wonder what kind of spirit you'll have, little oak seedling. (SEEDLING CHILD *enters, carrying rattle and stands beside real seedling, rubbing his eyes.*)

SEEDLING: Have I been planted yet? Where am I? (*Looking around*) Oh, how tall you all are.

1ST BIRCH: How adorable! It's a tiny new tree.

1ST PINE: Howdy, young fellow. You have just been planted in the finest grove in the forest.

2ND PINE: If we do say so ourselves!

OAK: Why, bless my acorns, you are an oak, like me!

RANGER: There you are, friends. Now, I must go back to the station and plant a thousand more just like him, all over the slopes of this preserve. (*He starts to exit right.*)

TREES (*Applauding him*): Cheers for the ranger! Happy Arbor Day!

RANGER (*To the audience*): Isn't that strange? I could have sworn I heard those trees say "Happy Arbor Day." I guess I've been in the woods too long. (*He shakes his head while trees lift arms and freeze in position as curtain falls.*)

THE END

All About Mothers

Characters

THREE NARRATORS, *boys*
FASHION COMMENTATOR
CAVE MOTHER
ROMAN MOTHER
ORIENTAL MOTHER
VICTORIAN MOTHER
VANESSA, *her daughter*

RECEPTIONIST
JUDGE
HANDY-LADY
HOSTESS
MOTHER OF THE FUTURE
CHORUS
TWO BOYS

TIME: *Mother's Day.*
SETTING: *Three chairs are at right. A small table is at one side of stage.*
AT RISE: *The* THREE NARRATORS *are sitting at right. Each rises when he speaks.*

1ST NARRATOR: Good afternoon, one and all. Today we are going to present a special kind of fashion show.

2ND NARRATOR: As you all know, there are fashions in hats and gowns, and houses and towns.

3RD NARRATOR: But did you know there are fashions in mothers, too?

1ST NARRATOR: And here is our Fashion Commentator to tell us all about it. (FASHION COMMENTATOR *enters left.*)

COMMENTATOR: Welcome to our Fashion Show of Mothers. We are going to show you a large variety of stylish

315

mothers from past ages to the present—and perhaps even beyond. Now, our first model will show us a real period piece—the earliest mother we know of—the Cave Mother. (CAVE MOTHER *enters, like a model, carrying baby in cradle made of twigs, which she sets down at center. Baby is dressed in leopard skin.*) Our Cave Mother sports a genuine hand-sewn leopard skin, carries a large knotty pine club, and wears matching mammoth bone in her hair.

1ST NARRATOR: Let us listen to the Cave Mother as she sings us an authentic lullaby from bygone days.

CAVE MOTHER (*Picking up baby and singing to tune of "Hush Little Baby"*):
Hush Stone Age baby, and don't you roar,
Mama's gonna catch you a dinosaur.
If that dinosaur's too fat,
Mama's gonna trap you a saber-toothed cat.
If that saber-toothed cat won't pounce,
Mama's gonna chisel you a rock to bounce.
That big rock will make you brave—
You'll be the best one in our cave!
(*She exits left with baby.*)

COMMENTATOR: And now we move on to later times. Our next model is truly elegant. (ROMAN MOTHER *enters left, carrying string shopping bag.*) Here is a Roman Mother, all done up in a fleecy white toga with sandals in natural leather. She carries a string shopping bag as she is on her way to the market place.

2ND NARRATOR: Tell us, madam, what are you shopping for?

ROMAN MOTHER: *Mater, Pater, filius et filia.*

3RD NARRATOR: I will translate. She said she is shopping for Mother, Father, and the son and daughter in her family.

2ND NARRATOR: And when you finish shopping in the market place, where else will you go?

ROMAN MOTHER: *Ad cup-ium coffee-ium in Forum!*

2ND NARRATOR: How about that? Even in ancient Rome, mothers had to have a cup of coffee, before they could start the day! (ROMAN MOTHER *exits right.*)

COMMENTATOR: Let us move on now to other times and other places. Here in the remote city of Sing-Song in the oriental country of Outer Ingolia, we find an Oriental Mother. (ORIENTAL MOTHER *enters with mincing steps, from right. She carries a fan and a crystal ball and pauses at center, gazing into ball.*)

1ST NARRATOR: Tell us, Madame Lotus Blossom, what are you doing?

ORIENTAL MOTHER: I am only doing my humble duty, O gracious narrator.

1ST NARRATOR: And what is your humble duty, please?

ORIENTAL MOTHER: Ah, so. (*Bowing*) I am doing what mothers in all times and places do for their children . . . I am baking cookies.

1ST NARRATOR: Baking *cookies?* But why are you gazing into a crystal ball? Why aren't you sifting flour and beating eggs?

ORIENTAL MOTHER (*Bowing again*): Ah, so. I am baking *fortune* cookies, honorable narrator! (*She fans herself rapidly and minces off left.*)

COMMENTATOR: On to modern times. A hundred years ago, mothers wore great billowy skirts, and sewed miles and miles of embroidery. It was the fashion to be very delicate and ladylike and to faint away at the drop of a hat. (VICTORIAN MOTHER *and* VANESSA *enter right.*)

2ND NARRATOR: Let us drop a hat and watch now, as a mother instructs her daughter in the fine art of swooning.

VICTORIAN MOTHER: Come, Vanessa, it is very important for you to learn how to swoon gracefully. Everybody swoons these days, so you might as well learn to do it correctly.

VANESSA (*Curtsying*): Yes, Mama.

VICTORIAN MOTHER: First you must make it clear that you feel faint. All the gentlemen in the room will rush to you, and you will be the center of attention. Won't that be fun? Now—announce your swoon.

VANESSA (*Sticking out her tongue, and waving her arms*): Aaaaak!

VICTORIAN MOTHER: No, no, no. You sound like a foghorn. You must flutter . . . flutter . . . flutter. (*She demonstrates.*) Oh—oh, dear. (*She sighs delicately.*) I feel so giddy. (*To* VANESSA) Now—you try it.

VANESSA (*Awkwardly*): Oh. Oh. Oh. I feel so giddy. (*She flops to the floor.*)

VICTORIAN MOTHER: Dear me, that is *not* a proper swoon at all. (*Helping* VANESSA *up*) Relax, Vanessa. You must look like a dying swan, not a dead duck. I will show you once more. (*Demonstrating*) Wrists leading . . . sink down . . . flutter your eyelids . . . and pass—right— out. (*She sinks down on floor.*)

VANESSA: Mama? (*Bending over her and fanning her with her hand*) Mama? Good heavens to Hepzibah! She really has fainted! Aaaak! (*She flops down on floor.* Two BOYS *run on and help take* VANESSA *and* VICTORIAN MOTHER *off right.*)

COMMENTATOR: We may all be very grateful that this kind of mother went out of fashion quickly. Can you imagine a modern mother swooning in the A & P, or in the middle of an expressway? This brings us to our modern mothers. Here is our verse choir bringing us up-to-date on mothers. (CHORUS, RECEPTIONIST *wearing headphones,* JUDGE *carrying gavel,* HANDY-LADY *carrying wrench,* HOSTESS *carrying lorgnette enter. All stand at center.*)

1ST NARRATOR: The modern mother! Really, there is no one like her.

2ND NARRATOR: Truly, she is not just one woman.

3RD NARRATOR: She is many women all rolled up into one.

CHORUS: Calling all mothers— Calling all mothers—

RECEPTIONIST (*Stepping forward and speaking into headphone set*): Good morning, a friendly mother speaking. This is your seven o'clock call, children. Up, John. Up, Mary. John, you have following appointments: after school, the dentist; then chores at home; then homework. Hello, Mary? I have an incoming call for you. Hello, dry cleaner? Will you deliver that suit now, please? Hello, will you switch that call to John, please? Hello, yes, I'll bake a dozen cookies for the class before noon. Hello, hello, friendly mother speaking. Hello, I'll connect you. Hold the line, please . . .

CHORUS: Mothers are legal eagles, too. They are the law!

JUDGE (*Going to table and rapping with gavel*): Ahem. The family court is now in session. Judge Maw Law is presiding. Daughter Mary, will you step into the witness box? Do you swear to tell the truth, the whole truth, and nothing but the truth? Now, you state that the accused over there—your lawful awful brother, John, struck you several times for no reason at all? John, how do you plead, guilty or not guilty? Guilty! John is herewith charged with assault and battery. I will now pass sentence. John, you will serve out a term of solitary confinement in your room for not less than one evening. Just a minute, Mary—you don't wiggle out of this so easily. For pestering John, I sentence you to hard labor, right now. Get in that kitchen and peel the potatoes for supper! Court adjourned!

CHORUS:

Can you fix my dolly?

Can you fix my cart?

Put it together,
Take it apart,
Mix it and fix it,
And make the thing start. . . .

HANDY-LADY (*Stepping forward*): I'm a handy-lady. A Mrs. Fixit. Is your faucet on the fritz? Leave it to me. I've put in more washers than you can shake a plumber at. Are your shingles loose? I'm your second-story woman. Leave it to me.

CHORUS: You can always leave it to a mother. But in the blink of an eye, she must change from blue denim to blue satin . . .

HOSTESS (*Stepping forward and speaking in cultured tones as she looks through lorgnette*): Good evening, dear children, and welcome to Mary's little birthday party. How are you, Sue and Lou and Ida Pru? Do come in, Cindy and Mindy and Wendy and Lindy. Take off your hats, Jean and Joan, and Jane and June. Did I forget anybody? Hm-m-m? Oh, dear. My own daughter. Happy birthday—um—um—oh, yes. Mary!

CHORUS:
Mothers are the busiest,
North or east or west,
Mothers are the whiz-i-est,
Mothers are the best.

NARRATORS:
Mothers zip you up, up, up,
And help you button down,
They buy you hats for Easter,
And patent shoes for town.

CHORUS:
They barber hair and bandage knees,
And cheer you when you're blue—

1ST SOLO:
But most of all, *they love you*—

CHORUS:

That's the best thing that they do.

COMMENTATOR: And so you see, in spite of changes in styles, we think that mothers will always be in fashion. They will go on forever. And, now, to finish our fashion show, we present the Mother of the Future. (MOTHER OF THE FUTURE *enters, holding baby in cradle shaped like rocket ship. Baby wears space helmet.*)

MOTHER OF THE FUTURE (*Singing to tune of "Rock-a-bye Baby"*):

Rocket by, baby,

On top of the stars,

Mommy will take you

To Venus and Mars.

When we're in orbit,

Far planets will call,

And off will zoom baby,

In a free fall.

(*She exits right.*)

2ND SOLO: What are mothers? (*All* MOTHERS *enter.*)

CHORUS:

They are watchers, they are listeners;

Mum's the word—for they can hide

All your secrets snug away,

And keep them safe inside.

3RD SOLO: What are mothers?

CHORUS:

They are workers, they are helpers,

They care when you're sick or sad.

They can wash and bake and sew,

They can keep you well and glad.

4TH SOLO: But what's the best thing that they do?

CHORUS (*Slowly*): They—love—you! (*All* MOTHERS *bow as curtain falls.*)

THE END

Operation Litterbug

Characters

DUDLEY D. DOO-BAD
PIGGY PETE PAPERSCRAPS
SADIE SCRAWL ⎱ *The Litterbugs*
ICKY EGBERT EMPTYBOTTLE
BAD BART BANANA-PEEL

GENERAL CLEANPARKS
LT. PAUL PICKUP
SGT. TOM TIDY ⎱ *The Orderly Army*
CPL. CLEM CLEANSER
AGENT SALLY SPOTLESS

SCENE 1

SETTING: *City Park. There are two trees, left and right. A ladder is against tree right. A brick wall, on which are cutout letters reading "City Park," stands between the trees. At right is a broken desk with sign "Department of Park Uglification" in uneven letters across front. In a wastebasket next to desk are signs on sticks.*

AT RISE: DUDLEY D. DOO-BAD *is speaking into a telephone made of two tin cans and a piece of string.*

DUDLEY: Department of Park Uglification, Dudley D. Doo-Bad, villain in charge, speaking . . . Give me Dirty

Dick, please. (*As he waits, he sails a paper airplane onto the park grounds.*) Hello, Dirty Dick? Did you get that load of choice garbage? (*Pause*) Good! (*Gleefully*) Three hundred pounds of old orange peels, apple scraps, and prune pits! This is what I want you to do with it. The Park here is having a celebration. The Mayor is going to make a speech about Keeping Our Parks Clean. Come and dump the garbage on the lawn in front of the speakers' stand. We want things one hundred per cent loathsome. (*Pause*) Now, to help things along, I want you to connect me with the Department of Dilapidation. . . . (*As he waits, he tears up a newspaper and tosses it over the apron of the stage. As he does this,* SALLY SPOTLESS *creeps in, climbs ladder and takes position in tree right. She has a pair of binoculars which she trains on the scene, and a notebook in which she writes things from time to time.*) Department of Dilapidation? Send me my Litterbugs on the double. We're going to make this Park the most unsightly in the district. (*As he puts down telephone,* LITTERBUGS *straggle in. As they come in,* PIGGY PETE, *who is leading the line, stops suddenly and they all bump into him.*) Ah, my trusty henchmen. Give the salute! (*With much shoving, they line up in a scraggly fashion and salute by holding their noses.*)

LITTERBUGS (*Speaking in unison*):
Scum for one
And scum for all.
The more—the messier!

DUDLEY: Now, down to work. Have you all done your bad deed for the day? Remember—the worst deed gets the famous Muddle of Honor. Let's hear from you, Piggy Pete.

PIGGY PETE: I did something terrible, chief. I emptied a wastebasket full of sticky ice cream cups on a sandbox full of nice, clean kiddies. (*All laugh and applaud.*)

DUDLEY: Not bad enough. How about you, Sadie Scrawl?

SADIE SCRAWL: I was horrible, chief. I put a big chalk mustache on that fresh, new picture of our Mayor. (*She goes into a fit of giggles and is slapped on the back by* BAD BART.)

DUDLEY: Not bad enough. You now, Icky Egbert Empty-bottle.

ICKY EGBERT: Aw, shucks. (*Shyly*) All I did was dump fifty bottles of ketchup in that beautiful fish pond. Now the fishermen will be catching their trout with ketchup already on them. (*All nod and clap hands.*)

DUDLEY: Not bad enough. You have one more chance, Litterbugs. It's up to you, Bad Bart Banana-Peel.

BAD BART (*Bragging*): Listen, none of you has come near my miserable deed. You know that cinder track where the boys have races in the schoolyard? (*All nod.*) I spread slimy, slippery banana peels all over it. And when the boys came out to race—you should have seen them. They fell down like ducks in a shooting gallery. You know who won that race? (*Boastfully*) Me. Big Bad Bart Banana-Peel!

DUDLEY: How splendidly horrible! This is what I like to hear about. Bad deeds with imagination. I hereby award you the Muddle of Honor! (*A brief fanfare is heard.* DUDLEY *takes the medal out of an old cigar box.*) Bad Bart Banana-Peel, this medal made from a genuine tomato can and the ribbon won by the prize pig at the county fair entitles you to be the Litterbug of the Month. (*Pins it on*)

SADIE SCRAWL: Three cheers!

ALL: Hip, hip, booo! Hip, hip, booo! Hip, hip, booo!

DUDLEY: Let's get down to business now. The Mayor is coming today to make a speech about keeping the parks clean. That means an all-out attack on *us*.

ALL (*Shuddering*): No! No!

DUDLEY: However, I have a special strategy. We'll ambush the Park. We'll make such a mussy, slummy, slovenly, sloppy, shambles of this Park that the Mayor won't dare show his face. After all, who is really in charge of this Park?

ALL: We are!

DUDLEY: Correct! Is the Park to be kempt or unkempt, my crumby crew?

ALL: Unkempt!

DUDLEY: Correct! Tidy or trashy, my filthy four?

ALL: Trashy!

DUDLEY: Correct! What is our cheer, my scummy chums? (*All take signs from wastebasket, march around.*)

ALL:

With an M
With an E
With a big double S
M-E-S-S—MESS!

Boooooo—Litterbugs! (*They slink off as* SALLY SPOTLESS *climbs down from tree.* LITTERBUGS *exit right.* SALLY *exits left, as the curtain falls.*)

* * *

SCENE 2

BEFORE RISE: *The* ORDERLY ARMY *enters from left, in front of curtain, led by* GENERAL CLEANPARKS, *and steps smartly to center. This* ARMY, *clad in white, is composed of* LT. PAUL PICKUP, *carrying a mop like a rifle;* SGT. TOM TIDY, *rolling behind him a large wire trash basket on a small wagon, labeled "Tank Corps"; and* CPL. CLEM CLEANSER, *who has a vacuum cleaner, labeled "Heavy Artillery." The* GENERAL *carries a pennant with "Orderly Army" written on it.*

GENERAL: *Squad—halt!* (*They halt and all exchange smart*

salutes. SALLY SPOTLESS *enters, out of breath, from left. She comes to a halt and salutes.*)

SALLY SPOTLESS: General Cleanparks! General Cleanparks! Agent Spotless of the Intelligence Corps reporting, sir. I have important news, sir! The Litterbugs under the command of Dudley D. Doo-Bad are in Sector C-five-zero-zero of City Park.

GENERAL: Great soaring scrub brushes! That's where the Mayor is today! Good work, Agent Spotless. We have no time to lose. We'll deploy our forces this way. Ladies first! Private Spotless—

SALLY SPOTLESS: Here, sir!

GENERAL: Your task is to wipe out Sadie Scrawl.

SALLY SPOTLESS: I'll erase her completely, sir! (*She takes a blanket from behind the basket.*)

GENERAL: Corporal Clem Cleanser—

CLEM CLEANSER (*Saluting*): Present and accounted for, sir.

GENERAL: Bear down on Piggy Pete with the heavy artillery.

CLEM CLEANSER: Right, sir!

GENERAL: Sergeant Tom Tidy—

TOM TIDY: I hear and obey, sir.

GENERAL: Get Icky Egbert and Bad Bart Banana-Peel and mow them down with that tank.

TOM TIDY: I will, sir.

GENERAL: Lieutenant Paul Pickup—

PAUL PICKUP: At your service, sir.

GENERAL: You must get the archvillain himself—Dudley D. Doo-Bad. Take him prisoner, and if he resists—mop him up!

PAUL PICKUP: It will be a pleasure, sir!

GENERAL: All right, squad. Begin the countdown! (*Everyone gets on hands and knees and begins countdown* with *"ten," loudly but with diminishing volume until they reach one, in a whisper. The curtain opens slowly.*)

*   *   *

SETTING: *The same as Scene 1.*

AT RISE: DUDLEY D. DOO-BAD *and the* LITTERBUGS *are in a tableau.* SADIE SCRAWL *has arm upraised at back wall, ready to write on it with chalk.* PIGGY PETE *holds scraps of paper, ready to scatter them by the tree.* BAD BART *has put a banana peel on each step of the ladder.* ICKY EGBERT *is up left, bent over, just putting bottle on ground, while* DUDLEY D. DOO-BAD *is at center, overseeing the job. As the* ORDERLY ARMY *comes to zero in the countdown, they jump up and shout.*

ORDERLY ARMY: Zero! (SALLY *races to back wall, flinging blanket over* SADIE SCRAWL, *who collapses on floor;* CLEM CLEANSER *gallops left with the vacuum cleaner.* CLEM *catches* PIGGY PETE'S *shirt in the suction tube.* PIGGY PETE *surrenders with hands in the air;* TOM TIDY *chases* BAD BART *with the tank. While* BAD BART *cowers on hands and knees,* TOM TIDY *wrestles with* ICKY EGBERT *and subdues him.* PAUL PICKUP, *brandishing the mop, chases* DUDLEY D. DOO-BAD *about the stage, finally flourishing mop in his face as* DUDLEY *goes on knees imploring.*)

DUDLEY: Spare me! Don't rub me out! We surrender! (LITTERBUGS, *with arms upraised, are marched to center. They turn and march toward left singing to tune of "The Volga Boatman.")*

LITTERBUGS:

We surrender!
We surrender!
Don't be mean,
We'll come clean

We surrender! (TOM TIDY *marches them offstage.*)

ORDERLY ARMY: Hooray! (TOM TIDY *returns and the* ORDERLY ARMY *lines up at center, marching in place, singing to tune of "Little Brown Jug."*)

We are the army of orderliness,

We march on dirt; we march on mess,

We scoop up scraps, we scrape up spots,

We swab and sponge and brush up blots. (SALLY SPOTLESS *runs offstage and brings in a large poster with picture of* GENERAL CLEANPARKS *pointing finger at audience. Sign says "The Orderly Army Needs You. Join Today."*)

Ha! Ha! Ha! Orderly,

Tidy, trim and spruce are we!

Ha! Ha! Ha! Join today.

Keep clean the Orderly Army way! (*All salute.* SALLY SPOTLESS *runs downstage, looks at the audience through her binoculars, first right, then left.*)

SALLY SPOTLESS: And if there are any litterbugs in this audience—look out! We'll get you, too! (*Curtain*)

THE END

The Franklin Reversal

Characters

MITEY FRANKLIN
CAL FRANKLIN
MAUD MARY FRANKLIN
MRS. FRANKLIN
MR. FRANKLIN
FOUR CHILDREN

BEFORE RISE: CAL *and* MITEY FRANKLIN *enter in front of the curtain and bow.*

MITEY (*To audience*): Mr. Mayor, Councilmen, gentlemen from the Pentagon and television networks—
CAL: Fellow citizens of Miller's Falls, we know that you are very upset about those weird happenings at our house—
MITEY: We know some pretty awful rumors are floating around about the Franklin family—
CAL: That's us—the Franklin twins.
MITEY: Our father is Cavendish Franklin, a direct descendant of Benjamin Franklin. He's a research scientist, and such a bug on science he even named us for his two favorite academic institutions—

CAL: I'm California Institute of Technology. They call me Cal for short—

MITEY: And I'm Massachusetts Institute of Technology. That's Mitey for short.

CAL: We really do want to set the record straight about yesterday. Contrary to popular opinion, we were not fooling around with nuclear fission.

MITEY: Or rockets—

CAL: It was just a little gilhooly I built for Mitey. He made a set of blueprints—

MITEY: Sure. It was just a little experiment in magnetic intensification, and everything seemed perfectly safe and foolproof.

CAL: Aw, come on, Mitey. Nothing is perfectly safe with Maud Mary around. (MAUD MARY *enters, clutching a large doll.*)

MITEY: Right! Maud Mary, in case you don't know it, is our sister.

CAL: When she was born, we all said—

CAL *and* MITEY: Boy! Another Marie Curie! (MAUD MARY *shakes her head.*)

MITEY: Dad kept watching for signs of scientific talent. He was going to name her "Polly" for Polytechnic.

CAL: But Mom put her foot down. So she's just plain old Maud Mary.

MITEY: Maud Mary. (*Sighs*) Does she take apart radios, or put together transistors like the rest of the Franklins? Does she even like arithmetic?

MAUD MARY: I like dolls.

CAL: She likes dolls. Oh, boy. It wouldn't be so bad if she would take them apart to see what makes them tick.

MITEY: There'd be hope for her if she set up an experiment to study the behavior patterns of dolls. But, no, she feeds them and rocks them and puts frilly clothes on them.

CAL: She's all girl.

MAUD MARY: I'm all girl.

MITEY: So what are you going to do?

CAL: You can't buck biology.

MITEY: Anyhow, the day those strange things happened, we had just come home from school.

CAL: Our mother was puttering around in the kitchen. (MAUD MARY *exits.*)

MITEY: And that pesky Maud Mary wasn't due home for another hour. (*The boys exit as the curtains open.*)

* * *

SETTING: *The Franklin living room. Down left, on a small table, is a glittering machine, with mirrors, dials, and a small handle.*

AT RISE: CAL *and* MITEY *enter left.* MITEY *carries school books, and* CAL *carries a large box wrapped as a present. They leave books and present on a chair, and go to the machine, which* MITEY *examines carefully.*

CAL: O.K., Mitey. I built the thing to your specifications. Now explain it. It looks like a kind of souped-up laser. What is the monster, anyhow?

MITEY: That's it—a monster. It's a magnetic oersted negative stimulated emitter of radiation. A live and kicking monster.

CAL: A magnetic laser, huh?

MITEY: Right. Remember my equations about the similarities of light and magnetism? Well, with this little instrument, I can magnify a magnetic field to infinity.

CAL: Wow! To infinity. Nobody has had an infinite field to work with—nobody!

MITEY: We have. (*Pats the machine*) Right here. The thing is, we have to be awfully careful. As the power zooms up, all the ordinary laws of physics will go right out the window. Nobody can even *begin* to predict what will happen. At a certain point the polarity will reverse, and socko!—the twilight zone.

CAL: Holy smoke, I feel like Columbus. How can we protect ourselves though? I mean, we could find ourselves sailing off to Alpha Centauri if we aren't careful.

MITEY: Well, look, we'll run the monster at very low intensity until Dad comes home. Will he be surprised! If this works half as well as I think it will, he'll take it right over to his lab.

CAL: It scares me. Shall I turn it on?

MITEY: Sure, you tooled it down to my scale, didn't you?

CAL: Yes, every time a step is passed it'll make a loud clicking sound.

MITEY: O.K., the first three steps are safe according to my calculations. After the third step—I wouldn't dare say.

CAL (*Setting dials*): One—two—three. (*He pulls up handle and there is a loud click and a humming sound. MRS. FRANKLIN enters right, carrying a small metal watering can.*)

MRS. FRANKLIN: Hello, boys. Home so soon? I just thought I'd water the African violets while I had the chance.

MITEY: Hi, Mom. (MRS. FRANKLIN *starts toward plants on table at right. The watering can seems to turn in her hand. She holds it stiffly at arm's length and seems to be pulled along by it toward the machine.*)

MRS. FRANKLIN: Oh! What in the world! (*She grabs hold of a chair, but the can drags her along to the table, where it slides along the top, and bangs into the machine.*) Stop it! Help!

MITEY: Turn it off, Cal. (CAL *pulls handle down, and MRS. FRANKLIN lets go of the can. The boys mop their foreheads.*) That's terrific magnetic pull! Unbelievable!

MRS. FRANKLIN: Another machine! Oh, Cal, Mitey, how many times have I told you those machines belong in the laboratory or down in the basement—not in my living room. Why, the ugly thing is positively possessed.

MITEY: No, Mom—it's negatively possessed. (MRS. FRANKLIN *fixes him with a stare and* MITEY *gives up.*) O.K., O.K. We'll move it when Dad comes home. It's really harmless, Mom, if you know how to work it.

MRS. FRANKLIN: Now, look, boys. I want you to come down to the basement right now with me and get that big box of party decorations. Maud Mary is having her birthday party this afternoon. I hope you remembered to get her a birthday present—?

CAL: Sure—it's in that box over there. We saw the greatest robot . . .

MITEY: It had a real dish antenna on its head, a fantastic remote control unit, and red searchlight eyes.

MRS. FRANKLIN (*Horrified*): You didn't! You didn't get that *sweet* little girl a robot!

CAL: No, Mom, we didn't. The salesgirl said she didn't think a girl-type-girl like Maud Mary would appreciate a robot.

MITEY: So we got her one of those big baby dolls with a stupid expression. We could still put a dish antenna on its head, though.

MRS. FRANKLIN: You two! You'll turn me gray yet. Come on now. There isn't too much time. (*She takes them by the shoulders and starts to push them off right.*)

CAL: Wait a minute, Mom. I think we ought to disassemble the machine.

MRS. FRANKLIN: No more arguments now. Maud Mary is at her dancing lesson, and she won't be back for an hour. We have to put up a roomful of balloons. Let's go, boys. (*They exit right as* MAUD MARY *enters left. She skips center, singing.*)

MAUD MARY (*Singing*):
Happy birthday to me,

Happy birthday to me,
Happy birthday, dear me-hee,
Happy birthday to me. (*She goes left, then right, calling.*) Hello? Hello? Cal? Mitey? Mama? Anybody? I'm home early. Where is everybody? (*She spots the machine.*) What's that? I know. It's a birthday present. They could have wrapped it, but I don't care. (*She circles it, then stands left, close to the table and pokes the motor gingerly.*) What is it? What does it do? Maybe it's a sewing machine. (*She squints down at it.*) Nope. There isn't any needle. I see a handle. Maybe it's a record player. Oh, goody, goody gumdrops. It is! It's a record player. I'll just pull up this handle. (*She pulls up the handle. The motor clicks slowly three times.*) That's funny. I don't hear any music. Maybe I should pull it up all the way. (*She does so. The machine clicks nine times, hums loudly.* MAUD MARY *backs away, frightened, then begins to turn around and around, arms outstretched. The lights blink on and off.* MAUD MARY *screams.* MRS. FRANKLIN, CAL *and* MITEY *rush in from right, stop in amazement as* MAUD MARY *halts, begins to spin rapidly in the opposite direction. The machine clicks rapidly, then stops, and there is a blackout.* NOTE: *During the blackout, as the dialogue proceeds,* MAUD MARY *lies on her back on the floor, arms outstretched. The wrapped present is removed, and a duplicate box, partially wrapped in the same paper, a large baby doll, cake plate, and pencil flashlight wrapped as a candle are put on stage in its place.*)

MRS. FRANKLIN: Maud Mary! What's happening? Cal—turn on the lights.

CAL: I can't, Mom. I think a fuse blew.

MITEY: She must have turned up the machine. I think she's spinning in an infinite field.

CAL: I knew we shouldn't have left the machine assembled. I knew it! (*The lights come on.*)

MRS. FRANKLIN: The lights. Oh, thank goodness! (*She runs to* MAUD MARY.) Maud Mary! Darling! Are you all right? (CAL *and* MITEY *rush to her, pick her up, one on each side.* MAUD MARY *remains stiff with arms outstretched. Once she is standing, she gives herself a shake, and looks from one to the other.*) Oh, she's all right. Thank heavens.

MAUD MARY: Happened what?

CAL: What did you say?

MAUD MARY: Happened what?

MRS. FRANKLIN: Maud Mary, stop teasing us. She's saying things backward. (MAUD MARY *walks backward to the machine and points at it.*)

MAUD MARY: That's what? Machine bad. Sick me made. Machine bad, bad!

MITEY: Backward. Of course. The polarity reversed, and the flow took Maud Mary with it. And it's still on. Mom—Cal—get out of range. (*He pulls them down right, as* FOUR CHILDREN, *walking backward, enter from left, birthday hats on their heads, each carrying a piece of cake.* MAUD MARY *walks backward, waving to them.*)

MAUD MARY: Bye good.

CHILDREN: Mary Maud, bye good. (*They wave.*)

MRS. FRANKLIN: But—it's the children we invited to the party. Why did they come so soon? And how did they get in? Mitey—Cal—what's going on?

MITEY: This gets more and more weird. I'm not sure what's happening, but I think that everything within range of the monster has been turned around in the fourth dimension.

CAL: Of course. It's like a film strip being run backward. Maud Mary's whole birthday party has been reversed.

(MAUD MARY *turns, puts the doll inside box, and quickly wraps up the birthday gift.*)

MAUD MARY: Present birthday a! Box the in what's?

CAL: Gee whiz, look what the kids are doing— (*The* Four CHILDREN *put their pieces of cake on the plate, so the four slices make a whole cake.* MAUD MARY *then switches on the flashlight candle and sets it in the cake.*)

CHILDREN (*Singing*):
You to birthday happy,
You to birthday happy,
Mary Maud, birthday happy,
You to birthday happy.

(MAUD MARY *takes a deep breath and holds it in puffed cheeks, then walks backward, bearing the cake off right, leaves it offstage and returns.* CHILDREN *walk backward off left again, waving hands in greeting to* MAUD MARY *as they start to exit.*) Mary Maud, hello. Mary Maud, birthday happy.

MAUD MARY: Body every, hello. Hello! (*They exit still waving.* MAUD MARY *holds her position.*)

MRS. FRANKLIN: Boys, I'm frightened. How long will this last?

CAL: I don't know. Maybe Maud Mary will go on unwinding until she's a little baby again.

MRS. FRANKLIN: How awful! Boys, you must do something. Please, Mitey, try to think of something to stop this. (MITEY *stands, scratching his head.*)

CAL: Well, gee, Mom, we're trying. It's just that we have twentieth century minds in a twenty-fifth century situation.

MITEY (*Brightly*): I have it. Stop worrying, everybody. This is a self-limiting reversal. It can't go much further. Watch— (MAUD MARY *walks backward to the machine and points to it.*)

MAUD MARY: That's what? Machine bad. Sick me made. Machine bad, bad.

MRS. FRANKLIN: Why—she said that before!

MITEY: Sure. Keep watching now. She's going backward to the place where she turned on the machine. Cal—get ready to pull out the plug.

CAL: O.K., Mitey.

MAUD MARY: Happened what? (*She shakes herself, then stands, arms outstretched, and plops down on the floor. The lights go out. The clicking starts again. The lights flash, come on again. MAUD MARY stands, spins, stops, spins the other way. Machine clicks slower, nine times. She slowly stops spinning, goes to the motor and pulls the handle half way down.*) That's funny. I don't hear any music. (*Motor clicks three times.*) Oh, boy. I'll just pull up this little handle— (*She pulls the handle, then rubs her eyes in a bewildered fashion.*)

MITEY: Now, Cal!

CAL: Got it! (*Pulls the plug out. CAL, MITEY and MRS. FRANKLIN rush over to MAUD MARY.*)

MRS. FRANKLIN: Maud Mary, are you hurt? How do you feel, dear?

CAL: Wow—what an experience. What was it like going backward, Maud Mary?

MITEY: Did you feel as if a terrific force grabbed you and pulled you into its power?

MAUD MARY: What? What's the matter with everybody? I just came home a little early and here's everybody asking me pesky questions. I don't know what you're talking about. I want my birthday party, please.

MRS. FRANKLIN: She doesn't remember. It's just as well, darling.

MITEY: Aw, too bad. We could have put her memoirs in the *Scientific American.*

MAUD MARY: Can I have my birthday party now? Can I? CAL: Her birthday party! Oh, no. O.K., Mitey—you were the mental giant who thought up the monster. Now you explain to Maud Mary that she's just *had* her birthday party.

MITEY: Aw, no. Aw, gee. Uh—Maud Mary, the fact is—

MAUD MARY: I'm going to have presents, and a cake and everything, aren't I, Mitey?

MITEY: Well, you see. The trouble is— What I mean is— Come on, Cal. You're in this as deep as I am. You explain to her. (*There is a terrific crash and banging off left, followed by outraged shouts from* MR. FRANKLIN. *He enters left, in a tattered jacket, with a shredded newspaper and hub cap in hand. He has a black eye.*)

MR. FRANKLIN: All right. Who did it? *Who did it?*

CAL (*Rushing to him*): What's the matter, Dad? Did you have an accident?

MR. FRANKLIN: No, I've been to a tea party. Now, all I want to know is—who did it, and *how* did you do it?

MITEY: Do what, Dad?

MR. FRANKLIN: Turn the entire house around, that's what. I drove up the driveway and sailed into what I thought was the garage. Ha!

MRS. FRANKLIN: Oh, Cavendish, what happened?

MR. FRANKLIN: Well, all I can tell you is—we're the only family in Miller's Falls with a station wagon rocking gently in the porch swing!

CAL: Front porch? My gosh! (*He runs off right.*)

MITEY (*Running left and peering out door*): The house is completely turned around! (CAL *re-enters right.*)

CAL: The front porch is where the garage used to be—

MITEY: You should see the garage. It's in the middle of Main Street. There's a whole line of cars backed up clear past the traffic light.

MAUD MARY (*Bawling*): I want my birthday party. I want my birthday party.

MR. FRANKLIN: Boys, it's one of those inventions again, isn't it? (*They nod, crestfallen.*) How many times have I told you to let me check them out before you fool with them? Oh, so help me, I'm going to make you eat those physics books page by page.

MRS. FRANKLIN (*Going to the window and looking out*): My kitchen. My kitchen is all over the front garden and the tulips are ruined. (*There is a knock at door right. MAUD MARY goes offstage and re-enters with the CHILDREN behind her.*)

CHILDREN: Hello, Maud Mary. Hello.

MAUD MARY: Hello, everybody. Look—they came. I'm going to have my party after all.

CAL *and* MITEY: Oh, no. Not now!

CHILDREN: Happy birthday, Maud Mary. (*There is a sound of tooting horns outside.*)

MRS. FRANKLIN (*Sobbing*): Oh, my lovely tulips!

MR. FRANKLIN: And you should see the car! Front fender all smashed in. Front porch, too. Looks like a tornado hit it. Not to mention the lawsuits I'm going to have because of that traffic jam out there.

MITEY (*Coming downstage*): Boy, oh, boy. Are we in trouble. (CAL *comes downstage.*)

CAL: You can say that again. (*Curtain closes behind them. To audience*) So, of course, our father made us—er— suggested to us that it might be a good idea if we explained to you folks in Miller's Falls just how our garage ended up out there on Main Street.

MITEY: That's the whole story. We're awfully sorry, and we won't do it again. I wanted to tell you there is a brighter side to all this—

CAL: Sure, the fellows from the Pentagon were real interested in the monster as a defensive weapon.

MITEY: Imagine a machine that reverses time. You plant a few of them on the perimeter of a country—

CAL: If anybody had a funny notion about sending over a few airplanes, the machine would send them right back home—without a scratch on them.

MITEY: Bullets would return to guns—tanks would run backward on their treads, and missiles would wind up right back on their launching pads.

CAL: I hope they can work things out.

MITEY: Before we go, we did want to explain about what happened to the waterfall.

CAL: Oh, yes. We're sure sorry about what happened to the Miller's Falls waterfall.

MITEY: We took another look at it today, and I'm afraid the damage is permanent.

CAL: But the Department of the Interior called us and said it's the most unusual tourist attraction since Old Faithful Geyser.

MITEY: Why, there isn't another town in the world that can boast a waterfall that falls—

CAL and MITEY (*Pointing to sky*): Upside down! (*They bow and exit.*)

THE END

All Points West

Characters

WAGONMASTER
JEB GREENFIELD
SARAH, *his wife*
CAL ⎫
DIGGER ⎪
SALLY ⎬ *their children*
CHAD ⎭
RIVERS
FEVER
TEXAS SIGNPOST ⎫
CALIFORNIA SIGNPOST ⎬ *two boys*
CHIEF EAGLEFEATHER
FLEETWING
TWO BRAVES
CHORUS

TIME: *A fine day in the summer of 1849.*
SETTING: *Albany, New York. Down center are two benches, placed diagonally, representing a covered wagon. Up center is a raised platform, or a pyramid of boxes painted to look like mountains.*
AT RISE: *The* CHORUS, *holding wood blocks and small drums, sits at the front of the stage. The* WAGONMASTER *stands beside benches, a long list in his hand.*

341

WAGONMASTER (*Calling offstage right*): Ho, you wagoners. Fasten your wagons. We're bound away by sunset.

CHORUS: Bound away. Bound away. Bound away West by sunset.

WAGONMASTER (*Speaking to audience*): Here I am again, leading another train out beyond the Alleghenies. Seems that there's no more north or south or east. Only one direction for folks these days—

CHORUS:
West.
Follow the sun
Over the river.
Follow the sun
Over the prairie.
Follow the sun
Over the mountains,
Down the great valleys,
Follow the sun
To the western sea!

WAGONMASTER: Year after year I lead them West. Never mind my name. Could be Boone or Carson or Fremont. Just call me Wagonmaster. I take them West.

CHORUS: West? West? Why go West?

1ST SOLO: Stay East.

2ND SOLO: Stay where the people are.

3RD SOLO: Stay where the towns are.

CHORUS: Stay East.

4TH SOLO: Stay home.

5TH SOLO: There are logs for the fire.

6TH SOLO: There is sugar for the tea.

7TH SOLO: There's a neighbor for the back fence.

CHORUS: Stay home!

8TH SOLO: Stay put.

9TH SOLO: A rolling stone gathers no moss.

10TH SOLO: Rivers may drown your bones.

11TH SOLO: The desert tells no tales.

CHORUS: Stay East! Stay home!

WAGONMASTER: Good advice. Sound counsel. Only trouble is—nobody took it. (CHAD *enters on the run, crossing to center.*)

CHAD (*Full of enthusiasm*): We're going West! We're leaving home. We're going to move along! (*He jumps up and kneels on nearest bench, facing left.*)

WAGONMASTER: Hello, tadpole. (CHAD *waves to him, as* JEB *enters from right with* SARAH *and* SALLY.) Are you on my wagon train muster?

JEB: You bet your rawhide boots we are. (*He sits on other bench also facing left.* SARAH *sits beside him, and* SALLY *kneels beside* CHAD.) Look under G for Greenfield. First wagon section. (CAL *and* DIGGER *enter right.* CAL *stands right and* DIGGER *left of benches.*)

WAGONMASTER (*Consulting his list and calling the roll*): Greenfield family. Point of origin: Albany, New York. Destination—

GREENFIELDS: West!

WAGONMASTER: Answer smartly when I call off your names. Jeb Greenfield.

JEB: Present. Father of this Greenfield family. Farmer by trade. Dreamer by nature. There's land in the West, free for the ploughing. When the wind blows off the hills I can almost taste the West, like wild honey. There's a sound in that wind that whispers—

CHORUS: Oregon . . . Oregon . . . Oregon.

WAGONMASTER: Sarah.

SARAH: Here. Mother of the Greenfields. Believer in the here and now, feet on the ground, and broom in the hand. But I believe in Jeb, too. If it's Oregon for him, then it's Oregon for me.

WAGONMASTER: Cal.

CAL: Accounted for. Cal, that's me. The loner. Albany is gettin' too big for me now. Too many people all pushing and jostling like minnows in a teacup. I'm scouting for a stretch of pure emptiness and a sky that only the mountains and I share.

WAGONMASTER: Digger.

DIGGER: Ready to go. They don't call me Digger for nothing. Gold. That's what I'm after. You know how a magnet pulls iron? That's how gold pulls me. I bought me a shovel and I don't aim to put it down until I hit California.

WAGONMASTER: Sally and Chad.

SALLY *and* CHAD: That's us.

SALLY: We came along for the ride.

CHAD: Some ride.

CHORUS: Some ride!

CHAD: They said we'd miss our schoolin', but shucks—you can't get a better teacher than the West.

SALLY: We'll write down the day's doings in a diary, and figure the miles by the rolling of the wheels.

CHAD: We'll reckon the mountains and the plains better than any old geography book. And as for history—

BOTH: We'll make our own history!

WAGONMASTER: All right now. It's time to move along. Start up the oxen.

JEB (*Pretending to shake reins*): Hey! Giddap. Move along, you molasses-footed critters. (WAGONMASTER, CAL *and* DIGGER *walk in place beside benches.*)

CHAD: We're heading West. (*Pointing left*) Yonder is the sun.

SALLY (*Pointing off right*): And back there is the city, getting smaller and smaller.

SARAH: Goodbye, city. You were mighty good to us, but it's time to move along.

CHORUS (*With wood blocks making sound of hoofs*):
    Clip-clop, move along, wagons,
    Clip-clop, move along West.
    Beat hoofs, carry us onward.
    Beat hoofs, over the trail.
    Clip-clop, move along, wagons,
    Clip-clop, move along West. (*The* RIVERS *enter and
    take their places on platform.* CHAD *shades his eyes and
    looks up at them.*)
CHAD: Something's over there. Something gliding and
    gleaming.
WAGONMASTER: Hold up the wagons. We're at the Rivers.
RIVERS:
    We are the Rivers,
    The broad and the shining,
    The great spills of water
    That surge to the sea.
    We are the Rivers,
    Undammed and unbridgeable,
    Wild and uncrossable.
    We are the Rivers,
    The Rivers, the Rivers,
    We are the Rivers
    That wind through the land.
    Who dares us?
    Who daunts us?
    Millraces of majesty,
    Father of Waters,
    And all of his kin.
WAGONMASTER (*To* RIVERS): We dare you. We daunt you.
    Know this, Father of Waters and all your forks and
    tributaries: We're going to cross you!
JEB: How are we going to cross a river so wide and so
    deep?
WAGONMASTER: Climb aboard the "Good Ship Wagon-

wheel." (CAL *and* DIGGER *sit on either side of bench with* CHAD *and* SALLY, *paddling.* WAGONMASTER *kneels beside* SARAH *and pantomimes paddling.*)

CHAD: Look at that. We're floating. We're floating like a corked bottle. And those oxen—why, they're swimming as if they had fins instead of horns. Rivers, we licked you. We licked you for sure!

WAGONMASTER: Don't get so cocky, son. There are worse things than rivers ahead of us. (*He resumes his place beside benches as do* CAL *and* DIGGER, *walking in place.* RIVERS *exit as* FEVER *enters and climbs up to the top of platform.*)

FEVER (*Shaking maracas*): I am the Fever, who comes from the lowlands where the mist is thick.

SARAH (*Wiping her brow*): Whatever has come over me? I feel so poorly.

SALLY: Me, too, Ma. I'm thirsty and hot as if it were noon.

FEVER (*Shaking the maracas*): I strike like a serpent that hides in the grass.

JEB: Don't want to move. My arms are so heavy. (*He hangs his head. All begin to slump.*)

CAL: Eyes sting and burn. (*He sits beside the wagon, head down.*)

DIGGER: Mouth like a ball of cotton. (*He sits, head down.*)

CHAD: Head splittin'. (*He slumps down.*)

FEVER (*Dancing and shaking the maracas triumphantly*):
Fever! Fever! Fever!
Beware, beware the Fever!
Coming like a brush fire
In the dead of night.
I'll take you and I'll shake you
Like a tambourine of bones.
You'll dance the Fever jig for me
And sing the Fever moan!

ALL: Water—give us water.

FEVER:

But I'll have you,
Yes, I'll have you,
You charred and burned-out embers,
You'll be trophies for the Fever.
Bow low. Bow low. Surrender.
Fever! Fever! Fever!
Fever is the king!

CHORUS:

Fever, Fever, Fever!
Fever is the king!

JEB: We're done for. Turn the wagon about. We're headin' home.

WAGONMASTER: Not by a jugful. (*He removes canteen hung around his shoulder and passes it around. Each pantomimes a swallow, and straightens up.*) There's quinine water in this canteen. It'll quench the fever. Put it out. (FEVER *shakes maracas more and more faintly, then exits at the end of* WAGONMASTER'S *speech.*) Stop it cold. (*All brighten up.*) There, you're feeling better already.

JEB: Like a new man. Gee-up, you lazy oxen! We're going on. (*The* SIGNPOSTS *enter left and right and stand on platform.*)

TEXAS SIGNPOST:

This way. This way.
This way to the open road,
This way to the lonesome road.
This way to the Texas trail.

CAL (*Pointing*): The Texas trail! That's my fork in the road. I'll be going now.

SARAH: Don't leave us, Cal. Think about Oregon a spell.

JEB: There's good farming in Oregon. We could use you, son.

TEXAS SIGNPOST (*As* CAL *wavers*):
This way to the Panhandle.
This way to the sky-wide desert.

CAL (*Going to* SIGNPOST, *and shading his eyes*): Glory!
Glory! Glory! Far as my eye can see. Plains upon blue
plains. Bare mountains shimmering with sun. The sky
goes on forever and then some. And see—there's only an
eagle wheeling in all that emptiness. Say! He's headed
southwest. Wait for me, eagle. Wait for me! (*He runs
off right. All wave goodbye.* SARAH *wipes her eyes.*)

CALIFORNIA SIGNPOST:
That way.
That way to the miners' camp
Veins of silver zigzag through the hills,
Nuggets of gold as big as hens' eggs on the ground,
Agates and turquoise and moonstones
That way. That way.

DIGGER: I've heard the call, and I'm off for California.

SARAH: Stop, son. How do you know it's not a fool's dream
and fool's gold?

JEB: Come along to Oregon. Farming's slow, but farming's
sure.

DIGGER (*Going up to* SIGNPOST): I can't stay. My blood is
restless. I've got to take the chance. See for myself. Dig
for myself. (*Looking out*) Far out there something is
hiding under the earth. Waiting for me. Listen!

CHORUS:
Gold in Californ-i-ay.
Gold in Californ-i-ay.
Gold in Californ-i-ay. (*All wave as* DIGGER *goes off left.*
SIGNPOSTS *exit right and left.*)

WAGONMASTER: Here now, folks. Don't look so downcast.
You've got your health and your wagons and your
young'uns. Some fine day Cal and Digger will show up
in Oregon, you wait and see. (*Drums begin to beat.*

CHIEF EAGLEFEATHER, FLEETWING *and* TWO BRAVES, *carrying bows, enter and stand on platform.*)

INDIANS:

Stop.

Go no further.

Stop.

Do not trespass.

Stop.

This is our land

We belong here.

Stop. Stop. Stop. (CHIEF *puts up his hand forbiddingly.*)

WAGONMASTER: We mean you no harm, Chief Eaglefeather. We must go through now, before the snow begins in the mountains.

CHIEF: Words. You speak words. Words no good. Do not pass.

INDIANS: Words no good. Do not pass. (*Drums beat fast, then stop.*)

WAGONMASTER: Chad, get out of the wagon.

CHAD: What for?

WAGONMASTER: You'll see. Chief, I offer you deeds instead of words. We will give you Chad to keep until we pass through your land. You will give us Fleetwing.

FLEETWING: No, Father. Do not send me away in the tepee that rolls.

CHIEF: Hush, my son. Do not show the white feather. It is a good plan. Go with them. Be brave. (FLEETWING *fearfully goes to sit beside* SALLY.)

CHAD: Pa—!

JEB: The Wagonmaster knows best. We can't turn back now. This is the only way we'll both trust each other. (CHAD *goes to Indians and is led off by* CHIEF, *the* BRAVES *following. Wood blocks begin to clip-clop. Those in the wagon begin to sway, as* CHORUS *chants. The lights dim.*)

CHORUS:
 Roll, wheels, roll,
 Over and over and over.
 Follow the sunset into the night,
 Roll through the darkness,
 Creaking along,
 Patient old oxen,
 Plodding the trail.
 Roll, wheels, roll,
 Roll, wheels, roll,
 Into the sunrise,
 Into the daylight,
 Over and over, turn the miles over,
 Over and over into the dawn. (*The lights come up.*)
SARAH: Look, Jeb—the mountains. (TWO BRAVES *steal up to the wagon, bringing* CHAD *back, and taking* FLEET-WING *away. They steal off as silently as they entered.*)
WAGONMASTER: Going up, folks. Everybody out of the wagons. They've got to be light on these mountain trails. (*All stand and walk in place behind the benches. At intervals they wipe their brows and pant as if the going were rough.*)
CHORUS:
 Going up . . . going up,
 Going up, going over, going through.
1ST SOLO:
 Where the trail is steeply rising—
2ND SOLO:
 Where the cliffs loom over chasms—
CHORUS:
 Toiling higher, snaking cloudward,
 Reaching, stretching, pulling, pulling.
 Worn-out wagons on the last mile,
 On the last rise, on the last day.
CHAD: Look, everybody! (*He goes up on platform, fol-*

lowed by the WAGONMASTER.) We're at the top of the mountain.

SARAH (*Going to the front of the benches and gazing out over the audience*): Down there—spread out like a green coverlet—trees and valleys and little streams. What is it, Jeb?

JEB: It's Oregon, I reckon. (*He joins her.*) Why, it's Oregon for sure! (SALLY *joins them.* SARAH *puts her arm around her.*)

SALLY: I can't wait to go down to it. We'll build us a cabin with a real board floor, and I'll fill it full of wild flowers.

CHAD (*Gazing out*): What's that blue line over there? That's the end of the land, isn't it? That blue is the Pacific Ocean.

WAGONMASTER: That's it, Chad. End of the trail. End of the journey. End of the rainbow. (CHAD *hangs head sadly.*) What's the matter?

CHAD: Why, it's over. All the adventuring and pioneering. Ma and Pa and Sally can be content with farming. But not me. Where can I go now I've come to the end of the circle? West was the last direction left.

WAGONMASTER: Look up, Chad.

CHORUS: Look up, Chad. (WAGONMASTER *points up and* CHAD's *eyes follow his finger.*)

WAGONMASTER: Out there's your new compass point. North, South, East, West—Up. Maybe you won't get there, or your children. But one fine day a descendant of yours will find a way to put a shoulder of wind to a wagon, and you'll see the Greenfields heading out on a trail past the moon. And I'll tell you something, Chad. There'll be no stop to that direction. It'll be a new West. A West without end.

CHORUS:

Look up. Look up.

Look up. Look out. Look afar.

There's a trail along the far, far horizon.
Wingèd oxen, prairie schooners heading out,
Heading out—heading out beyond the fields of glowing
  stars,
To a West beyond a West beyond a West,
To a West that stretches endless in the sky.
To a West without a boundary or an end!
(WAGONMASTER *puts hand on* CHAD's *shoulder and both
gaze up, holding pose.* SARAH, *arm around* SALLY, *and*
JEB *look out at audience, as if gazing toward Oregon.
All hold pose as curtains close.*)

THE END

Production Notes

SMALL CRIMSON PARASOL

Characters: 6 male; 4 female; 5 or more boys or girls for Chorus. (Note: Yin, Yan, and Grandmother are nonspeaking parts.)

Playing Time: 20 minutes.

Costumes: Appropriate Japanese costumes. Sukoshi carries a red parasol. Woodcutter has large cardboard axe. Kirai wears a flowered kimono and carries two large fans. Chotto's shell may be a tub painted like a tortoise shell, and worn on the back of the actor, who enters on hands and knees, wearing green hood and green socks on hands and feet. Zin-Zin wears yellow and black striped costume, and has a long tail and a hood with ears. The members of Chorus have wood blocks, flute or recorder, drum, gong, etc.

Properties: Large book with "Little Red Riding Hood" printed on cover, scroll with "Small Crimson Parasol" printed on it, two large gold discs, tea table, cups, teapot, straw basket, kimono, kerchief, quilt, blanket, medal on ribbon, pillow, three bamboo trees, two screens.

Setting: The stage is bare, except for mats down left on which Chorus kneels. Yin and Yan carry on and off articles used for set-ting, as indicated in text.

Lighting: No special effects.

PETER, PETER, PETER!

Characters: 8 male; 4 female.

Playing Time: 25 minutes.

Costumes: Peter wears blue jeans, sports shirt, and baseball cap; Joey wears a baseball uniform, and Skinny, who is barefoot, wears blue jeans, ragged at the knee, a polo shirt, and a straw hat. Miss Oolong wears a long black dress, rope beads, heels, black hat, and spectacles. Jane the Brain is dressed in a skirt, white lab jacket, horn-rimmed glasses, and has ribbons on her braids. Mr. Whistle wears a Scoutmaster's uniform with hat. Peter Prime wears Scout uniform and cap; Peter the Second is dressed in beret, short pants, knee socks, white shirt with flowing tie, and Peter the Third wears overalls, polo shirt, and carries handyman's pail.

Properties: Wrist watch, baseball bat, knapsack, two fishing poles, book labeled "Atomic Physics Made Difficult," four baseballs, violin, signs for three houses in Scene 3, music stand, three telephones and telephone tables, hammer, shingles, notebook, pencil, reverse duplicator (portable hair-dryer), newspaper, smelling salts, large folding screen.

Setting: Scene 1 is a street. The scene may be played before the curtain. Scene 2 is the home of The Brain. Down right is a chair, and upstage is a machine labeled "Super-Duper-Duplicator" (large cardboard carton with folding screens standing at either end). At one side of machine are a crank and a hopper; there is a dial at center, and at other side is an opening and a basket to catch baseballs. Wires, bulbs, and tape reels complete the machine. Scene 3 is Peter's street. Down right is a sign reading "Plunk Residence" and a chair, music stand, and telephone on a table. Down left is sign "The Whistles Live Here." Beside it are the Clubhouse and a telephone on a table. Sign reading "Parmenter" is at center, with chair, telephone, table with drawer, and newspaper.

Lighting: If desired, lights may be flashed on and off while duplicators work.

Sound: Knocking on doors, gongs, telephone ringing, and, if desired, noises while machines operate.

ANYWHERE AND EVERYWHERE

Characters: As many boys and girls as desired. Children may play two parts if necessary, and all parts may be taken by either boys or girls.

Playing Time: 15 minutes.

Costumes: Chorus wears everyday dress. Others may wear appropriate costumes, or carry props suggesting their roles.

Properties: Seven signs, shaped like arrows, as indicated in text; handlebars; bicycle bell; wheels; steering wheel; horn; hand bell; con-

fetti; large cutout of ship; whistle.

Setting: A bare stage, with chairs for Chorus. The backdrop is a scene of the earth and moon, with a rocket ready to blast off. Rocket is made of cardboard, and is controlled by a string so that it can rise at end of play.

Lighting: No special effects.

THE WONDERFUL CIRCUS OF WORDS

Characters: 3 male; 1 female; 24 boys or girls. All-boy cast may be used, if desired.

Playing Time: 15 minutes.

Costumes: Jamie wears everyday school clothes. Grammarian wears ringmaster's costume. Jim wears a baseball uniform and cap. "Throws" is dressed as a discus thrower, "Runs" as a runner, "Brings" as a weight lifter, "Leaps" in a Superman costume with cape, and "Makes" as a carpenter. "Slowly" wears a turtle costume, "Quickly" a rabbit costume, "Clumsily" a bear costume, "Skillfully" a monkey costume and "Happily" a canary costume. Other words wear costumes indicating the meaning of their words: kimono for "Japan," a silver costume with glitter for "Sparkling," red clown outfit and red balloon for "Red," etc. Period wears black, with a sandwich sign which has a large black dot on the front and "The End" printed on the back. "Article" wears black, with a sandwich sign marked "A, An," on the back and "The" on the front. Pennant bearers wear colorful costumes. If desired, the characters may wear name cards, rather than special costumes.

Properties: Book, pencil, paper,

whistle, pennants marked "Nouns," "Verbs," "Adjectives" and "Adverbs," small drum and drumsticks, pail with tennis balls, satchel with baseballs, cardboard discus, dumbbells, hammer, colorful juggling balls, tissue-covered hoop.
Setting: Jamie's living room. A living room set may be used, or the stage may be bare except for a desk and chair.
Lighting: No special effects.

THE BIG SHOO

Characters: 8 male; 1 female; 5 boys or girls for crows; as many extras for Farm Folk as desired.
Playing Time: 15 minutes.
Costumes: The children, Big Dan'l, Jabez, and Farm Folk men wear blue jeans and bright shirts. Farm women wear colorful country dresses. Phineas and the Professor wear cutaway suits, and Phineas has a gaudy vest and derby, carries a bandanna in his pocket. The Professor has white hair, mustache and goatee, and wears a top hat. Tattersall wears a ragged, oversized suit stuffed with straw, stuffed socks on his feet, floppy gloves, and a shapeless felt hat. He may wear clown make-up. Samson's body is a foil-covered box, his arms and legs are wrapped in foil, and he wears heavy gloves and stiff boots. His head is a foil-covered box or bag, with antennae on top, and he carries concealed nuts and bolts for "tears." The crows wear black tights and sweaters, closely-fitting black hoods, and yellow nose cones, black crepe paper wings.
Properties: Large red bandanna, easel with sign, "Tonight Only! The Great Big Shoo!", two white sheets, bag of grain, stop watch, nuts and bolts.
Setting: A recently harvested cornfield. There is a backdrop with corn stacks and harvest moon. Upstage is a banner reading, "Harvest Festival Tonight! Come One. Come All." There may be one or two real corn stacks on stage as well. There is a T-shaped frame at right for Tattersall, a raised platform at left for Samson. Benches are placed diagonally right and left.
Lighting: Lights may be flickered on and off when Samson frightens the crows.
Sound: Bells, thunder, recorded square dance music as indicated in text.

SPACESHIP SANTA MARIA

Characters: 12 male; 3 female; 1 male voice (loudspeaker).
Playing Time: 20 minutes.
Costumes: Commentator, Dr. Vector, and Dr. Quantus wear suits and ties. Dr. Theorembus is dressed in a frock coat and top hat, and Dr. Archivista wears a tweed suit. All five wear neck mikes. Commander Smith's military uniform has four stars; Technician and Radar Man wear white lab coats. President Inuk and Aides wear boots and parkas. The space crew are dressed in space suits and carry helmets. Phoebe carries a guitar.
Setting: A blockhouse at the New Palos Rocket Complex, Palos, Spain. On risers up center is a television "screen" large enough to accommodate four chairs. For opening scene, it has a morning sky background, in front of which is a cutout rocket which can move upward at time of launch. For scene with spaceship crew,

the sky and rocket are removed (by prop boys or the technicians, if desired), revealing four chairs with wide seat belts. In front of the screen at center is a table with four chairs. A large standing microphone is at one side of the table. Up right is radar equipment, and up left is a computer. There is an exit at one side.

Lighting: Lights may be flickered as rocket is launched.

Sound: Loudspeaker for countdown, etc. (This may be an offstage mike or megaphone); beeps and hums for radar, computer; high-pitched sound for laser.

PENNY WISE

Characters: 3 male; 1 female; 13 boys or girls for Eight Pennies, Nickel, Dime, Quarter, Half Dollar, and Dollar.

Playing Time: 15 minutes.

Costumes: Pennies wear brown shirts and trousers or skirts. Penny Bright wears brown trousers and shirt, a copper helmet, and has copper disks front and back. Old Timer wears dull brown trousers and shirt and has tarnished copper disks. He has white hair and a beard and carries a cane. Other coins wear clothes of appropriate colors and disks of appropriate size. Quarter wears silver helmet with wings. Dollar has long rectangle, worn lengthwise, representing dollar bill. Values should be clearly printed on all coins. Sally Spender wears pinafore with large pocket containing coins. Savin' Steven wears school clothes.

Properties: Tambourines covered with copper foil, piggy bank, coins.

Setting: Ten chairs are arranged in a semicircle at one side of stage.

Down right is a basket of balloons with a sign reading, BALLOONS 5¢. Beside basket is pay telephone on a pole, with sign reading, TELEPHONE HERE 10¢. Down left is red and white gumball machine, with sign reading, GUMBALL MACHINE—ONE PENNY. Machine should be box large enough for Penny Bright to climb into (upstage side of box may be open, concealing ladder) and should contain large red beach ball (the gumball). There should be a slot in top of box, a hole in center (for gumball), and an opening at side, for Penny to roll out of.

Lighting: No special effects.

Sound: Piano accompaniment for "Farmer in the Dell," if desired.

SCAREDY CAT

Characters: 6 male; 3 female; 1 male or female for Shadow.

Playing Time: 15 minutes.

Costumes: Modern everyday dress for Mrs. Reese and Tony, appropriate costumes for Terry, Walter, and Linda. In Scene 2, the Reeses wear bathrobes. Dr. Blunder wears a dark suit and glasses, and has a goatee and mustache. Pockets and Willy wear old clothes, and the Police Officer is in uniform. Shadow wears a black cat costume.

Properties: Crayon or marking pen for Mrs. Reese, basket with toy kitten, black medical bag containing pills, two sacks containing silverware, etc., toy gun for Police Officer.

Setting: The living room of the Reese home. A sofa is up center, with end tables holding bric-a-brac at either end. A card table, covered with a sheet that hangs to the floor in front, is at center.

Other chairs, lamps, etc., complete the furnishings. An exit at right leads to rest of house, and door at left, to the outside.

Lighting: The room may be slightly darkened in Scene 2.

Sound: Doorbell, clock chimes, as indicated in text.

THE WAYWARD WITCH

Characters: 1 female; 2 male or female for Cats; as many boys and girls as desired for chorus and Children.

Playing Time: 15 minutes.

Costumes: Winnie and Witches wear traditional black costumes. Winnie has large spectacles, and carries a broom. At end she wears bunny ears and a powder puff tail. Wizards also wear black and have conical orange hats with tassels. Cats wear black shirts and tights, and have on masks. First group of Children wear bathrobes, others wear everyday clothes. At end all Children wear witches' hats and masks.

Properties: Orange and black book covers; small twig broom with bent handle, wand, talcum powder, large black handkerchief for Winnie. The portable properties for the Cats to take on and off are: two cardboard pumpkins; a "wigwam" of sticks for the fire, with red cellophane and a torch type flashlight for greater effect; a cardboard stand-up Christmas tree, large enough to hide Winnie; large stockings with tape attached; cardboard wreath; a large valentine envelope with a red heart in the center (the heart should have loosely taped red net backing so that Winnie can come through easily); large, round, red firecracker mounted on a bunting-draped wagon (the firecracker

should have a large fuse with red paper flame inside).

Setting: A living room. Simple cardboard silhouettes—a large orange moon, witches in flight, mountains and trees—may be taped to back curtain. At center is a three-dimensional cardboard fireplace with an entrance at back for Winnie. In front of the fireplace is a stool. A row of chairs extends diagonally from either side of the fireplace.

Lighting: No special effects.

Sound: Music, as indicated in text.

Special Effects: A black thread may be attached to one end of Winnie's wand; the other end should be held by someone offstage. Winnie should hold the wand loosely when she waves it, and it may then be pulled off. Talcum powder thrown in air gives the effect of white smoke. When Winnie throws her "magic" powder, one of the "sleeping" cats turns off the flashlight in the fireplace.

THE RUNAWAY BOOKMOBILE

Characters: 4 male; 3 female; 1 female voice (Aunt Polly); 15 or more boys and girls for Chorus. Solos may be doubled if fewer Chorus members are desired.

Playing Time: 20 minutes.

Costumes: Dragger and Bookworm wear school clothes and caps. Biblio wears a pointed hat made of newsprint and a fantastic costume with book pages sewn on it. Medusa wears a Grecian robe, and a cap of snakes. She should have dead-white make-up, fangs, and claws. Queen Elizabeth is dressed in an Elizabethan costume, and carries a scepter and handkerchief. Tom Sawyer wears jeans, checked shirt, straw hat, and carries a fishing pole. The Librarian wears a suit.

Properties: Books for Bookworm, including one with *The Runaway Bookmobile* printed on the cover; two large hand mirrors; library card, stamp and stamp pad.

Setting: The interior of a bookmobile. There are shelves of books up right and left, and a desk and chair up center.

Lighting: No special effects.

THE INSATIABLE DRAGON

Characters: 6 male; 1 female; as many extras for Brothers and Sisters as desired. The Dragon hand puppet may be worked by the actor who plays the Big Dragon, or by another boy.

Playing Time: 15 minutes.

Costumes: Chinese dress. San-Su wears a robe with sash and sandals. The men wear tunics, trousers, and sandals. Lum-Fu has two stones in one pocket. Wang is dressed in a brightly-colored silk robe. Dragon wears a red robe, red gloves with long fingernails, and a fierce dragon mask. The puppet wears the same costume, and the Brothers and Sisters should be similarly dressed.

Properties: Stick with piece of fish, four sticks for torches, buckets.

Setting: The house of Wang the magician. Folding screens with Oriental designs form the backdrop. Down center is a cardboard box cut to resemble a low table. It is covered with a cloth that reaches to the ground to hide the puppeteer, and a second cloth is draped over one side. A shallow brass-colored bowl is on the table, and bowl, table and cloth have holes cut in them so the puppet may be worked from beneath. To the left of the table is a basket containing charcoal, and to the right is another basket containing rolled-up paper scrolls. There is an exit at one side and another behind the folding screens for the entrance of the Brothers and Sisters.

Lighting: No special effects.

Sound: Offstage gong as indicated; music for dance, if desired.

MEET THE PILGRIMS!

Characters: 6 male; 4 female.

Playing Time: 15 minutes.

Costumes: Appropriate Pilgrim costume for boys and girls. Towami wears Indian costume. Francis Billington may wear slightly different costume to set him apart from other Pilgrim children.

Properties: Tin trays with wooden spoons; large platters and tureens; nine wooden bowls; large metal tablespoons; long white tablecloth; metal pitcher; platters with turkey, fish, pies, pastries, etc.; carving set, large wooden table, benches, parchment scroll.

Setting: A clearing in Plymouth, Massachusetts. Autumn foliage encloses clearing; benches and table are at left side of stage. Table is laden with cooking utensils and platters of food. At one side a fire is laid, with a tripod crane holding a large pot.

Lighting: No special effects.

Sound: If desired, appropriate Thanksgiving music may be used as soft background accompaniment when Pilgrim characters introduce themselves at beginning of play, when Thanksgiving table is being set, and when Love Brewster reads parchment at end of play.

THE CHRISTMAS REVEL

Characters: 8 male; 8 female; as many players as desired for Other Boys and Girls.

Playing Time: 35 minutes.

Costumes: Appropriate dress of the Elizabethan period. In Scene 2, Walter wears a small scabbard which contains a jeweled knife. In Scene 3, he and Katherine wear masks and peasant costumes. Titania also wears a mask. Sir Thomas is dressed as the Lord of Misrule.

Properties: Box containing gloves, fan, marionette, basket containing two bags of gold sovereigns, yule log, firebrand, three dolls.

Setting: Warwickshire, England. Scene 1 takes place in a village square, and may be played before the curtain if desired. Scenes 2 and 3 take place in the Great Hall at Charlecote. A fireplace with large mantel is up center. In Scene 2, Lady Joyce's fan is on a table. In Scene 3, benches are placed about the room, and there is a dais set beside the fireplace; at rise, Betsy and Nan's marionette is on the mantel. If desired, traditional mummers' pantomime or other appropriate Christmas program material may be added to the opening festivities of Scene 3.

Lighting: No special effects.

STAR BRIGHT

Characters: 8 male; 3 female; male and female extras (as many as desired) for Children of All Nations.

Playing Time: 20 minutes.

Costumes: Zodiac is dressed as a wizard, with conical hat and flowing robe. King Conifer wears green. The stars wear white robes with five-pointed foil stars on the fronts of their costumes. Cometta has a tiara with a flowing rainbow-colored veil at back. Globulo has a tall crown, Polaris, a silver hat with large magnet on front, and Vesper, a crescent moon hat. Meteorus has red streamers on his star, and a silver Roman helmet with a red plume. Astra has a low silver crown. The sailors wear dungarees, white polo shirts, sailor hats. The children should wear costumes from nations around the world.

Properties: Stars and whistle for Zodiac, scroll for King Conifer, paddles for sailors.

Setting: The midnight sky. There is a dark blue backdrop covered with stars, comets, etc. Down left is a "cloud bank" large enough to conceal King Conifer. A stool is behind the cloud bank. Six pedestals are arranged in a semicircle upstage.

Lighting: A spotlight on Astra, as indicated in the text.

Sound: Offstage bells.

MOTHER GOOSE'S CHRISTMAS SURPRISE

Characters: 7 male; 6 female.

Playing Time: 20 minutes.

Costumes: Nursery rhyme characters are dressed in appropriate costumes. Miss Muffet has lacy doilies or snowflake ornaments in her pocket; Boy Blue has a horn with him; Bo-peep carries a shepherd's crook with a red ribbon wound around it (it may be red-and-white striped). Humpty Dumpty has eggs covered with gold and silver glitter; strings are attached so eggs may be hung on tree. Mary Contrary has silver bells in her pocket; Mother Hubbard carries an empty purse, and

360 PRODUCTION NOTES

Dog Tray wears brown costume, neck ruff, and clown hat of red and green. Dr. Foster has medical bag containing two bottles, one filled with green liquid, one with red. Mother Goose wears green witch's hat, red cape, red dress, and green apron. Santa wears traditional costume.

Properties: Large, sparkling star on a long pole, broom decorated with bells and red and green streamers, Christmas tree on a stand, bag for Santa (containing can of spray, alarm clock, leash with five collars, large bottle marked GLUE, joke book, water wings, package of handkerchiefs, large gift certificate, package of dog biscuits, "deed" rolled up like a scroll).

Setting: Mother Goose's living room. At rise, chairs are arranged in a semicircle behind large panel painted to resemble a book with words "The Christmas Surprise Party, by M. Goose" written on it. There may be a boy standing behind Christmas tree who can lift Christmas star into place, as indicated in text.

Lighting: No special effects.

Sound: Tinkling of bells, and, if desired, medley of carols as Mother Goose and Santa Claus enter, and accompaniment for song at end of play.

A CLEAN SWEEP

Characters: 9 male; 9 female; Bad Days and Good Days may be either boys or girls.

Playing Time: 15 minutes.

Costumes: Old Year Sweeps wear patched clothes and have smudged faces. New Year Sweeps are dressed in white; boys wear silver bow ties; girls wear silver sashes. Bad Days are dressed in black; if parts are played by girls, they may be dressed in witches' costumes. Easter is dressed as a bunny. Fourth of July wears red, white, and blue cheerleader's costume. New Year wears top hat, tuxedo, and ribbon over his shoulder with date of new year on it; he carries bag of confetti. Other holidays wear appropriate costume. Good Days may be dressed in pastel-colored robes.

Properties: 6 old brooms; 6 new brooms; flower basket filled with petals or small hearts; basket of Easter eggs; cheerleader's pompons; Halloween mask; small Christmas tree decorated with snowflakes, candles, and bells; three tambourines; large book with blank pages.

Setting: Twelve chairs are arranged in a row upstage. Concealed beneath each chair may be a small bag of ribbon confetti. The numbers of old year are pinned to backdrop.

Lighting: No special effects. If desired, lights may be dimmed when holidays leave stage and brought up full when New Sweeps stand.

Sound: Chimes; songs and musical accompaniment, as indicated in text. If desired, "Auld Lang Syne" may be played at beginning and at end of play.

THE MARVELOUS TIME MACHINE

Characters: 6 male; 4 female.

Playing Time: 20 minutes.

Costumes: Father Time wears a white tunic and sandals, a beard, and a white shaggy wig. Tic Toc wears an elfin costume. Necessity, Priscilla, Mother and Grandfather Jonas wear Colonial outfits. Ned, Gramps, Patsy and Mrs.

Jonas wear modern everyday clothes.

Properties: Scroll, quill pen, stack of large envelopes, straw broom, carving knife, coils and pieces of wire, vacuum cleaner, two Time Machines.

Setting: In front of the curtain at left there is a small desk with a sign which says, "Office of Father Time." A small stool is at side of desk. The stage is divided into two sets. On the right is a Colonial cottage. There is a fireplace containing a kettle. A musket is over the fireplace. There is a table with some benches around it. A window is at back. Necessity's Time Machine is down center. Ned Jonas' living room is at left. There are a dinette table and chairs, an easy chair and lamp, and a television set. A window is at back. Ned's Time Machine is down center, next to Necessity's. Screens may be used to divide stage.

Lighting: Lights come up and go out on front of curtain and sides of stage as indicated in text.

Sounds: Time Machines cranking and humming, war whoops, banging on door, auto horn, musket shot, thunder, as indicated in text.

Young Abe's Destiny

Characters: 5 male; 2 female. Fortunato is a nonspeaking part.

Playing Time: 20 minutes.

Costumes: Children wear winter coats, mufflers, stocking caps, etc. Abe does not wear a hat. Dr. Fate wears a purple robe and a pointed hat with zodiacal signs on it. Fortunato is dressed as a jester. He carries a rattle with bells on it and has a knapsack on his back.

Properties: Books, pocketknife, covered basket, deck of cards, large pocket watch, knapsack containing brass ring on string, silk hat, and shawl.

Setting: A clearing beside a cabin in Spencer County, Indiana, in the early 1800's. The backdrop shows a cabin, bare trees, and a cloudy sky. A rail fence is across the stage up right. A large flat rock is down left and a large bare tree is down right. Exits are at right and left.

Lighting: Lights dim and spotlight shines on Abe during oath, if desired.

Sounds: Owl hoots; drums; bells; recordings of "Hail to the Chief" and "The Battle Hymn of the Republic," as indicated in text.

The "T" Party

Characters: 5 male; 6 female.

Playing Time: 10 minutes.

Costumes: Lady Tiddliwinks and Countess Truffles wear oversized garden hats and afternoon dresses. Both carry purses. Maid wears a dark dress, white frilly apron and cap; Footman wears a page's costume. Thumbelina and Tinker Bell wear tights and ballet-type dresses of various colors. Tiny Tim wears trousers, a red, double-breasted jacket, wing collar and cravat and dark cap; Tom Thumb wears a black suit, white tie, top hat and monocle; Toby Tyler is in a clown suit, but no make-up; the Mystery Guest wears all black, with a top hat, short black cape, and half mask. There is a black "T" on his forehead.

Properties: Purses, fans, watch, lorgnettes, cardboard telephone (T-shaped), tray with teapot, tureen and foodstuffs, large blank business card.

Setting: A garden. At center are two chairs and small table, on which are bell, quill, inkstand, and paper. Six chairs stand diagonally right of center, and at left is a large tree, made of cardboard, with a straight, fat trunk in which is a door large enough to permit the entrance of the guests. The foliage of the tree is cut horizontally, to resemble a letter T.

Lighting: No special effects.

CUPIVAC

Characters: 10 male; 6 female; Cupivac, Pages and Trolls may be male or female.

Playing Time: 20 minutes.

Costumes: Pixies wear red tights, and shirts. Cutt, Drye and Dr. Mentor wear white lab coats. Cupid wears a safari outfit and a pith helmet. Storybook characters wear appropriate costumes.

Properties: Order book and pencil, purple computer program cards, litter, stretcher.

Setting: Cloud Nine. A long table with three chairs is up center with a sign, "Department of Romance." Three telephones are on the table. The backdrop is covered with hearts in all shapes, sizes and colors. The computer, a large cardboard flat covered with dials, cranks, and wires, has a slot for cards and a heart-shaped button. It is carried in and placed so that characters may enter unseen from offstage and appear from behind. Computer's voice may come from offstage, or a person may be hidden behind flat. Exits are at right and left.

Lighting: No special effects.

Sound: Telephone bells, computer

noises and music played by chime, as indicated in text.

A TALE OF TWO DRUMMERS

Characters: 9 male; 3 female.

Playing Time: 20 minutes.

Costumes: Appropriate dress of the Revolutionary War period. American officers wear rough cloaks over their uniforms. British soldiers wear red coats, tricorn hats, and white breeches. Aide carries sword, Sergeant-Major a staff, and Pvt. Hopkins a musket. Dame Helena has a lace handkerchief. Beauchamps puts on cloak when he exits.

Properties: Colonial marching drum, drumsticks, map.

Setting: The parlor of the Channing town house on Bloomington Road, New York. Bay window with a hinged windowseat is up center. In the windowseat are the drum and drumsticks. A fireplace with clock on mantel is at left. A long table with chairs stands at left, and a chair is up left. A water pitcher and glass are on the table. Up center near window is a coat rack. An exit up right leads to the street, and an exit down right leads to the kitchen. Another exit down left leads to the upstairs.

Lighting: No special effects.

Sound: Clock chiming, offstage drum rolls, as indicated in text.

THE EXTERIOR DECORATOR

Characters: 3 male; 1 female; 16 male or female.

Playing Time: 15 minutes.

Costumes: Madame Frost is dressed in white winter cape and green ankle-length frock. Jacques Frost wears white winter coat and scarf over green shirt and white trousers and boots. Dr. Equinox is dressed in a black frock coat with green flower in buttonhole. Monsieur Printemps wears light green smock, beret, green trousers, and slippers. He has green, waxed mustache and Vandyke beard. Greensmocks wear darker green smocks and berets; Bluesmocks, light blue smocks and berets. Sunlighters wear gilded slickers, boots and fire hats. West Winds are dressed in green ten-gallon hats, shirts and trousers, yellow neckerchiefs and boots. Robins wear red polo shirts and green trousers. Two extra robes for Monsieur and Madame Frost are sewn with crepe paper flowers.

Properties: Two signs reading, "Chateau Glacé" and "Chateau Soleil," doctor's bag, large outdoor thermometer, large prescription pad and crayon, large calling card, patch of paper grass, paper grass and flower border, crepe paper leaves, white paper clouds, gold disc for sun, gold dustcloths, two large fans, four flutes or whistles, four music stands, two garlands.

Setting: The Chateau Glacé. Downstage are two sheet-draped lawn chairs. Down right is a sign reading "Chateau Glacé." There are cardboard trees and bushes at stage right and left. At rise there is a backdrop of gray clouds, later replaced by blue one with cutout white disc for sun.

Lighting: Dim, coming up full at end.

Sound: Recorded music as indicated in text.

LION TO LAMB

Characters: 11 male; 11 female. (5th, 10th, 13th, 14th Solos are girls; 4th, 6th, 12th, 20th Solos are boys. Other solo parts may be taken by either boys or girls.)

Playing Time: 15 minutes.

Costumes: Boys in chorus wear black trousers, white shirts, and large red bow ties. 12th Solo is dressed as a sailor; 20th Solo is dressed as a miller. 5th and 6th Solos wear hats. Girls in chorus wear black skirts, white blouses, and red neckerchiefs. Lion Wind wears brown tights, polo shirt, has a tail, and has hood with name on it. He carries a fan, which may be tucked in his belt. Lamb Wind wears white tights, white woolly sweater, and has hood with white lamb ears.

Properties: Umbrella for 4th Solo, newspaper for 7th Solo, shingles for 9th Solo, kite for 11th Solo, sailboat for 12th Solo, laundry basket containing clothes strung on clothesline, four red bandannas for 15th, 16th, 17th, and 18th Solos, small windmill for 20th Solo, basket of crepe paper flowers and petals.

Setting: Ten chairs are at each side of stage, and a weather vane is at center. Upstage is a backdrop representing the sky, with clouds, a hook for kite, and, if desired, lighted "stars" which may be turned off, when Wind "blows them out." A small ladder is beside backdrop.

Lighting: Stars may go out, as indicated in text.

CINDER-RILEY

Characters: 2 male; 5 female; at least 3 male for prop boys; as many male and female as desired to be Dancers.

Playing Time: 20 minutes.

Costumes: The Leprechaun wears a brown tunic, tights, a cap and a kerchief. He carries a stick and has a red handkerchief in one pocket. The Stepmother and Stepsisters wear long gowns, crowns, and comical putty noses. The Stepmother wears a cloak. Cinder-Riley wears a long gown, a crown, and silver slippers (the gown should be expendable, since it must be cut). The Fairy Godmother wears a housedress, two aprons, two mob caps, and two pairs of shoes. Jack wears a crown of potatoes, a tattered shirt, and breeches decorated with green patches. The Dancers may wear green and white costumes; the boys may wear gold ties and the girls, gold kerchiefs.

Properties: Large portable screen decorated with a coat of arms or other royal device; light card table covered with long tablecloth; papers, quill pen and inkstand (on top of table); broom; reticule containing huge shears for Fairy Godmother.

Setting: The stage is bare, and all necessary furnishings are brought on and removed as indicated in the text. The backdrop may be hung with drawings of large knives, forks, spoons and skillets.

Lighting: No special effects.

Sound: Piano or recorded music, clock chimes, as indicated in text.

THE SNOWMAN WHO OVERSTAYED

Characters: 6 male; 5 female; as many boys and girls as desired for Chorus.

Playing Time: 15 minutes.

Costumes: Snowman wears white costume, with top hat. Tree is dressed in a brown kimono, and has branches with leaves and flowers hidden in sleeves. Chorus wear green kimonos and hoods, and have yellow hats hidden under hoods. Spring wears a flowing pastel dress and carries a wand. Sprinkle carries a watering can. Others wear appropriate costumes.

Properties: Wand, watering can.

Setting: A bare garden. A backdrop of blue sky with fluffy clouds may be used.

Lighting: No special effects.

Sound: Music for Sprinkle's dance, as indicated in text.

ALL HANDS ON DECK

Characters: 6 male; 5 female.

Playing Time: 30 minutes.

Costumes: Early 19th century dress. The girls and Aunt Patience wear long dresses. Aunt Patience has white hair and wears old-fashioned spectacles. She walks with a cane. Betty Apple wears an apron over her dress. Ramu Singh wears a turban, brocaded tunic and trousers, fancy slippers and jewels. Matey and Squid have on faded bell-bottom trousers and jerseys. Sailor wears bell-bottoms, striped jersey and a round hat. Captain Dread's uniform is black, without insignia, and he has a black beard. Officer wears a more elaborate uniform, with gold braid, insignia, etc.

Properties: Pillowslip, thimble, thread, needles, partially embroidered coverlet with ship's flag marked in ink, sewing basket containing ribbons and spyglass, newspaper, feather duster, wicker hamper with catch, handcuffs for Sailor.

Setting: The parlor of Captain Bristow's home in Salem, Massachusetts. There is a large window at right which looks out on the harbor. At the beginning of the play, heavy curtains are drawn across it and are later opened. The window itself is open so that

flag may be hung outside. Up left are a grandfather's clock and a long, old-fashioned hooded cradle large enough to hold a boy. A baby blanket is draped over its side. A rocking chair is at center, and near it is a stool. A fireplace with a mantel and bookcases holding a number of books are at the back. The exit at right leads outside, and the one at left to Aunt Patience's room. Other chairs, sea chests, tables, etc., may complete the furnishings.
Lighting: No special effects.

THE CROCUS WHO COULDN'T BLOOM

Characters: 9 male; 10 female.
Playing Time: 20 minutes.
Costumes: Mother Nature wears a green dress, apron, and sunbonnet. Father Nature wears green overalls. Robins have appropriate bird costumes; when they return they wear spring hats. Katy Caterpillar wears a blue-green burlap bag and a green hood with antennae. Later she puts on sequined butterfly wings, black bathing cap with glitter dust, and antennae. Flowers wear brown cloth or paper seed cases, which cover them entirely except for their faces; under the cases they wear green tights and shirts, and long white socks. Their heads are covered with green bathing caps, on which are sewn large crêpe-paper flowers, folded in green wrapping. Weed has black seed case. March Winds are dressed as lions. Miss Shower wears silver raincoat and hat. Mr. Sun wears yellow cardboard disk. Gertie wears red overalls, red plaid shirt, and gloves with large, green thumbs.
Properties: Three flags, marked "Autumn," "Winter," and

"Spring"; triangle and striking rod, New Year's noisemaker, and bicycle siren. Cocoon is made of brown burlap and mosquito netting. Mother and Father Nature have a wheelbarrow, several burlap sheets, and four white sheets. Mother Nature has a mirror and a sign reading "Do Not Disturb Flowers until Spring," and Father Nature has a red kerchief and a small whistle. Robins have small valises and Miss Shower has a sprinkling can with aluminum raindrops.
Setting: A garden. There is a stone wall running across the back, strong enough for the Robins to stand on. A tree stands in front of the wall, close to the right exit. On the wall, attached to the tree, is a large nest. The tree has detachable leaves, green on one side and red or yellow on the other, and it has green buds which can be opened into pink flowers. At left is a flower bed, suggested by stakes with twine. There are two lawn chairs near center and clock-calendar, a large disk, down left.
Lighting: No special effects.
Sound: Chimes, music, noisemaker, siren, as indicated in text.

SUN UP!

Characters: 4 male; 1 female; 16 or more Puddle Jumpers (male or female).
Playing Time: 15 minutes.
Costumes: Puddle Jumpers, Coaxer and Commander wear bright summer clothes under raincoats and rain hats. They carry umbrellas. Commander has epaulets on raincoat and badge on hat; Coaxer may wear white or pastel rain clothes. Witch wears black rain cape, black kerchief or

peaked hat, and witch make-up. Father Time has white hair and beard. He wears toga and sandals, and carries toy scythe. Sun has laugh wrinkles and wide smiling mouth, and wears straw boater.

Properties: Umbrellas, toy scythe, large calendar for Father Time.

Setting: An outdoor scene. There is a blackdrop showing city skyline over which are gray clouds. There are two large tagboard clouds which can be removed to reveal blue sky, rainbow, and large gold disc, in center of which is cut out for Sun's "face."

Lighting: No special effects.

THE PUNCTUATION PROCLAMATION

Characters: 9 male; 3 female; boy and girl extras for Other Courtiers.

Playing Time: 15 minutes.

Costumes: Heralds wear tunics, tights, berets, and boots; Ho has a coin in his pocket. Tutor is dressed in academic robe and wears mortarboard; Storyteller wears long robe, conical magician's hat and glasses; Scribe wears cloak over his trousers and has quill pen behind his ear. Treasurer wears long black cloak, and hat with gold coins on it. Cook wears a white apron. Others wear appropriate court costume.

Properties: Coin, quill pens, scrolls, cardboard hourglass, easel, lesson pad, lesson book, large book for Storyteller, large menu, wooden spoon, small abacus.

Setting: The throne room of King Pish-Posh. At center is a large, decorated throne, and diagonally to the left and right are chairs for the Courtiers. At left is a small table, on which are a large cardboard hourglass, scrolls, and quill pens. Down right are two stools.

Lighting: No special effects.

TERRIBLE TERRY'S SURPRISE

Characters: 4 male; 3 female; 8 male or female for April Fool and Little Follies.

Playing Time: 15 minutes.

Costumes: School clothes and sneakers for Terry; housedress, spectacles, and white wig for Grandma; jester's costume for April Fool; jesters' costumes or elf suits for Little Follies; suits or dresses for "students."

Properties: Knitting needles, yarn, stocking, notebook, report card, whistle, men's shoes, apple, pitch pipe, chalk, portable blackboard, six chairs, five small desks and one larger one, 5 paper planes.

Setting: A living room with window and drapes. Downstage is a rocker, and at left are a chair and table, on which are a fountain pen, paper, and ink. Exits are at right and left.

Lighting: Flashing lights when April Fool and Follies enter and exit.

Sound: Offstage recording or piano music; school bell.

TROUBLE IN TREE-LAND

Characters: 5 male; 1 female; 9 girls and boys for tree parts. Note: If an all-boy cast is desired, the parts of Lucy and the female trees may be changed to boys' roles.

Playing Time: 10 minutes.

Costumes: Pines, Maples, and Birches wear tree costumes. Pines should have pine needles on sleeves; Maples should have large "roots," if possible; and Birches should have long branches. Trees may wear signs indicating their names. Oak wears brown academic robe, green mortarboard, and horn-rimmed glasses. Seedling Child wears green baby bonnet, brown tights, and pixie tunic. Others wear appropriate modern dress.

Properties: Spade, seedling wrapped in burlap, signs for trees, rattle, toy axe, box of matches, sticks, picnic basket (filled with food, paper cups, napkins, etc.), camping equipment.

Setting: A forest grove. There may be a backdrop of a forest scene and platforms for the trees. At rise, sticks of wood are spread on ground near trees, and there may be acorns on ground near oak.

Lighting: If desired, lights may be flickered menacingly when trees chant.

ALL ABOUT MOTHERS

Characters: 5 male; 11 female; 5 or more boys and girls for Chorus. If desired, all parts may be played by girls.

Playing Time: 15 minutes.

Costumes: Commentator wears stylish outfit. Receptionist wears headphones. Judge wears black robe. Handy-Lady wears blue jeans or overalls, a plaid shirt, and a cap. Hostess wears glamorous dress. Oriental Mother wears kimono; Victorian Mother and Vanessa wear shawls and long dresses with full skirts. Mother of the Future wears astronaut's coveralls and space helmet. Other mothers wear appropriate costume, as described in the text.

Properties: Cradle made of twigs, baby doll dressed in leopard skin, club, string shopping bag, fan, crystal ball, gavel, lorgnette, wrench, cradle shaped like rocket ship, baby doll with space helmet.

Setting: Three chairs are at right and a small table is at one side of stage.

Lighting: No special effects.

Sound: Piano accompaniment for songs; appropriate music for mothers' entrances, if desired.

OPERATION LITTERBUG

Characters: 8 male; 2 female.

Playing Time: 15 minutes.

Costumes: Dudley D. Doo-Bad wears a patch over one eye, a black mustache, battered top hat, patched pants. Piggy Pete wears hobo make-up, oversized pants, checked vest, ragged shirt. Sadie Scrawl wears an old housedress. Icky Egbert wears a T-shirt with holes, ragged blue jeans. Bart Banana-Peel wears blue jeans, patched cowboy shirt, ten-gallon hat. General Cleanparks and Orderly Army are all dressed in white.

Properties: Paper airplane, newspaper, tin can telephone, binoculars, notebook and pencil, cigar box containing medal, pastel chalks, bucket with crumpled paper, bag with old bottles, two banana peels, mop, large trash basket in wagon marked "Tank Corps," blanket, vacuum cleaner with sign on it saying "Heavy Artillery," wastebasket, Orderly Army pennant, General Cleanparks poster, and four signs, "Keep Your City Filthy," "Make Your Park a Mess," "Expert Litter—Dirt Cheap," "This Is Your Park—Keep It Dirty."

Setting: A city park. A brick wall

on which are cutout letters reading "City Park" stands between two trees. A ladder leans against one of the trees. Stage right is a broken desk with sign "Department of Park Uglification" in uneven letters across front.

Lighting: No special effects.

Sound: Fanfare, as indicated in text.

THE FRANKLIN REVERSAL

Characters: 3 male; 2 female; 4 boys or girls for party guests.

Playing Time: 20 minutes.

Costumes: Modern everyday dress. Mr. Franklin's jacket is torn and dirty, and he has a black eye. The 4 children wear suitable party clothes, and wear paper birthday hats on first appearance. Cal and Mitey wear lab coats.

Properties: Large baby doll, large box wrapped as present, duplicate box partially wrapped with the same paper; school books, small metal watering can for Mrs. Franklin, large cake plate, pencil flashlight wrapped as candle, birthday hats, four pieces of cake, shredded newspaper, hub cap.

Setting: The Franklin living room. Down left is a small table on which is a glittering machine, which has a cord plugged into wall, and which should click loudly and hum when handle is moved. There are chairs right and left, potted plants on table at right. Lamps, pictures, bookcases complete furnishings. There is a window up left, and door left leads to outside; another, at right, leads to rest of house.

Lighting: Flickering lights and blackouts as indicated in text.

Sound: Offstage crash, auto horns.

ALL POINTS WEST

Characters: 11 male; 2 female; 3 male or female for Rivers and Fever. As many boys and girls as desired for Chorus, other Rivers and additional Indians.

Playing Time: 20 minutes.

Costumes: Appropriate dress of the period for Wagonmaster and pioneers. Wagonmaster has a canteen slung over one shoulder. Rivers wear blue and green togas and carry tridents; Fever wears red leotard, mask, and carries maracas. Texas Signpost is dressed as a cowboy, and carries a sign reading "Texas"; California Signpost is dressed as a miner and carries a sign reading "California." Indians wear appropriate costumes, and Braves may carry bows and arrows. Boys in Chorus may wear jeans, straw hats, brightly colored shirts, etc., and girls may wear long skirts, sunbonnets, white blouses. They have wood blocks or drums.

Properties: List, shovel, canteen, maracas, tridents, bows and arrows, wood blocks, drums.

Setting: Two wooden benches, representing a covered wagon, are placed diagonally down center, so action is clearly visible to audience. Up center is a platform or a pyramid of boxes, painted to look like mountains.

Lighting: Lights may dim following scene with Indians, as indicated in text.